Introduction to the Unitary Patent and the Unified Patent Court

Introduction to the Unitary Patent and the Unified Patent Court

The (Draft) Rules of Procedure of the Unified Patent Court

Pieter Callens and Sam Granata

Wolters Kluwer
Law & Business

Published by:
Kluwer Law International
PO Box 316
2400 AH Alphen aan den Rijn
The Netherlands
Website: www.kluwerlaw.com

Sold and distributed in North, Central and South America by:
Aspen Publishers, Inc.
7201 McKinney Circle
Frederick, MD 21704
United States of America
Email: customer.service@aspenpublishers.com

Sold and distributed in all other countries by:
Turpin Distribution Services Ltd.
Stratton Business Park
Pegasus Drive
Biggleswade
Bedfordshire SG18 8TQ
United Kingdom
Email: kluwerlaw@turpin-distribution.com

Printed on acid-free paper.

ISBN 978-90-411-4757-8

Printed and bound by CPI Group (UK) Ltd., Croydon, CR0 4YY

About the Authors

Pieter Callens (1980) is an attorney-at-law specialising in intellectual property law (with a special focus on patent law) at the Belgian law firm Eubelius. He has developed extensive expertise in different matters of intellectual property law and unfair competition. He obtained a Master in Law at the Catholic University of Louvain (Belgium) and a Master in Economic Law at the Université Libre de Bruxelles (Belgium). During his law education, Pieter studied US patent law as an exchange student at Duke University (North Carolina, USA). In his previous professional life, Pieter was advisor to the Belgian Minister of Economy with respect to intellectual property matters. Pieter advised the Belgian Presidency of the European Union in 2010 when the European Council reached a political compromise on the language regime of the unitary patent.

Pieter is a member of AIPPI and the Advisory Board for Intellectual Property to the Federal Belgian Ministry of Economy. He has written several publications on Belgian intellectual property law.

Sam Granata (1970) is a Judge at the Commercial Court of Antwerp (Belgium), external member of the Enlarged Board of Appeal of the EPO and member of the Advisory Board for Intellectual Property Rights to the Federal Belgian Ministry of Economy. Throughout his academic and professional career, Sam has proven to have a strong interest in patent law. He obtained a Master in Law at the Catholic University of Louvain (Louvain, Belgium), a Master in Intellectual Property Law at Franklin Pierce Law Center (now University of New Hampshire, New Hampshire, US) and a Master of Arts in Interactive Multimedia at the University of London (London, UK).

In his previous professional life, Sam was a research fellow at the Center for Intellectual Property of the Catholic University of Louvain (Louvain, Belgium) and has worked as an attorney-at-law specialising in intellectual property law and mediator in Brussels and Antwerp (Belgium). He is a frequent speaker at IP related events.

Table of Contents

PART 5
GENERAL PROVISIONS (R. 260 – R. 365)

Foreword

This book describing the functioning of the new Unitary Patent and the to be established Unified Patent Court will be most welcome for patent practitioners, lawyers, patent attorneys, IP specialists in companies in Europe and abroad.

At a time when Europe's long awaited patent reform has been finally agreed, there is an urgent need for practitioners to become familiar with the new system. Although the system is not expected to come into operation before spring 2014 at the earliest, practitioners will need to start reflecting on how to adapt their patent prosecution and litigation strategies and practices in the future. This book contains the necessary practical information to help them to get a better understanding on how the system will work.

The new system means change, change for the better, reducing the high costs, complexity and legal insecurity of the current fragmented patent system in Europe. But for practitioners change is always a challenge. This book should contribute to meeting this challenge, in particular by providing a description of the different options patent holders and litigants will have in the future.

It is very useful that this book, beyond a description of the new system, also gives an overview of the history of patent reform in Europe and of the complicated political decision-making process that led to the final adoption of the patent package. Some of the political and legal choices legislators made and some of the provisions both in the EU Regulations creating the unitary patent and in the Agreement creating the Unified Patent Court, can be fully understood only against this background.

It is further helpful, and not only for historical reasons, to understand the importance of the breakthrough under the Belgian Presidency of the Council of the European Union in the second half of 2010, which led to the establishment of enhanced cooperation among 25 Member States of the European Union on the unitary patent. The book describes in detail the process and the elements of compromise developed by the Belgian presidency, which paved the way for the enhanced cooperation. One of the authors of this book, working at the time for the Belgian presidency, is in a very good position to provide this information.

Finally, the book contains a description of the draft Rules of Procedure of the Unified Patent Court, with flowcharts to facilitate their understanding. Although the Rules of Procedure are still in the making, it is important that practitioners become familiar with them at an early stage. This will not only allow them to better assess how the Unified Patent Court is supposed to work in practice, but will also put them in a better position to contribute to further work on the draft Rules of Procedure and to participate in the forthcoming public consultation. This is further value added by this much-needed and welcome book.

Margot Froehlinger

Acknowledgement

The study of the Rules of Procedure would not have been possible without the input from Mr. Willem Hoyng allowing insight in the drafting process and keeping us updated regarding the last drafts.

Introduction

The call from industry for a harmonised European patent system, consisting of an EU-wide patent title and a unified court system, is something most patent practitioners in Europe (irrespective of their period of service) have been hearing for a very long time. This is no surprise when one considers that ever since the Treaty of Rome establishing the European Economic Community was signed in 1957 and entered into force on 1 January 1958, there have been numerous attempts and propositions to create a unified European patent system.

But in 2012, finally, 25 EU Member States – Spain and Italy do not take part for language reasons – agreed to get started with a unified patent system on their territories. Two European Regulations of 17 December 2012 created the European patent with unitary effect (the "unitary patent"). One Regulation concerns the unitary patent itself, while the second Regulation relates to the translation regime of the unitary patent.

Since the 1970s, a European application procedure for patents exists, covering 38 European countries resulting in the so-called "European patent". The European Patent Office (the "EPO"), with its headquarters in Munich, examines European applications and decides whether or not to grant a patent. However, the disadvantage of the classic European patent is that, after approval, the patent proprietor only obtains a bundle of national patents. To have effect in some or all of the 38 participating European countries, the patent proprietor has to "validate" the European patent in the different countries. This means that the patent proprietor needs to pay the renewal fees of the countries where patent protection is wanted and, if required, translate the patent into the official language(s) of the countries concerned. Therefore, obtaining patent protection for an invention in a great number of European countries (e.g. all EU countries) is very costly. A European patent is twelve times more expensive than a US patent.

The new unitary patent intends to get rid of the disadvantages of the classic European patent. As soon as the two European Regulations regarding unitary patent protection come into operation, a unitary patent proprietor shall only have to pay one renewal fee and translate the text of the patent into at most one additional language (other than the language of the EPO procedure), for its invention to be protected in 25 EU Member States.

Another disadvantage of the current system is the parallel litigation. Today, after the opposition proceedings before the EPO, it is not possible for an alleged infringer to invalidate with a single court decision a European patent in all Member States where the patent is valid. On the other hand, the current system can cause conflicting decisions on the validity and/or infringement of a patent. Parallel litigation is again very costly and certainly not effective. The 25 EU Member States wanted a complete reform of the current patent system and therefore choose to deal with these disadvantages. On 19 February 2013, the 25 EU Member States that are participating in the unitary patent system shall have the opportunity to sign a treaty ("Agreement") to establish a Unified Patent Court. The Unified Patent Court installs a patent jurisdiction with effect in all Participating Member States. This will, amongst other things, enable a unitary patent proprietor to obtain a cease-and-desist order or a preliminary injunction effective in all Participating Member States. It will also enable a defendant to obtain revocation of a unitary patent with effect in the Participating Member States.

In this publication we shall describe into detail all the new provisions of the two Regulations regarding the unitary patent and the Agreement on a Unified Patent Court. Since both the Regulations and the Agreement are not yet in operation, it is not our intention to take up any positive or negative position regarding the new system but rather provide interested parties with an introduction to the new patent and litigation system.

In the first place the interested parties are patent practitioners (patent attorneys, IP lawyers, researchers, judges, members of the national patent offices and the EPO, etc.). But this book is equally intended to be read and used by entrepreneurs, tech transfer officers, engineers, company lawyers, public servants and all other persons interested in the new system. At the same time, this publication can be a working tool for the EPO, the Participating Member States and the Unified Patent Court to set up the new system in the best possible conditions.

The book consists of two parts. The first part gives an overview in plain text of all rules regarding the unitary patent and the Unified Patent Court. First, the reader is informed on how to obtain a unitary patent, the (translation) requirements for a unitary patent and all the consequences of the unitary patent title. Then, the reader can get acquainted with the organisation and functioning of the future Unified Patent Court. We shall discuss the different divisions of the Court, the judges and panels deciding the cases, the competence and powers of the Court, the language regime, etc. The second part of the book deals with the draft Rules of Procedure of the Unified Patent Court.

The subsequent stages of the proceedings are represented in flowcharts and, where necessary, further explained in plain text. Finally, the language issues of the proceedings are analysed in detail. Compared to the Regulations and the Agreement, the Rules of Procedure are not yet final since they have to be adopted by the (Administrative Committee of the) Court itself. The authors hope that the second part of this book can be used by all different stakeholders as a working tool during the process of finalising the Rules of Procedure.

The manuscript of this book was submitted for publication on 31 December 2012. The study of the unitary patent provisions is based on the Regulations Nos. 1257/2012 and 1260/2012, as approved by the European Council and the European Parliament on 17 December 2012. However, for the Unified Patent Court, the text of this book is based on the version of the Agreement on a Unified Patent Court submitted to the delegations of the Participating Member States for final linguistic remarks on 17 December 2012. Therefore, it is possible that this book does not include minor linguistic changes which have been included in the signed version of the Agreement. The version of the draft Rules of Procedure which has been used for the second part of this book, is the fourteenth draft, dated 31 January 2013. The fourteenth draft was intended for public consultation.

THE UNITARY PATENT

Chapter I
History of the EU Patent Title

A. THE COMMUNITY PATENT CONVENTION

The proposition by the French Senator Henri Longchambon to the Council of Europe in 1949 (known as the "Longchambon plan")[1] marked the beginning of discussions on a European patent law system. After the entry into force of the Treaty of Rome in 1958, many people feared that patent rights would replace the prohibited quantitative restrictions, since Article 36 of the Rome Treaty had mentioned "the protection of industrial and commercial property" as a prohibition or restriction that was still possible under the Treaty. Some critics claimed that instead of customs authorities, bailiffs would be present at the borders to block goods from other countries based on industrial property rights.[2] For this reason, the Court of Justice developed in those years the first jurisprudence on the Community exhaustion of rights.

This fear led in 1960 to the creation of three Working Parties with the intention of seeking solutions in the field of patents, trademarks and design rights. In 1962, the Working Party on patents put together a preliminary draft convention, which contained the substance of the future European Patent Convention and the Community Patent Convention. But due to political problems, this project was put on hold for several years.

The patent activities resumed in 1969 on the initiative of France, which suggested splitting the project up in two parts: the European Patent Convention (EPC) and the Community Patent Convention (CPC). The EPC would be open to all European countries (including EEC non-Member States). The CPC would only be open to EEC Member States. The EPC intended installing a centralised granting procedure for patent rights in the Contracting Member States, while the CPC wanted to create a unified patent title for the common

1. H. Longchambon, "Creation of a European Patents Office", Report of the Committee on Economic Affairs and Development of the Council of Europe, 6 September 1949, Doc 75, assembly.coe.int
2. B. Schwab, "The Community Patent" in P. Vancraesbeeck (ed.), *Problems of Patent Law*, Kluwer, Diegem, 1994, p. 245

market. The Community Patent Convention built further on the basis of the European Patent Convention.

Two preparatory conferences were convened in Luxembourg in the beginning of the 1970s, which led to the conclusion of the EPC in Munich in October 1973[3] and the CPC in Luxembourg in December 1975.[4]

Everyone expected the two Conventions to enter into force more or less simultaneously. In reality the EPC entered into force on 7 October 1977, but the CPC never did. To enter into force, the CPC had to be ratified by all nine signatory EEC Member States. However, Denmark and Ireland came across national obstacles during the ratification process.

While awaiting the entry into force of the CPC, the interim Committee in charge of the preparatory work drafted three Protocols. One was the draft Protocol on litigation. This Protocol formed the first step towards unified patent litigation.

In order to finalise and adopt the Protocols and find a solution to the deadlock on the ratification of the CPC, a second Conference was convened in Luxembourg in December 1985. The Conference wanted to explore the possibility of putting the CPC progressively into force by a smaller number of ratifications than all signatory parties. The Conference adopted the Protocol on litigation,[5] but failed to reach a solution on the problem of entry into force of the CPC.

Finally, in 1989, a third Conference in Luxembourg found an agreement on the entry into force concerning Community Patents. Article 10 of the Agreement concerning Community Patents[6] provides that the Agreement would enter into force upon ratification of twelve Member States. But at the same time a separate Protocol was agreed which provided that if the ratification by the twelve Member States had not taken place by 31 December 1991,[7] a new Conference would be convened. This Conference would then be able to amend the number of ratifications needed. The entry into force of the Protocol was again subject to twelve ratifications.[8] If the Protocol would not have entered into force on the 31 December 1991, the EEC Member States declared that "a Conference of Representatives of the Governments of the Member States of

3. Convention on the Grant of European Patents, 5 October 1973
4. Convention for the European Patent for the Common Market (Community Patent Convention) of 15 December 1975, *OJ* L 17/27, 26 January 1976
5. Protocol on the settlement of litigation concerning the infringement and validity of Community patents (Protocol on Litigation), *OJ* L 401/4, 30 December 1989
6. Agreement 89/695/EEC relating to Community patents of 15 December 1989, *OJ* L 401/01, 30 December 1989
7. Article 1 of the Protocol on a possible modification of the conditions of entry into force of the Agreement relating to Community patents, *OJ* L 401/51, 30 December 1989
8. Article 4 of the Protocol on a possible modification of the conditions of entry into force of the Agreement relating to Community patents, *OJ* L 401/51, 30 December 1989

the European Economic Community shall be convened by the Presidency of the Council of the European Communities in order to find unanimously the means of ensuring that the Community patent system is implemented at the time of the completion of the Internal Market".[9]

Despite all efforts, neither the CPC, nor the Agreement or Protocol of 1989 ever entered into force.

B. PROPOSAL FOR COUNCIL REGULATION ON THE COMMUNITY PATENT

After the many difficulties encountered by the CPC, the European Commission gave new impetus to the matter by presenting a proposal for a Council Regulation on the Community Patent[10] on 1 August 2000. In the accompanying press release,[11] the Commission gave a comparison of the costs of a US patent, a Japanese patent and a patent delivered under the EPC. The comparison showed that the costs of an EPC patent amounted to EUR 49,900, while a US patent would only cost EUR 10,330 and a Japanese patent EUR 16,450.

In 2001, the Belgian presidency tried to find an agreement within the European Council on the Community Patent Regulation, but failed.[12] In the following years, further attempts were made, but at the Council meeting of 11 March 2004 it became clear that the prospects for a Community Patent were still remote. Commissioner Bolkestein stated: "I can only hope that one day the vested, protectionist interests that stand in the way of agreement on this vital measure will be sidelined by the over-riding importance and interests of European manufacturing industry and Europe's competitiveness. That day has not yet come."[13]

One of the major obstacles to finding a compromise was the translation requirements for the Community Patent.

---

9. "Declaration on a possible modification of the conditions of entry into force of the Agreement" in the Joint Declaration Agreement relating to Community patents, OJ L 401/57, 30 December 1989
10. Proposal for a Council Regulation on the Community Patent, COM/2000/0412, *OJ* C 337E, 28 November 2000
11. Press release of 5 July 2000, "Commission proposes the creation of a Community Patent", ec.europa.eu/internal_market/indprop/patent/comp-council_en.htm
12. Press release of 20 December 2001, " Results of the Internal Market Council on the Community Patent", ec.europa.eu/internal_market/indprop/patent/comp-council_en.htm
13. Press release of 11 March 2004, "Results of the Competitiveness Council of Ministers, Brussels, 11 March 2004 Internal Market, Enterprise and Consumer Protection issues", europa.eu/rapid/press-release_MEMO-04-58_en.htm?locale=fr

C. COMMUNICATION "ENHANCING THE PATENT SYSTEM IN EUROPE"

The patent file reappeared on the European radar in 2007 with a Communication from the Commission regarding the European patent system.[14] In the Communication, the Commission pointed out that it strongly believed that an improved patent system was vital if Europe were to fulfil its potential for innovation. The purpose of the Communication was to revitalise the debate on the patent system in Europe to encourage Member States to work towards consensus and real progress on the issue.

Making the Community patent a reality (the Commission called it "a key objective for Europe")[15] and at the same time improving the existing fragmented patent litigation system would, according to the Commission, make the patent system significantly more accessible and bring cost savings for all who have a stake in the patent system. In parallel, supporting measures to maintain and, where necessary, improve the quality and efficiency of the current system, together with targeted measures to improve SME access, should ensure that Europe's patent system will play its role in boosting innovation and competitiveness in Europe.

Annex I of the Communication gives an overview of the cost structure of direct patent filings and maintenance in 2003. It calculates the costs of a European patent validated in three and in 13 Member States and compares it to US and Japanese patents. The procedural cost with translation for a European patent validated in 13 countries amounts to EUR 20,175, while a US patent only costs EUR 1,856 and a Japanese patent EUR 1,541.[16] If the costs for maintaining the patent are included, the difference in costs becomes even more striking: EUR 129,183 for a European Patent maintained for 20 years in 13 Member States, against EUR 14,556 for a US patent and EUR 17,341 for a Japanese patent.

Annex IV of the Communication compares patent litigation costs in France, UK, Germany and the Netherlands in 2003. The costs for first instance proceedings would amount to 150,000 to 1,500,000 EUR in the UK, EUR 50,000 to 200,000 in France, EUR 60,000 to 200,000 in the Netherlands and EUR 50,000 in Germany. Appeal proceedings in the UK would cost

---

14. Communication from the Commission to the European Parliament and the Council, "Enhancing the patent system in Europe", 3 April 2007, COM/2007/0165
15. Communication from the Commission to the European Parliament and the Council, "Enhancing the patent system in Europe", 3 April 2007, COM/2007/0165, p. 4
16. Communication from the Commission to the European Parliament and the Council, "Enhancing the patent system in Europe", 3 April 2007, COM/2007/0165, Annex I

between EUR 150,000 and 1,000,000, EUR 40,000 to 150,000 in France and the Netherlands and EUR 90,000 in Germany.[17]

D. COUNCIL CONCLUSIONS UNDER THE SWEDISH PRESIDENCY

After the Communication of the Commission, the Council, under Swedish presidency, approved in December 2009 a number of political conclusions with respect to the patent litigation system and the unitary patent title. At this stage the title of the unitary patent was changed from "Community patent" to "EU patent," due to the entry into force of the Lisbon Treaty on 1 December 2009.

Regarding the translation arrangements, the Council concluded that "the EU Patent Regulation should be accompanied by a separate regulation, which should govern the translation arrangements for the EU patent adopted by the Council with unanimity in accordance with Article 118 second subparagraph of the Treaty on the Functioning of the European Union. The EU Patent Regulation should come into force together with the separate regulation on the translation arrangements for the EU patent."[18]

Meanwhile the Council had requested an opinion of the European Court of Justice[19] on the compatibility of the envisaged agreement on a European and Community Patents Court in July 2009.[20] This did not prevent the Council of paying great attention to the creation of an "integrated specialised and unified jurisdiction for patent related disputes"[21] in the Council conclusions of December 2009. The Council took decisions on the composition of the panels,[22] jurisdiction in respect of actions or counterclaims for revocation,[23]

17. Communication from the Commission to the European Parliament and the Council, "Enhancing the patent system in Europe", 3 April 2007, COM/2007/0165, Annex IV
18. Council of the European Union "Enhanced patent system in Europe – Council conclusions", Doc 17229/09, 7 December 2008, register.consilium.europa.eu/pdf/en/09/st17/st17229.en09.pdf, point 36
19. Request for an opinion submitted by the Council of the European Union pursuant to Article 300(6) EC, Opinion 1/09, 2009/C 220/15, *OJ* 12 September 2009
20. Council Working Document on a revised Presidency text of the Draft Agreement on the European and Community Patents Court and Draft Statute, Doc 7928/09 of 23 March 2009.
21. Council of the European Union "Enhanced patent system in Europe – Council conclusions", Doc 17229/09, 7 December 2008, register.consilium.europa.eu/pdf/en/09/st17/st17229.en09.pdf, second recital
22. Council of the European Union "Enhanced patent system in Europe – Council conclusions", Doc 17229/09, 7 December 2008, register.consilium.europa.eu/pdf/en/09/st17/st17229.en09.pdf, point 13-19
23. Council of the European Union "Enhanced patent system in Europe – Council conclusions", Doc 17229/09, 7 December 2008, register.consilium.europa.eu/pdf/en/09/st17/st17229.en09.

languages of the proceedings,[24] transitional period,[25] principles on the financing[26] and accession.[27]

With these conclusions, Swedish presidency had the clear intention of reaching an agreement on the non-sensitive issues of the EU patent.

E. FAILURE TO REACH UNANIMITY ON THE LANGUAGE REGIME

In the second half of 2010, the Belgian presidency was given the difficult task of finding a compromise on the language regime for the EU patent. Article 118, paragraph 2 of the Treaty on the Functioning of the European Union (hereafter "TFEU"), as amended and renamed by the Treaty of Lisbon of 13 December 2007, provides that for regulations establishing language arrangements for European intellectual property rights, the Council should act unanimously after consulting the European Parliament.

In the past it appeared impossible to find unanimity for a language regime that would enhance the patent system. The reason is quite simple. The EPO has three official languages of proceedings: French, German and English. But because of the system of the European Patent Convention, patent proprietors need to translate their patent in the official languages of the Member States in which they wish to validate their patent rights. One of the objectives of an EU patent title has always been to abolish, as much as possible, the costly translation requirements.

Traditionally most of industry was in favour of using only one official language, namely English. The Scandinavian countries and some Eastern European countries were of the same opinion. After all, English is nowadays the language which is customary in the field of international technological research and publications. However, for France and Germany it was difficult to give up their national language, which made it equally difficult for other

pdf, point 20

24. Council of the European Union "Enhanced patent system in Europe – Council conclusions", Doc 17229/09, 7 December 2008, register.consilium.europa.eu/pdf/en/09/st17/st17229.en09.pdf, point 21-23
25. Council of the European Union "Enhanced patent system in Europe – Council conclusions", Doc 17229/09, 7 December 2008, register.consilium.europa.eu/pdf/en/09/st17/st17229.en09.pdf, point 24-26
26. Council of the European Union "Enhanced patent system in Europe – Council conclusions", Doc 17229/09, 7 December 2008, register.consilium.europa.eu/pdf/en/09/st17/st17229.en09.pdf, point 29-34
27. Council of the European Union "Enhanced patent system in Europe – Council conclusions", Doc 17229/09, 7 December 2008, register.consilium.europa.eu/pdf/en/09/st17/st17229.en09.pdf, point 35

countries such as Spain and Italy to see French and German as an official patent language and not Spanish or Italian. Positions were much more nuanced and differentiated than that, but in a nutshell this was the challenge for the Council to overcome. Behind these language arguments economical and protectionist arguments were also hidden. In Spain, for example, translation activities by patent attorneys for non-EU applicants were considered of great economic value.

In June 2010, as a starting point for negotiations under the Belgian presidency of 2010, the Commission presented a proposal for a Council Regulation on the translation arrangements for the European Union patent.[28] This proposal started from the existing official languages for granting European patents (French, German and English),[29] but added two elements. First, a system of machine translations for EU patent specifications into all official EU languages would be put in place by the time the Regulation applied. Such machine translations would serve for information purposes only and would have no legal effect. Secondly, applicants filing a European patent application in an official EU language other than French, German or English,[30] would be entitled to full reimbursement of their translation costs.

One of the problems of the Commission's proposal was that automatic machine translations were not yet operational for all languages and their quality could not be guaranteed.

The Belgian presidency added the following compromise elements to the Commission proposal in order to obtain unanimity:

(i) speeding up the development of automatic machine translations by the EPO:
   In October 2010, the EPO's Administrative Council gave the green light to accelerating, in conjunction with the European Commission, the creation of patent-specific machine translation services from and into English for all the languages of the Member States of the EPO. German and French would follow at a later stage.[31] On 30 November 2012, the EPO and Google signed a Memorandum of Understanding to use Google's machine translation technology to translate patents

28. Proposal for a Council Regulation on the translation arrangements for the European Union patent, COM 2010/350, 2010/0198 (CNS), 30 June 2010
29. Article 3 of the Commission proposal: "After the publication of the EU patent specification in accordance with Article 14, paragraph 6, of the Convention on the Grant of the European Patents of 5 October 1973, as amended (hereinafter referred to as the "EPC"), no further translations are required."
30. Article 14.2 EPC
31. EPO, Patent Information News Issue 4/2010, www.epo.org

into the languages of the 38 countries that it serves.[32] The EPO would put technical texts in the various languages at Google's disposal, and Google then uses these texts to "train" its machine translation software;

(ii) translation costs for European patent applications submitted in other than the three official EPO languages, should be reimbursed immediately and not by way of a fee reduction;

(iii) granting EU patents by means of the existing EPC procedure:
If the choice between a classic European patent or an EU patent were placed at the end of the EPO granting procedure, the use of the three existing official EPO languages for the EU patent would be more justifiable;

(iv) during a transitional period, the applicant should provide a full English translation of patents where the language of the proceedings is French or German.

In the Competitiveness Council of 10 November 2010, the presidency added two extra elements for compromise:

(i) besides the English translation, the applicants of patents of which the language of the proceedings was English, should provide a full translation of the specification of the patent into any other official language of the Union;

(ii) protection of third parties acting in good faith:
In the event of a dispute concerning a claim for damages, the competent court should be able to take into consideration whether the alleged infringer acted without knowing or without reasonable grounds for knowing, that he was infringing the European patent with unitary effect before being provided with a translation into an official language of either the Member State in which the alleged infringement took place or the Member State in which the alleged infringer was domiciled.

Both elements were a clear concession to Spain and Italy. The Spanish delegation kept insisting on Spanish as an official language and granting more than one language legal value. The first element would have made it possible to have Spanish translations of patents granted in English. The second element would allow a judge to take into account whether or not an infringer was provided with a translation in its own language for the calculation of damages.

---

32. EPO Press release, "European Patent Office and Google sign memorandum on translation of patents", 30 November 2010, www.epo.org

Despite all efforts to find a unanimous compromise with the 27 Member States of the European Union, the Council of 10 November 2010 established that the objectives of the EU patent could not be attained within a reasonable period by the Union as a whole.

F. ENHANCED COOPERATION

Ironically, the conclusion of the Council of 10 November 2010 was not the end of the EU patent title, but the real starting point for political compromise.

If Member States cannot reach an unanimous agreement on a subject matter within a reasonable period, the European Treaties provide, as a last resort, the possibility to enter into "enhanced cooperation" with a group of at least 9 Member States. The principle of enhanced cooperation is laid down in Article 20 of the Treaty on European Union (hereafter the "TEU").

According to Article 20 TEU, enhanced cooperation should aim to further the objectives of the Union, protect its interests and reinforce its integration process. Such cooperation shall be open at any time to all Member States. Acts adopted in the framework of enhanced cooperation shall bind only Participating Member States and shall not be regarded as part of the *acquis* which has to be accepted by candidate states for accession to the Union.[33]

The decision authorising enhanced cooperation can only be adopted by the Council as a last resort, when it has established that the objectives of such cooperation cannot be attained within a reasonable period by the Union as a whole, and provided that at least nine Member States participate in it.[34]

The details of enhanced cooperation are elaborated on in Articles 326-334 TFEU. Article 326 TFEU states that enhanced cooperation may not undermine the internal market or economic, social and territorial cohesion, and shall not constitute a barrier to or discrimination in trade between Member States, nor shall it distort competition between them.

Article 329.1 TFEU describes the procedure that needs to be followed by Member States which intend to embark on enhanced cooperation:

> "Member States which wish to establish enhanced cooperation between themselves in one of the areas covered by the Treaties, with the exception of fields of exclusive competence and the common foreign and security policy, shall address a request to the Commission, specifying the scope and objectives of the enhanced cooperation proposed. The Commission may submit a proposal to the Council to

33. Article 20.4 TEU
34. Article 20.2 TEU

> that effect. In the event of the Commission not submitting a proposal, it shall inform the Member States concerned of the reasons for not doing so.
>
> Authorization to proceed with the enhanced cooperation referred to in the first subparagraph shall be granted by the Council, on a proposal from the Commission and after obtaining the consent of the European Parliament."

Following this procedure, twelve Member States (Denmark, Estonia, Finland, France, Germany, Lithuania, Luxembourg, the Netherlands, Poland, Slovenia, Sweden and the United Kingdom) addressed requests to the Commission by letters dated 7, 8 and 13 December 2010 indicating that they wished to establish enhanced cooperation between themselves in the area of the creation of unitary patent protection, on the basis of the existing proposals supported by these Member States during the negotiations. The Member States requested the Commission to submit a proposal to the Council to that end. It was important that France, Germany and UK were part of the initial group of Member States requesting enhanced cooperation to ensure the strength of the enhanced cooperation.

The requests were confirmed at the meeting of the Council on 10 December 2010. Afterwards, 13 more Member States, namely Belgium, Bulgaria, the Czech Republic, Ireland, Greece, Cyprus, Latvia, Hungary, Malta, Austria, Portugal, Romania and Slovakia wrote to the Commission indicating that they also wished to participate in the envisaged enhanced cooperation. Eventually, a total of 25 Member States requested enhanced cooperation. Only Spain and Italy did not take part.

On 14 December 2010, the Commission presented its proposal for a Council decision authorising enhanced cooperation in the area of the creation of unitary patent protection.[35] The proposal was accompanied by an "explanatory memorandum", which recalled the history of the EU patent proposals, key elements that should ideally form part of the envisaged implementing measures, assessment of the legal conditions for enhanced cooperation and an impact assessment of the enhanced cooperation.

Finally, on 10 March 2011 the European Council gave a green light to the enhanced cooperation,[36] authorising the 25 Member States to establish enhanced cooperation between themselves in the area of the creation of unitary

35. Proposal for a Council decision authorising enhanced cooperation in the area of the creation of unitary patent protection, COM(2010) 790, 2010/0384, 14 December 2010
36. Council decision of 10 March 2011 authorising enhanced cooperation in the area of the creation of unitary patent protection, 2011/167/EU, *OJ* L 76/53, 22 March 2011

patent protection, by applying the relevant provisions of the Treaties. By deciding that the conditions laid down in Article 20 TEU and in Articles 326 and 329 TFEU were fulfilled, the opponents to the new patent system (namely Spain and Italy) were sidelined.

Spain and Italy did not leave it at that, and, on 8[37] and 17 June 2011[38] respectively, initiated actions before the Court of Justice of the European Union (the "CJEU") for annulment of the Council decision of 10 March 2011 authorising enhanced cooperation in the area of the creation of unitary patent protection. Article 263 TFEU stipulates that the CJEU can review the legality of acts of the Council on grounds of lack of competence, infringement of an essential procedural requirement, infringement of the Treaties or of any rule of law relating to their application, or misuse of powers. If the action is well founded, the Court of Justice of the European Union can declare the act concerned to be void.[39]

In the annulment cases (which were joined by the CJEU),[40] Spain and Italy invoked six pleas to annul the decision authorising enhanced cooperation. They claimed that the Council lacked competence to establish enhanced cooperation with a view to creating a unitary patent, the Council had misused its powers, the judicial system of the Union was not respected, the 'last resort' condition of Article 20.2 TEU was not met and Articles 118, 326, 327 and 328 TFEU and Article 20.1 TEU were infringed.

Although both cases have not yet been decided by the ECJ, on 11 December 2012 the Advocate-General proposed that the CJEU would dismiss the actions of Spain and Italy.[41]

---

37. ECJ, case C-274/11, *Kingdom of Spain v. the Council of the European Union*
38. ECJ, case C-295/11, *Italian Republic v. the Council of the European Union*
39. Article 264 TFEU
40. Order of the President of the Court of Justice of 10 July 2012 to join the cases C-274/11 and C-295/11
41. Opinion of Advocate-General Bot, 11 December 2012, joined cases C-274/11 and C-295/11, *Kingdom of Spain and Italian Republic v. Council of the European Union*, www.curia.europe.eu

Chapter II
Legal Instruments for Unitary Patent Protection

For the establishment of enhanced cooperation in the area of the creation of unitary patent protection within the 25 Participating Member States (hereafter referred to as "Participating Member States"), two legal instruments were adopted.

All substantive provisions regarding the European patent with unitary effect are included in Regulation No. 1257/2012 of the European parliament and of the Council of 17 December 2012 implementing enhanced cooperation in the area of the creation of unitary patent protection (hereafter referred to as "Unitary Patent Regulation"). This Regulation was adopted by means of the EU co-decision procedure. Since the Lisbon Treaty that took effect on 1 December 2009, this renamed ordinary legislative procedure became the main legislative procedure of the EU´s decision-making system. The co-decision procedure gives the same weight to the European Parliament and the Council of the European Union, which both have to adopt the Regulation.[42] Article 118.1 TFEU provides that the ordinary legislative procedure needs to be followed for establishing measures for the creation of European intellectual property rights to provide uniform protection of intellectual property rights throughout the Union.

However, Article 118.2 TFEU provides that for establishing language arrangements for the European intellectual property rights, a special legislative procedure needs to be followed. For such measures, the Council shall act unanimously after consulting the European Parliament. As mentioned earlier, this was the main reason why the language arrangements for the unitary patent protection were included in a different Regulation.

On 17 December 2012 the Council adopted the Regulation No. 1260/2012 implementing enhanced cooperation in the area of the creation of unitary patent protection with regard to the applicable translation arrangements (hereafter referred to as "Translation Regulation").

42. Articles 289 and 294 TFEU

Chapter III
Unitary Patent

A. LEGAL STATUS OF UNITARY PATENT REGULATION

The Unitary Patent Regulation is not only an instrument of Union law, but at the same time it constitutes a special agreement within the meaning of Article 142 of the EPC.[43]

Article 142 EPC stipulates that any group of Contracting States of the EPC, which has provided by a special agreement that a European patent granted for those States has a unitary character throughout their territories, may provide that a European patent may only be granted jointly in respect of all those states. By means of such "special agreement", the 25 Participating Member States could avoid a revision of the EPC and/or (in an earlier stage where all EU Member States participated) the accession of the EU to the EPC. The special agreement enables a group of Contracting States of the EPC to give additional tasks to the EPO[44] and to set up a special department within the EPO for that purpose.[45]

Besides a special agreement under the EPC, the Unitary Patent Regulation is also to be considered as a regional patent treaty within the meaning of Article 45(1) of the Patent Cooperation Treaty of 19 June 1970 ("PCT") (as last modified on 3 February 2001) and a special agreement within the meaning of Article 19 of the Convention for the Protection of Industrial Property, signed in Paris on 20 March 1883 (and last amended on 28 September 1979).[46]

Article 45(1) of the PCT stipulates that any treaty providing for the grant of regional patents and giving to all persons who are entitled to file international applications the right to file applications for such patents, may provide that international applications designating or electing a state party to both the regional patent treaty and the PCT may be filed as applications for such patents. Although the Unitary Patent Regulation is technically not

43. Article 1.2 Unitary Patent Regulation
44. Article 143.1 EPC
45. Article 143.2 EPC
46. Recital 6 of the Preamble to the Unitary Patent Regulation

a treaty, the reference to Article 45(1) PCT is included in the Unitary Patent Regulation to ensure that patent applicants can, as is currently the case for European patents, keep using the international (PCT) application procedure to obtain a unitary patent.

In Article 19 of the Paris Convention for the Protection of Industrial Property, the countries of the Paris Union reserve the right to make separately between themselves special agreements for the protection of industrial property, in so far as these agreements do not contravene the provisions of the Paris Convention.

B. ADDITIONAL LAYER OF PATENT PROTECTION

Recital 26 of the Preamble to the Unitary Patent Regulation stipulates that the Regulation should be without prejudice to the right of the Participating Member States to grant national patents and should not replace Participating Member States' laws on patents.

This means that, when the Unitary Patent Regulation applies, patent applicants shall have the choice to obtain in Europe:

- a national patent;
- a European patent taking effect in one or more of the Contracting States to the EPC;
- a unitary patent; or
- a unitary patent validated in addition in one or more other Contracting States to the EPC which are not among the Member States participating in the Unitary Patent Regulation.

The last situation shall occur when a patent proprietor chooses to have a unitary patent in the 25 Participating Member States, but additionally also validates its European patent in other countries of the European Patent Organisation which are not unitary patent Member States (Italy, Spain, Switzerland, Turkey, Norway, Iceland, etc.). The patent proprietor shall then have both a unitary patent and a European patent for the non-Participating Member States.

The unitary patent is not a substitute for the existing European patent. It is an additional patent protection system, which can only be "activated" once the EPC patent application procedure has been successfully completed. After grant, the patent proprietor shall have to choose to obtain either a European patent for the 25 Participating Member States (i.e. a bundle of national patents) or a unitary patent (i.e. one patent title with immediate effect in all 25 Participating Member States). Since there are more countries participating in the EPC than in the Unitary Patent Regulation, the patent proprietor can still validate its European patent in non-unitary patent countries. Then there will be a sort of co-existence between a European and unitary patent. The invention shall be protected in France and Germany by a unitary patent, for example, while (if validated) the same invention shall be protected in Switzerland by a European patent.

C. GRANTING PROCEDURE

To obtain a unitary patent title for all Participating Member States, the normal EPC procedure, should be completed. Hence, the task of examining applications, which eventually leads to unitary patents, shall be carried out by the European Patent Office.

It is important to note that the request for unitary effect can only be submitted in the post-grant phase, i.e. after the grant of the European patent. The patent proprietor can submit the request for unitary patent protection up to one month after the publication of grant of the European patent in the *European Patent Bulletin*.[47] Such request shall be submitted in the language of the proceedings of the EPO[48] in which the European patent application is filed or into which it is translated.[49] During the transitional period (*infra*), the request should be submitted together with the translations required by Article 6 of the Translation Regulation.[50]

When such a request is submitted to the EPO together with the necessary translation within the one month deadline, the applicant shall (in case of grant) obtain a European patent with unitary effect ("unitary patent").[51] The name "European patent with unitary effect" has been used ever since the enhanced cooperation procedure was initiated by the 25 EU Member States. The name "EU patent" could not be maintained because two of the 27 EU Member States (Spain and Italy) did not participate in the enhanced cooperation.

The EPO shall administer the requests for unitary effect by proprietors of European patents and ensure that the unitary effect is indicated in the Register for unitary patent protection.[52] Consequently, the EPO shall examine the request as to formal requirements and then register the unitary effect or reject the request, which in both cases must be communicated to the patent

47. Article 9.1(g) Unitary Patent Regulation
48. Article 14.1 EPC
49. Article 14.3 EPC
50. Article 9.1(h) Unitary Patent Regulation
51. Article 2(c) Unitary Patent Regulation
52. Article 9.1(h) Unitary Patent Regulation

proprietor. The Register for unitary patent protection shall be included within the European Patent Register.[53]

The EPO shall also be responsible[54] for the reimbursement of translation costs for applicants filing patent applications in one of the official languages of the Union which is not an official language of the EPO. For many Participating Member States it was important that patent applicants would still be able to file their European applications (leading to unitary patents) in its national language without any additional cost (*infra* IV.A.). The EPO has the task of administering a compensation scheme for the reimbursement of all translation costs up to a ceiling, for applicants filing patent applications[55] at the EPO in an official language of the Union other than French, English or German.[56] Such reimbursement shall only be available for SMEs, natural persons, non-profit organisations, universities and public research organisations having their residence or principal place of business within a Member State. The compensation scheme shall be funded through the renewal fees for unitary patents and additional fees for their late payment.[57]

D. EQUAL CLAIMS

A unitary patent can only be obtained if the European patent is granted with the same set of claims in respect of all the Participating Member States. A European patent granted with different sets of claims for different Participating Member States cannot benefit from unitary effect.[58]

The European patent with the same set of claims in all Participating Member States benefits from unitary effect only if its unitary effect has been entered in the Register for unitary patent protection.[59]

E. UNITARY CHARACTER

A unitary patent shall have a unitary character, which means that it shall provide uniform protection and shall have equal effect in all the Participating Member States.[60]

53. Article 9.1(h) Unitary Patent Regulation
54. Article 9.1(f) Unitary Patent Regulation
55. Article 14.2 EPC
56. Article 5.1 Translation Regulation
57. Article 5.2 Translation Regulation
58. Article 3.1 Unitary Patent Regulation
59. Article 3.1 Unitary Patent Regulation
60. Article 3.2 Unitary Patent Regulation

It is important to note that during a first phase the unitary character and effect shall only occur in those Participating Member States for which the Agreement on a Unified Patent Court has entered into force at the date of publication of the grant of the European patent. Consequently, the unitary character and effect shall depend on the ratification of the Agreement on a Unified Patent Court and shall therefore, gradually occur for the 25 Participating Member States.[61]

The unitary effect of a European patent shall be deemed not to have arisen if the European patent has been revoked or limited.[62] If an opposition procedure against a granted European patent (for which a request for unitary effect has been submitted and registered), leads to the revocation or limitation of the patent, the unitary patent shall be deemed to never have existed in case of revocation and deemed to be equally limited in case of limitation. This is called the accessory nature of the unitary effect, meaning that the effect should be deemed not to have arisen to the extent that the basic European patent has been revoked or limited.[63]

A major point of discussion during the negotiations for the Unitary Patent Regulation was whether the unitary character should mean that unitary patents can only be transferred or licensed as a whole, or if it should be possible to, for example, split up the ownership per Member State and/or grant licences limited to certain territories. As a matter of compromise, it was decided that unitary patents should always be transferred (and limited) as a whole, but licences to certain (parts of the) territories of the Participating Member States should remain possible. In this respect, Article 3.2 of the Unitary Patent Regulation clearly stipulates that a unitary patent may only be limited, be transferred, be revoked or lapse, in respect of *all* the Participating Member States, but may be licensed in respect of the *whole or part of the territories* of the Participating Member States.[64]

F. DATE OF EFFECT

According to Article 4.1 of the Unitary Patent Regulation, a unitary patent shall take effect (retroactively) in the Participating Member States on the date of publication by the EPO of the grant of the European patent in the *European Patent Bulletin*. This article is the equivalent of Article 64.1 EPC by which a European patent confers on its proprietor from the date on which the mention

61. Article 18.2 Unitary Patent Regulation
62. Article 3.3 Unitary Patent Regulation
63. Point 7 of the Preamble to the Unitary Patent Regulation
64. Article 3.2 Unitary Patent Regulation

of its grant is published in the *European Patent Bulletin*, in each Contracting State in respect of which it is granted, the same rights as would be conferred by a national patent granted in that State.

There is no "unitary" provisional protection, since the Unitary Patent Regulation does not include any arrangements regarding provisional protection. It shall remain an aspect of national law to determine the provisional protection of published European patent applications.[65] Today, many EPC Member States provide provisional protection for patent applications. Such protection shall of course extent to European patent applications that eventually lead to unitary patents.

When the unitary effect of a European patent has been registered and extends to the territory of the Participating Member States, the Participating Member States should ensure that the European patent is deemed not to have taken effect on their territory as a national patent on the date of publication of the grant in the *European Patent Bulletin*, so as to avoid any duplication of patent protection.[66] Most likely, the national patent legislation of a number of Participating Member States shall have to be amended to ensure the absence of effect of the European patent as a national patent, once the unitary patent takes effect.

G. EFFECT

The draft versions of the Unitary Patent Regulation included three articles dealing with the effect and the consequences of unitary patent protection. The fact that the right for the patent proprietor to prevent direct use of the invention (ex. Article 6), the right to prevent indirect use of the invention (ex. Article 7) and the limitations of the effects of the patent (ex. Article 8), formed part of an EU Regulation, was heavily criticised by practitioners and patent judges. In particular, patent judges from countries already having specialised courts with expertise in patent litigation were reluctant to include provisions of substantial patent law in EU legal instruments. On 23 September 2011, an international conference regarding the unitary patent protection took place in Warsaw.[67] At this conference, the reputed judges Lord Robin Jacob (UK) and Robert Van Peursem (Netherlands) pleaded for the deletion of Articles 6-8 in the draft Regulation.

65. Article 67 EPC
66. Article 4.2 Unitary Patent Regulation; point 8 of the Preamble
67. "The future unified patent litigation system in the EU", organised by ERA (*Europäische Rechtsakademie*), the Polish ministry of Economy and the Polish EU presidency, Warsaw, 23 September 2011.

The reason for this criticism was that by introducing these patent rights and limitations in Union law, the Court of Justice of the European Union would become competent to interpret these provisions of material patent law and render preliminary rulings regarding these articles. The judges not only feared that too many preliminary rulings would slow down proceedings, but more importantly judges did not feel comfortable about the CJEU ruling on patent matters. It was said that the CJEU would not have sufficient expertise in intellectual property rights and would not be able to answer preliminary questions with quality rulings. Moreover, judge Van Peursem explicitly formulated the fear that by interpreting the provisions on direct and indirect use and limitations of unitary patents, the CJEU would in the long run also (indirectly) influence the interpretation of these rights and limitations for classic European patents. On 2 November 2011 the general assembly of the Intellectual Property Judges Association (IPJA) in San Servelo called on the European Council to delete Articles 6-8 from the draft Regulation. The call was supported by judges from 24 EU Member States.

Nevertheless, in a first phase the European Council upheld Articles 6-8 of the draft Regulation. The legal reason for this was that the legislation procedure stipulated in Article 118.1 TFEU can only be followed for the "creation of European intellectual property rights to provide uniform protection of intellectual property rights throughout the Union". Therefore, Article 118.1 TFEU can only be used as a legal basis for a unitary patent regulation if the regulation contains a minimum set of "uniform protection". In Warsaw, the German Professor Dr. Winfried Tilmann explained that in his opinion the regulation should at least include one sanction, the injunction claim, in order to fulfil the requirement of "uniform protection".[68] Prof. Tilmann even went a step further and advocated the inclusion of an autonomous and harmonised damage sanction in the Regulation. Because of the very diverse national rules on damages, it would be difficult for the Unified Patent Court to apply the national rules to grant damages.[69]

---

68. W. Tilmann, "Moving towards completing the European Patent System – Overview of the draft Agreement on a European and EU Patents Court (EEUPC): "This Lisbon article provides the legal basis for (I quote) 'measures for the creation of European intellectual property rights to provide uniform protection of intellectual property rights'. In order to be based on art. 118 TFEU the Regulation must contain, as it does, at least one sanction, one measure to provide 'uniform protection', the injunction claim. The Regulation cannot leave the uniform protection to the Agreement. That would mean risking a decision of the ECJ that the Regulation cannot be based on art. 118."

69. "This small degree of involvement of the ECJ is unavoidable, because, as I said, art. 118 TFEU may be used as a legal basis for the Regulation only if the Regulation contains a minimum set of 'uniform protection'. I would go even further than the draft-Regulation and the draft-Agreement and advocate an inclusion also of an autonomous and harmonized damage-sanction in the Regulation. Despite the existence of art. 13 of the Enforcement Directive and its repetition

Other authors, such as, for example, Prof. Dr. Rudolf Krasser, contested this thesis. According to Krasser, it is sufficient that Union law creates an intellectual property right which is unitary for all (participating) Member States, to apply Article 118.1 TFEU. If the invention is identical in all Participating Member States and the invention is exclusively attributed to a specific legal subject in all Participating Member States and accordingly this legal subject can forbid the use of the subject matter of the right without the owner's consent in all these Member States, there is a uniform protection.[70]

Because of the cases Italy and Spain had initiated against the enhanced cooperation in the field of unitary patent protection, many Member States found it dangerous to open legal discussions regarding the application of Article 118.1 if Articles 6-8 were deleted from the project.

Despite this threat, the UK stressed the practical importance of the deletion during the negotiations preceding the Council of 29 June 2012. In the end, the Council of 29 June 2012[71] agreed to "suggest" that Articles 6-8 of the Regulation to be adopted by the Council and the European parliament would be deleted. The European Parliament was not happy with this decision and immediately postponed its vote on the patent package to further negotiate on this aspect.

Finally, on 19 November 2012, Council and Parliament agreed on a compromise text. The compromise consisted in removing the former Articles 6-8

---

in art. 41 of the draft-Agreement it would be difficult for the Patent Court to apply the still widely differing or not even existent national civil laws on damages of the participating member states."

70. R. Krasser, "Effects of an inclusion of regulations concerning the content and limits of the patent holder's rights to prohibit in an EU regulation for the creation of unitary European patent protection", Munich, 18 October 2011, www.eplawpatentblog.com: "The minimum requirement for the application of the authorization is, according to Art. 118 Para. 1 of the TFEU, merely that an intellectual property right is created by Union law. This itself achieves the necessary minimum harmonization at least if the subject matter and core effect of the right in question is established identically in the law of the (participating) Member States. In the case of patents, the subject matter of the law consists of a technical invention, the core effect in the fact that the invention is exclusively attributed to a specific legal subject and accordingly this legal subject can forbid the use of the subject matter of the right without his consent. For this reason, the proposed Regulation can be restricted to creating the basis for the grant of unitary patents for the participating Member States. Thanks to the granting act under Union law, which is unitary for all participating states, a bond based on Union law is established with respect to the invention – as defined in the patent claims – to which it relates, which is closer than in the case of the grant of a ('bundle') patent based only on the European Patent Convention (EPC). This is reflected in the fact that the patent can only be limited, licensed or transferred or can only be cancelled uniformly for all participating states, as laid down in Art. 3 (2) of the proposed Regulation. As we have already said, it is sufficient for the uniform protection required by Art. 118 Para. 1 of the TFEU and the 'same effect' of Art. 3 (2) of the proposed Regulation that the aforesaid core effect is unitary."

71. Conclusions of the European Council of 28 and 29 June 2012, EUCO 76/12, p. 2, www.consilium.europa.eu/uedocs/cms_data/docs/pressdata/en/ec/131388.pdf

from the draft Regulation and inserting them in the Agreement on the Unified Patent Court.[72] The current Article 5 of the Unitary Patent Regulation provides that the unitary patent shall confer on its proprietor the right to prevent any third party from committing acts against which the patent provides protection throughout the territories of the Participating Member States in which the patent has unitary effect, subject to applicable limitations.[73] The scope of this right and its limitations shall be uniform in all Participating Member States in which the patent has unitary effect.[74]

Paragraphs 1 and 2 of Article 5 provide a cease and desist claim open to all proprietors of unitary patents in all Participating Member States.

To determine which acts specifically can be prohibited, Article 5.3 provides that the acts against which the unitary patent provides protection and the applicable limitations shall be those defined by the law applied to unitary patents in the Participating Member State whose national law is applicable to the unitary patent as an object of property in accordance with Article 7 Unitary Patent Regulation.

At first sight, one could believe that the prohibited acts would be those provided by the national law applicable to the unitary patent as an object of property. In reality, Article 5.3 Unitary Patent Regulation is nothing but a disguised referral to the Agreement on a Unified Patent Court. The Unified Patent Court is a court common to the Contracting Member States and thus part of their judicial system.[75] Irrespective of the national law indicated by Article 7 Unitary Patent Regulation, the articles of the Agreement regarding the right to prevent direct and indirect use of the invention[76] and limitations[77] shall be applicable as the law common to all jurisdictions. Instead of directly referring to the Agreement, the Regulation first refers to a national law of which the articles of the Agreement form part.

The intention of the European legislator (or should we say of the UK) was to make sure that the CJEU did not have any competence over the acts of infringement (direct and indirect use) and the limitations of the effect of unitary patents. Because the articles regarding the rights of the patent proprietor and the limitations thereof are included in a treaty, which is not an instrument of European Union law, the CJEU would not have any competence. However, the question remains as to whether this goal is reached with the new Article 5 of the Unitary Patent Regulation.

---

72. Articles 25-28 of the Agreement on a Unified Patent Court
73. Article 5.1 Unitary Patent Regulation
74. Article 5.2 Unitary Patent Regulation
75. Recital 7 of the Preamble to the Agreement on a Unified Patent Court
76. Article 25-26 of the Agreement on a Unified Patent Court
77. Article 27 of the Agreement on a Unified Patent Court

On 29-30 November 2012, the *Europäische Rechtsakademie* organised another international conference regarding unitary patent protection, which took place in Paris.[78] At this conference, Professor Tillman explained that it cannot be fully assured that Article 5 of the Unitary Patent Regulation excludes any competence of the CJEU to interpret the articles of the Agreement regarding direct and indirect use and limitations. It all depends on how the CJEU copes with the camouflaged referral by Article 5. In a formalistic or "international" interpretation, the construction can be seen as a clear split between the articles of Union law (which are to be found in the Regulation) and the articles of international law (which are to be found in the Agreement). However, in an "incorporating" interpretation, the referral by Article 5 of the Unitary Patent Regulation to the Agreement can be seen as incorporating the application of the articles of the Agreement into the Unitary Patent Regulation, which would mean that they become part of Union law.[79] Following the "incorporating" interpretation, there is still a chance that the CJEU declares itself competent to interpret Articles 25 et seq. of the Agreement.

Paragraph 4 of Article 5 Unitary Patent Regulation provides that the Commission shall evaluate the functioning of the applicable limitations in the report the Commission shall present to the European Parliament and the Council no later than three years from the date on which the first unitary patent takes effect, and every five years thereafter,[80] and, where necessary, shall make appropriate proposals for amending it.[81] According to Recital 11 of the Preamble to the Unitary Patent Regulation, the proposals from the Commission shall take into account the contribution of the patent system to innovation and technological progress, the legitimate interests of third parties or the overriding interests of society.

To avoid any interference to this competence for the Commission, Recital 11 states that the Agreement on a Unified Patent Court does not preclude the European Union from exercising its powers in this field.

With respect to damages, Recital 13 of the Preamble to the Unitary Patent Regulation provides that the regime applicable to damages shall be governed by the laws of the Participating Member States, in particular the provisions implementing Article 13 of Directive 2004/48/EC of the European Parliament and of the Council of 29 April 2004 on the enforcement of intellectual property rights (hereafter the "Enforcement Directive"). Consequently, the Unified

---

78. "The Creation of Unitary Patent Protection in the European Union", organised by ERA (*Europäische Rechtsakademie*), Paris, 29-30 November 2012
79. , "Overview of the Regulation on unitary patent protection and the applicable translation arrangements", lecture of Prof. Dr. W. TILMANN at the ERA conference in Paris
80. Article 16.1 Unitary Patent Regulation
81. Article 5 Unitary Patent Regulation

Patent Court shall have to apply national law in cases where it has to decide on damages.

H. EXHAUSTION

The rights conferred by a unitary patent shall not extend to acts concerning a product covered by that patent which are carried out within the Participating Member States in which that patent has unitary effect after that product has been placed on the market in the Union by, or with the consent of, the patent proprietor, unless there are legitimate grounds for the patent proprietor to oppose further commercialisation of the product.[82]

The principle of exhaustion laid down in the Unitary Patent Regulation is a codification of the case law of the CJEU regarding exhaustion.[83]

I. UNFAIR COMPETITION AND COMPETITION LAW

Article 15 of the Unitary Patent Regulation provides that the Regulation shall be without prejudice to the application of competition law and the law relating to unfair competition. This means that besides claims based on the infringements of the Unitary Patent Regulation, it remains possible to invoke parallel actions regarding competition law or unfair competition. Such actions shall be subject to the national laws of the Participating Member States.

J. OBJECT OF PROPERTY

1. Applicable Law

As an object of property, a unitary patent shall be treated in its entirety and in all the Participating Member States as a national patent of the Participating Member State in which that patent has unitary effect and in which, according to the European patent register:

(a) the applicant had his residence or principal place of business on the date of filing of the application for the European patent; or

(b) where point (a) does not apply, the applicant had a place of business on the date of filing of the application for the European patent.[84]

82. Article 6 Unitary Patent Regulation
83. Recital 12 of the Preamble to the Unitary Patent Regulation
84. Article 7.1 Unitary Patent Regulation

Where two or more persons are entered in the European Patent Register as joint applicants, point (a) shall apply to the joint applicant indicated first. Where this is not possible, point (a) shall apply to the next joint applicant indicated in the order of entry. Where point (a) does not apply to any of the joint applicants, point (b) shall apply accordingly.[85] Consequently, it shall become more and more important for patent applicants to make arrangements on who shall be mentioned first as the applicant. If a Dutch company and a French based researcher jointly apply for European patent protection (which can become a unitary patent), the law governing the licences to such patent shall be determined by French law, if the researcher is mentioned first in the application, or by Dutch law if the company is mentioned first.

Where no applicant had his residence, principal place of business or place of business in a Participating Member State in which that patent has unitary effect, Article 7.3 Unitary Patent Regulation stipulates that the unitary patent as an object of property shall be treated in its entirety and in all the Participating Member States as a national patent of the State where the European Patent Organisation has its headquarters. The headquarters of the European Patent Organisation and the EPO is of course located in Munich. This article has ensured Germany of a certain amount of patent litigation since all disputes regarding transfers and licences of unitary patents applied for by companies not having any place of business in the Participating Member States shall fall under German law. This rule shall not only apply to, for example, US and Chinese applicants, but also to Spanish and Italian applicants. Spain and Italy do not participate in the enhanced cooperation, but their residents can of course apply a unitary patent with effect in 25 EU Member States.

Article 7.4 Unitary Patent Regulation provides that the acquisition of a right may not be dependent on any entry in a national patent register. This article wants to prevent that by imposing an obligation to register the unitary patent in a national patent register, Participating Member States would still be able to have control over the rights conferred by the unitary patent on their territory. Imposing national requirements would be contrary to the intentions of the unitary patent.

The EPO must to be informed of any limitations, licences, transfers or revocations of unitary patents.[86]

Previous draft versions of the Unitary Patent Regulation contained provisions regarding minimum requirements for the transfer of unitary patents,[87]

85. Article 7.2 Unitary Patent Regulation

86. Article 9.1(h) Unitary Patent Regulation

87. Article 15 of the proposal for a Council Regulation on the Community patent, Working Document 13706/09 of 29 September 2009, register.consilium.europa.eu/pdf/en/09/st13/st13706.en09.pdf

rights *in rem*[88] (e.g. unitary patent as a security), levy of execution,[89] insolvency proceedings,[90] contractual licensing[91] and compulsory licences,[92] but the Participating Member States eventually agreed to delete these articles and leave all these aspects of property to national law.

2. Offer for Licences with Renewal Fee Reduction

In order to promote and facilitate the economic exploitation of an invention protected by a unitary patent,[93] Article 8 of the Unitary Patent Regulation sets up a new licensing model. Currently, patent proprietors need to find interested parties for licences by themselves, with no help from the EPO.

The proprietor of a unitary patent shall be able to file a statement at the EPO notifying that the proprietor is prepared to grant a licence. The patent proprietor to some extent makes a "licence offer" public through the EPO. Article 8.1 Unitary Patent Regulation provides that the proprietor of a European patent with unitary effect may file a statement with the EPO to the effect that the proprietor is prepared to allow any person to use the invention as a licensee in return for appropriate consideration.

The EPO shall make sure that statements on licensing are registered.[94] The Unitary Patent Regulation does not stipulate a specific register for such statements, but, in our opinion, such statements should be included in the Register for unitary patent protection and be available online in order to give third parties the opportunity to get in contact with the patent proprietor for a licence. The compensation shall remain a matter of negotiation between the parties, the only requirement the Unitary Patent Regulation sets is that the consideration should be "appropriate".[95] The term "consideration" makes it

88. Article 16 of the proposal for a Council Regulation on the Community patent, Working Document 13706/09 of 29 September 2009, register.consilium.europa.eu/pdf/en/09/st13/st13706.en09.pdf
89. Article 17 of the proposal for a Council Regulation on the Community patent, Working Document 13706/09 of 29 September 2009, register.consilium.europa.eu/pdf/en/09/st13/st13706.en09.pdf
90. Article 18 of the proposal for a Council Regulation on the Community patent, Working Document 13706/09 of 29 September 2009, register.consilium.europa.eu/pdf/en/09/st13/st13706.en09.pdf
91. Article 19 of the proposal for a Council Regulation on the Community patent, Working Document 13706/09 of 29 September 2009, register.consilium.europa.eu/pdf/en/09/st13/st13706.en09.pdf
92. Article 21-22 of the proposal for a Council Regulation on the Community patent, Working Document 13706/09 of 29 September 2009, register.consilium.europa.eu/pdf/en/09/st13/st13706.en09.pdf
93. Recital 15 of the Preamble to the Unitary Patent Regulation
94. Article 9.1(c) Unitary Patent Regulation
95. Article 8.1 Unitary Patent Regulation

clear that not only financial compensation can be granted for the licence, but also other forms of consideration, such as, for example, a cross-licence.

The EPO shall also register the licensing commitments undertaken by the proprietor of the European patent with unitary effect in international standardisation bodies and the withdrawal of licensing statements.[96] The former shall be the case if agreement is reached within a specific sector on the use of the invention as an international standard.

A licence obtained by means of the new system shall be treated as a contractual licence.[97]

Recital 15 of the Preamble and Article 11.3 of the Unitary Patent Regulation state that in case the patent proprietor files a licensing statement, the patent proprietor should benefit from a reduction of the renewal fees as from the EPO's receipt of such statement. Since the patent proprietor in our understanding remains free after submitting a licensing statement to grant a licence or not (depending, for example, on the appropriate consideration), the question is what happens if a patent proprietor files a statement for the sole purpose of receiving a renewal fee reduction and never actually concludes licences with third parties. If no security mechanism is put into place, the chances are that every patent proprietor of a unitary patent will file a licensing statement to pay lower renewal fees.

The Unified Patent Court shall have competence over disputes regarding the compensation of the licences granted following a statement to the EPO (*infra*, V.C.3).

3. Compulsory Licences

Compulsory licences for unitary patents shall be governed by the laws of the Participating Member States as regards their respective territories.[98]

K. ROLE OF THE EPO

Within the framework of the unitary patent system, the European Patent Organisation and the EPO play an important administrative role.

The EPO shall have the following tasks with respect to the unitary patent:[99]

- administer requests for unitary effect by proprietors of European patents;

96. Article 9.1(c) Unitary Patent Regulation
97. Article 8.2 Unitary Patent Regulation
98. Recital 10 of the Preamble to the Unitary Patent Regulation
99. Article 9.1 Unitary Patent Regulation

- set up the Register for unitary patent protection within the European Patent Register and administer the Register for unitary patent protection;
- receive and register statements on licensing referred to in Article 8 Unitary Patent Regulation, their withdrawal and licensing commitments undertaken by the proprietor of the unitary patent in international standardisation bodies;
- publish the translations referred to in Article 6 Translation Regulation during the transitional period referred to in that article;
- collect and administer renewal fees for unitary patents, in respect of the years following the year in which the grant is published in the *European Patent Bulletin*;
- collect and administer additional fees for late payment of renewal fees where such late payment is made within six months of the due date, as well as to distribute part of the collected renewal fees to the Participating Member States;
- administer the compensation scheme for the reimbursement of translation costs in case of applications submitted in an official language other than French, German and English;
- ensure that a request for unitary effect by a proprietor of a European patent is submitted in the language of the proceedings no later than one month after the grant is published in the *European Patent Bulletin*; and
- ensure that the unitary effect is indicated in the Register for unitary patent protection, where a request for unitary effect has been filed and, during the transitional period, has been submitted together with the translations referred to in Article 6 Translation Regulation, and that the EPO is informed of any limitations, licences, transfers or revocations of European patents with unitary effect.

In fact, the EPO shall act as a centralised one-stop-shop for administrating unitary patents.

The Participating Member States shall ensure effective legal protection before a competent court of one or several Participating Member States against the decisions of the EPO in carrying out the aforementioned tasks.[100] This role shall be taken up by the Unified Patent Court, since the Agreement on a Unified Patent Court provides for such protection in Article 33(1), §2.

To ensure the governance and supervision of the EPO tasks, the Participating Member States shall set up a select committee of the Administrative Council

100. Article 9.3 Unitary Patent Regulation

of the European Patent Organisation (hereinafter "Select Committee").[101] The possibility to set up a select committee of the Administrative Council by members of the European Patent Organisation is stipulated in Article 145 EPC. Article 145 EPC clarifies that the EPO places the staff, premises and equipment at the disposal of such Select Committee as may be necessary for the performance of its duties.

The Select Committee shall consist of 25 representatives of the Participating Member States and a representative of the Commission as an observer, as well as alternatives who will represent them in their absence.[102] The members of the Select Committee may be assisted by advisers or experts. Decisions of the Select Committee shall be taken with due regard for the position of the Commission and with a majority of three-quarters of the votes.[103]

Besides governing and supervising the special tasks of the EPO, the Select Committee shall also set the level of renewal fees and the share of distribution of the renewal fees (*infra*).

L. COOPERATION WITH NATIONAL OFFICES

Under the Swedish presidency, the Council agreed in 2009 to set up an "enhanced partnership" (not to be confused with the enhanced cooperation).[104] The aim of the enhanced partnership has always been to promote innovation by enhancing the efficiency of the patent-granting process through avoiding duplication of work. The idea was to make use of the national industrial property offices' existing expertise to strengthen the capacity of the EPO, and so enhance the overall quality of the European patent system in the future.[105] In reality, the enhanced partnership was also meant to take away the fear of national patent offices of the Member States that they would disappear or at least have a less important role to play, once the unitary patent was in place.

In the Unitary Patent Regulation itself, there are no articles relating to enhanced partnership with national offices, but the political commitment has been included in Recital 22 of the Preamble to the Unitary Patent Regulation: "An enhanced partnership between the EPO and central industrial property

101. Article 9.2, §2 Unitary Patent Regulation
102. Article 9.2, §3 Unitary Patent Regulation
103. Article 9.2, §4 Unitary Patent Regulation with reference to Article 35(2) EPC
104. Council of the European Union "Enhanced patent system in Europe – Council conclusions", Doc 17229/09, 7 December 2008, register.consilium.europa.eu/pdf/en/09/st17/st17229.en09.pdf, point 41 – 49
105. Council of the European Union "Enhanced patent system in Europe – Council conclusions", Doc 17229/09, 7 December 2008, register.consilium.europa.eu/pdf/en/09/st17/st17229.en09.pdf, point 41

offices of the Member States should enable the EPO to make regular use, where appropriate, of the result of any search carried out by central industrial property offices on a national patent application the priority of which is claimed in a subsequent European patent application. All central industrial property offices, including those which do not perform searches in the course of a national patent-granting procedure, can play an essential role under the enhanced partnership, inter alia by giving advice and support to potential patent applicants, in particular small and medium-sized enterprises, by receiving applications, by forwarding applications to the EPO and by disseminating patent information."

M. RENEWAL FEES

1. Level of Renewal Fees

Instead of paying renewal fees in every Participating Member State (as for classic European patents), patent proprietors shall only pay one single annual renewal fee for a unitary patent.

Renewal fees for unitary patents and additional fees for their late payment shall be paid to the European Patent Organisation by the patent proprietor. Those fees shall be due in respect of the years following the year in which the grant of the European patent which benefits from unitary effect is published in the *European Patent Bulletin*.[106]

Following the general rules on renewal fees, a unitary patent shall lapse if a renewal fee and, where applicable, any additional fee have not been paid in due time.[107]

The Regulation itself does not set the level of renewal fees. Setting the level of renewal fees is the responsibility of the Select Committee of the Administrative Council of the European Patent Organisation. But the Unitary Patent Regulation does provide a number of requirements which have to be respected by the Select Committee when determining the renewal fees.

The renewal fees for unitary patents should be:

- progressive throughout the term of the unitary patent protection;
- sufficient to cover all costs associated with the grant of the European patent and the administration of the unitary patent protection; and

---

106. Article 11.1 Unitary Patent Regulation
107. Article 11.2 Unitary Patent Regulation

- sufficient, together with the fees to be paid to the European Patent Organisation during the pre-grant stage, to ensure a balanced budget of the European Patent Organisation.[108]

The Unitary Patent Regulation provides that the level of the renewal fees shall be set, taking into account, among other things, the situation of specific entities such as small and medium-sized enterprises, with the aim of:

- facilitating innovation and fostering the competitiveness of European businesses;
- reflecting the size of the market covered by the patent; and
- being similar to the level of the national renewal fees for an average European patent taking effect in the Participating Member States at the time the level of the renewal fees is first set.[109]

With resepct to the first objective of facilitating innovation and fostering competitiveness, Recital 19 of the Preamble to the Unitary Patent Regulation explicitly states that the situation of specific entities such as small and medium-sized enterprises should be taken into account, for example in the form of lower fees.

In order to attain the aforementioned objectives, Article 12.3 Unitary Patent Regulation provides that the level of renewal fees shall be set at a level that:

- is equivalent to the level of the renewal fee to be paid for the average geographical coverage of current European patents;
- reflects the renewal rate of current European patents; and
- reflects the number of requests for unitary effect.

2. Distribution of Renewal Fees

The EPO shall retain an amount of 50% of the renewal fees.[110] In this respect, Article 146 EPC provides that where additional tasks have been given to the EPO, the group of Contracting States shall bear the expenses incurred by the European Patent Organisation in carrying out these tasks. Where special departments have been set up in the EPO to carry out these additional tasks, the group of Contracting States shall bear the expenditure on staff, premises and equipment chargeable in respect of these departments.

108. Article 12.1 Unitary Patent Regulation
109. Article 15.2 Unitary Patent Regulation
110. Article 10 Unitary Patent Regulation

After the 50% retained by the EPO, the remaining amount of renewal fees shall be distributed among the Participating Member States[111] and are to be used for patent-related purposes.[112] One of the possibilities could be that Participating Member States use the share of renewal fees to finance the costs of their local division of the Unified Patent Court. Hence, during the first seven years, the facilities and administrative support staff for a local division of the Court need to be financed by the Member States where the local division is located.[113]

The appropriate level and distribution of renewal fees shall be determined in order to ensure that, in relation to the unitary patent protection, all costs of the tasks entrusted to the EPO are fully covered by the resources generated by the unitary patents and that, together with the fees to be paid to the European Patent Organisation during the pre-grant stage, the revenues from the renewal fees ensure a balanced budget of the European Patent Organisation.[114]

The share of distribution of the renewal fees between the Participating Member States shall be set by the Select Committee.[115] The share of distribution of renewal fees to be set by the Select Committee shall be based on the following fair, equitable and relevant criteria:[116]

(a) the number of patent applications;
(b) the size of the market, while ensuring a minimum amount to be distributed to each Participating Member State;
(c) compensation to the Participating Member States which have:
  (i) an official language other than one of the official languages of the EPO,
  (ii) a disproportionately low level of patenting activity, and/or
  (iii) acquired membership of the European Patent Organisation relatively recently.

3. Administration by EPO

The EPO shall be responsible for the collection and administration of the renewal fees for unitary patents, in respect of the years following the year in which the grant is published in the *European Patent Bulletin*, and the distribution of the part of the collected renewal fees to the Participating Member States. The EPO shall also collect and administer additional fees for late

111. Article 13.1 Unitary Patent Regulation
112. Recital 21 of the Preamble to the Unitary Patent Regulation
113. Article 15 of the Agreement on a Unified Patent Court
114. Recital 20 of the Preamble to the Unitary Patent Regulation
115. Article 9.2 Unitary Patent Regulation
116. Article 13.2 Unitary Patent Regulation

payment of renewal fees where such late payment is made within six months of the due date.[117]

The European Commission shall establish a close cooperation through a working agreement with the EPO in the fields covered by the Unitary Patent Regulation.[118] This cooperation shall include regular exchanges of views on the functioning of the working agreement and, in particular, on the issue of renewal fees and their impact on the budget of the European Patent Organisation.

N. FOLLOW-UP

Not later than three years from the date on which the first unitary patent takes effect, and every five years thereafter, the Commission shall present to the European Parliament and the Council a report on the operation of the Unitary Patent Regulation and, where necessary, make appropriate proposals for amending it.[119]

Besides this report, the European Commission shall regularly submit to the European Parliament and the Council reports on the functioning of the renewal fees, with particular emphasis on compliance with Article 12 of the Unitary Patent Regulation.[120] It is to be seen in practice how the term "regularly" is interpreted by the European Commission.

O. ENTRY INTO FORCE AND APPLICATION

The entry into force of the Unitary Patent Regulation takes place on the twentieth day following that of its publication in the *Official Journal* of the European Union.[121] Consequently, the Unitary Patent Regulation entered into force on 20 January 2013.

However, the Unitary Patent Regulation shall only apply from 1 January 2014 or the date of entry into force of the Agreement on a Unified Patent Court, whichever is the later.[122] Since the Agreement on a Unified Patent Court shall be signed in spring 2013 and 13 ratifications are necessary for its entry

117. Article 9.1(e) Unitary Patent Regulation
118. Article 14 Unitary Patent Regulation
119. Article 16.1 Unitary Patent Regulation
120. Article 16.2 Unitary Patent Regulation
121. Article 18.1 Unitary Patent Regulation
122. Article 18.2, §1 Unitary Patent Regulation

into force, chances are small that the Unitary Patent Regulation shall be applicable in January 2014.

Moreover, the territorial scope of unitary patent protection shall in a first phase most likely be limited because of the link with the ratification of the Agreement on a Unified Patent Court. A European patent for which unitary effect is entered in the Register for unitary patent protection shall have unitary effect only in those Participating Member States in which the Unified Patent Court has exclusive jurisdiction with regard to unitary patents.[123] Consequently, the territory of unitary patent protection shall in the beginning be limited to those Member States where such patent can be litigated before the Unified Patent Court. In this respect, Recital 25 of the Preamble to the Unitary Patent Regulation states that establishing a Unified Patent Court to hear cases concerning the unitary patent is essential in order to ensure the proper functioning of that patent, consistency of case law and hence legal certainty, and cost-effectiveness for patent proprietors. According to the Preamble, it is therefore of paramount importance that the Participating Member States ratify the Agreement on a Unified Patent Court and take the necessary steps for that Court to become operational as soon as possible.

Each Participating Member State shall notify the Commission of its ratification of the Agreement on a Unified Patent Court at the time of deposit of its ratification instrument. The Commission shall publish in the *Official Journal* of the European Union the date of entry into force of the Agreement and a list of the Member States who have ratified the Agreement at the date of entry into force. The Commission shall thereafter regularly update the list of the Participating Member States that have ratified the Agreement and shall publish such updated list in the *Official Journal* of the European Union.[124]

Before the Unitary Patent Regulation can apply to a Member State, the Member State has two important tasks to fulfil. The first is to ensure that the measures referred to in Article 9 Unitary Patent Regulation are in place by the date of application of this Regulation.[125] Therefore, the Member State shall need to grant the EPO its new tasks regarding unitary patents. The second task is individual to the Member State, namely to ensure that, where the unitary effect of a European patent has been registered and extends to its territory, that European patent is deemed not to have taken effect as a national patent in its territory on the date of publication of the grant in the *European Patent Bulletin*.[126] In other words, the Member State has to adapt its national law to ensure that the national effect of a European patent is reversed as soon as the

123. Article 18.2, §2 Unitary Patent Regulation
124. Article 18.3 Unitary Patent Regulation
125. Article 18.4 Unitary Patent Regulation
126. Article 18.5 Unitary Patent Regulation

unitary effect has been registered. In the case of a Participating Member State in which the Unified Patent Court does not have exclusive jurisdiction with regard to unitary patents on the date of application of this Regulation, the national law should be modified by the date from which the Unified Patent Court has such exclusive jurisdiction in that Participating Member State.

Unitary patent protection may be requested for any European patent granted on or after the date of application of the Regulation.[127]

127. Article 18.6 Unitary Patent Regulation

Chapter IV
Translation Regime of the Unitary Patent

A. REIMBURSEMENT OF TRANSLATION COSTS FOR APPLICATION

As mentioned above, in order to receive a unitary patent, the applicant first has to obtain a European patent. Therefore, the same granting procedure before the EPO needs to be followed.

Currently, the applicant can file a European patent application in one of the official languages of the EPO (i.e. French, German or English).[128] But natural or legal persons having their residence or principal place of business within an EPC Member State having a language other than English, French or German as an official language, and nationals of that Member State who are resident abroad, may file their patent application in an official language of that Member State.[129] However, a translation into an official language of the EPO needs to be filed within two months of filing the European patent application.[130] Such persons filing in a language other than the three languages of the EPO, are entitled to a reduction of the filing fee.[131]

For unitary patents, the Translation Regulation goes a step further. If SMEs, natural persons, non-profit organisations, universities or public research organisations having their residence or principal place of business within a Participating Member State, file a European patent application at the EPO in one of the official languages of the Union that is not an official language of the EPO (i.e., any official EU languages other than French, German or English), these applicants shall be entitled to a reimbursement of all translation costs up to a ceiling.[132]

The Translation Regulation gives the EPO the task of administering a compensation scheme for the reimbursement of all translation costs up to a

128. Article 14.2 EPC
129. Article 14.4 EPC
130. Article 14.2 EPC *juncto* Rule 6.1 of the Implementing Regulations to the EPC
131. Rule 6.3 of the Implementing Regulations to the EPC
132. Article 5.1 Translation Regulation

ceiling. The compensation scheme shall be funded through the renewal fees for unitary patents.[133]

B. GENERAL PRINCIPLE: NO TRANSLATIONS

As a general principle, Article 3 Translation Regulation provides that where the specification of a European patent, which benefits from unitary effect, has been published in accordance with Article 14.6 EPC, no further translations shall be required.

Article 14.6 EPC provides that, for European patents, the specification shall be published in the language of the proceedings and shall include a translation of the claims in the other two official languages of the European Patent Office. If this is done well, as a general rule, no additional translations are required if the patent proprietor decides to file a request for unitary effect. A request for unitary effect[134] shall be submitted in the language of the proceedings before the EPO.[135]

There are two exceptions to this general rule: translations in case of a dispute and translations during a transitional period.

C. FIRST EXCEPTION: TRANSLATION IN THE EVENT OF A DISPUTE

In case of an infringement dispute, the Translation Regulation provides two different sorts of protection for the defendant. At any time during the dispute, the defendant can request a full translation of the unitary patent into an official language of either the Participating Member State in which the alleged infringement took place or the Participating Member State in which the alleged infringer is domiciled.[136] Consequently, the defendant can request a full translation when he receives a cease-and-desist letter.

Secondly, when legal proceedings have commenced, the competent court for disputes concerning unitary patents (which shall be the Unified Patent Court) can impose a full translation of the patent into the language used in the proceedings of that court.[137]

133. Article 5.2 Translation Regulation
134. Article 9 Unitary Patent Regulation
135. Article 3.2 Translation Regulation
136. Article 4.1 Translation Regulation
137. Article 4.2 Translation Regulation

The cost of translations in case of a dispute shall be borne by the patent proprietor.[138] To avoid the patent proprietor using the automatic translation software of the EPO, Recital 8 of the Preamble to the Translation Regulation stipulates that such translations may not be carried out by automated means.

One of the very important elements in finding a compromise for the language regime was that certain Member States that do not have an official language of the EPO in their country, sought to protect alleged infringers which were not aware of the patent claims. Therefore, Article 4.4 of the Translation Regulation provides that, in the event of a dispute concerning a claim for damages, the court hearing the dispute shall assess and take into consideration, in particular where the alleged infringer is an SME, a natural person or a non-profit organisation, a university or a public research organisation, whether the alleged infringer acted without knowing or without reasonable grounds for knowing, that he was infringing the unitary patent before having been provided with the translation that can be requested by the alleged infringer in case of dispute.[139]

D. SECOND EXCEPTION: THE TRANSITIONAL PERIOD

The key to the political compromise regarding the language regime was the setting up of a transitional regime. The reason for the transitional regime is that the software for machine translations is not yet available for all official languages of the European Union. For as long as automated translations could not provide alleged infringers with the necessary information regarding patents, the Participating Member States felt that, during a transitional period, manual translations still had to be available.

The transitional period shall start on the date of application of the Translation Regulation.[140]

Six years after the date of application of the Translation Regulation and every two years thereafter, an independent expert committee shall carry out an objective evaluation of the availability of high-quality machine translations of patent applications and specifications into all the official languages of the Union, as developed by the EPO.[141] This expert committee shall be established by the Participating Member States in the framework of the European Patent Organisation and shall be composed of representatives of the EPO and of the non-governmental organisations representing users of the European patent

138. Article 4.3 Translation Regulation
139. Article 4.4 Translation Regulation
140. Article 6.1 Translation Regulation
141. Article 6.3 Translation Regulation

system invited by the Administrative Council of the European Patent Organisation as observers.[142]

On the basis of the first of the evaluations and every two years thereafter on the basis of the subsequent evaluations, the European Commission shall present a report to the Council and, if appropriate, make proposals for terminating the transitional period.[143]

If the transitional period is not terminated on the basis of a proposal of the Commission, it shall lapse twelve years from the date of application of the Translation Regulation.[144] In practice, the chances are small that the transitional period shall be terminated earlier than twelve years from the date of application because the 25 Participating Member States have to take a unanimous decision to terminate the transitional period.

1. German or French to English

During the transitional period, a request for unitary effect shall have to be submitted together with a full translation of the specification of the European patent into English, where the language of the proceedings before the EPO is French or German.[145]

Recital 12 of the Preamble to the Translation Regulation explains that this should ensure that, during a transitional period, all unitary patents are made available in English, which is the language customarily used in the field of international technological research and in publications.

2. English to Other Official Language

Where the language of the proceedings is English, a full translation of the specification of the European patent into any other official language of the Union shall have to be submitted together with the request for unitary effect.[146]

This would ensure that, with respect to unitary patents, translations would be published in the other official languages of the Participating Member States.[147]

The question remains as to the sanction on a patent proprietor for submitting a request for unitary effect without the appropriate translation. A literal reading of the term "together" in Article 5 Translation Regulation leads to the

142. Article 30.3 EPC
143. Article 6.4 Translation Regulation
144. Article 6.5 Translation Regulation
145. Article 6.1(a) Translation Regulation
146. Article 6.1(b) Translation Regulation
147. Recital 12 of the Preamble to the Translation Regulation

conclusion that if no request and a manual translation of the specification are submitted within the first month after grant of the European patent, no unitary effect shall be obtained.[148]

3. Publication by EPO

During the transitional period, the EPO shall have the task of publishing the translations as soon as possible after the date of the submission of a request for unitary effect as referred to in Article 9 of the Unitary Patent Regulation.[149]

4. For Information Purposes Only

Just as for automated machine translations, the text of the manual translations during the transitional regime shall have no legal effect and shall be for information purposes only.[150] Only the specification of the patent in the language of the proceeding shall have legal effect.

Nevertheless, such translations may not be carried out by automated means. Their high quality should even contribute to the training of translation engines by the EPO and would also enhance the dissemination of patent information.[151]

E. ENTRY INTO FORCE

The arrangements for the entry into force and application of the Translation Regulation are of course the same as for the entry into force of the Unitary Patent Regulation. The Regulation entered into force on the twentieth day following that of its publication in the *Official Journal* of the European Union, i.e., 20 January 2013.[152]

The Translation Regulation shall apply from 1 January 2014 or the date of entry into force of the Agreement on a Unified Patent Court, whichever is the later.[153]

To overcome the current shortcomings of the whole of the European patent system, the 25 Member States participating in the enhanced cooperation

---

148. "The European Patent with unitary effect and the role of the EPO" lecture by Dr. Pierre Treichel at the conference "The Creation of Unitary Patent Protection in the European Union", organised by ERA (*Europäische Rechtsakademie*), Paris, 29-30 November 2012
149. Article 6.2 Translation Regulation
150. Article 6.2 Translation Regulation
151. Recital 12 of the Preamble to the Translation Regulation
152. Article 7.1 Translation Regulation
153. Article 7.2 Translation Regulation

felt that it was not enough to install a new patent with lower translation costs and a one-stop-shop for renewal fees. The Participating Member States decided that in order to improve the patent system it was necessary to also install a pan-European patent court. Because the Participating Member States see the Unified Patent Court as an integral part of the unitary patent package, they linked the application of the Unitary Patent Regulation and the Translation Regulation to the application of the Unified Patent Court.

THE UNIFIED PATENT COURT

Chapter I

Legal Status of the Agreement and the Unified Patent Court

A. TREATY BETWEEN 25 EU MEMBER STATES

On 19 February 2013, the 25 EU Member States participating in the enhanced cooperation regarding unitary patent protection shall have the opportunity to sign the Agreement on a Unified Patent Court (the "Agreement").

The Agreement is nothing more or less than a treaty that can be ratified by Austria, Belgium, Bulgaria, Cyprus, the Czech Republic, Denmark, Estonia, Finland, France, Germany, Greece, Hungary, Ireland, Latvia, Lithuania, Luxembourg, Malta, the Netherlands, Poland, Portugal, Romania, Slovakia, Slovenia, Sweden and the United Kingdom (the "Contracting Member States").

Other than the two Regulations regarding the unitary patent, the Agreement is not an instrument of Union law. It is not a European Union treaty, but merely an international agreement between the participating countries which are also Member States of the European Union.

B. CJEU OPINION ON CONFORMITY WITH EU TREATIES

The legal status of the Agreement and the Court were a major issue during the negotiations of the Agreement. The Member States were looking for a way to fit the new litigation system into the existing legal order of Union law and determine its position with respect to national law and to other international treaties (e.g. the EPC). The biggest difficulty appeared to be the match with Union law. Therefore, on 6 July 2009 the Council requested an opinion of the CJEU on the question of whether "the envisaged agreement creating a Unified Patent Litigation System[154] is compatible with the provisions of the Treaty establishing the European Community".

154. At the time of the request named "European and Community Patents Court"

The CJEU took two years to form its opinion, which paralysed negotiations on the draft Agreement. But meanwhile, the Council used the time to find a political comprise on the language regime for the unitary patent (*supra*, Unitary Patent, I.E-F).

The opinion of the CJEU (the "Opinion") was delivered on 8 March 2011,[155] and was negative. According to the full Court of Justice, the envisaged agreement creating a unified patent litigation system was not compatible with the provisions of the TEU and TFEU.

The CJEU had major concerns about the respect for some basic principles of Union law, such as the primacy of Union law and the liability of the Member States in case of infringement of Union law. Luckily, the CJEU itself gave some guidance in its Opinion as to how the basic principles of Union law could be respected by an international court system by giving the example of the Benelux Court of Justice.[156] Based on the CJEU Opinion, the Council amended the Agreement.

1. Primacy of Union Law

In its Opinion, the CJEU stressed that the founding treaties of the European Union had established a new legal order, for the benefit of which the Member States limited their sovereign rights. The essential characteristics of the European Union legal order are in particular its primacy over the laws of the Member States and the direct effect of a whole series of provisions which are applicable to the Member States themselves and to their nationals.[157]

The Member States are obliged, *inter alia* by the principle of sincere cooperation,[158] to ensure, in their respective territories, the application of and respect for European Union law.[159] The national court, in collaboration with the Court of Justice, fulfils a duty to ensure that the interpretation and application of the Treaties the Union law is observed.[160]

The draft Agreement as it was presented to the CJEU, described a court system which was outside the institutional and judicial framework of the European Union, and to which even non-EU Member States could adhere. The patent court as it was first developed was an organisation with a distinct legal personality under international law. The problem for the CJEU was that through this system the courts of the EU Member States would be divested

155. Opinion 1/09 of the (full) Court of Justice, 8 March 2011, www.curia.europa.eu
156. Opinion 1/09 of the (full) Court of Justice, 8 March 2011, www.curia.europa.eu, point 82
157. Opinion 1/09 of the (full) Court of Justice, 8 March 2011, www.curia.europa.eu, point 65
158. Article 4.3 TEU
159. Opinion 1/09 of the (full) Court of Justice, 8 March 2011, www.curia.europa.eu, point 68
160. Opinion 1/09 of the (full) Court of Justice, 8 March 2011, www.curia.europa.eu, point 69

of certain powers with respect to patent law and the envisaged patent court would have the duty to interpret and apply EU law.[161]

According to the CJEU, the envisaged court would interpret and apply the future regulation on the Community patent (now the unitary patent) and other instruments of European Union law, in particular regulations and directives in conjunction with which that regulation would, if necessary, have to be read – namely provisions relating to other bodies of rules on intellectual property, and rules of the TFEU concerning the internal market and competition law.

The CJEU earlier ruled that international agreements creating a court responsible for the interpretation of the provisions of its own agreement, are not in principle incompatible with European Union law. An international agreement may even affect the own powers of the CJEU provided that the indispensable conditions for safeguarding the essential character of those powers are satisfied and, consequently, there is no adverse effect on the autonomy of the European Union legal order.[162]

As an example of an international agreement which respects the aforementioned principles, the CJEU referred to the Benelux Court of Justice. Since the Benelux Court is a court common to a number of Member States, situated, consequently, within the judicial system of the European Union, the CJEU was of the opinion that the decisions of the Benelux Court are subject to mechanisms capable of ensuring the full effectiveness of the rules of the European Union.[163]

Therefore, according to the CJEU Opinion, the Member States re-designed the legal status of the Unified Patent Court in the image of the Benelux Court of Justice. In the current Agreement it is no longer possible for non-EU countries (e.g. Switzerland) to be a member of the Unified Patent Court system. Additionally, the current Agreement clarifies that the Unified Patent Court is a court "common to the Contracting Member States".

To this respect paragraph 7 of the Preamble to the Agreement states that "the Unified Patent Court should be a court common to the Contracting Member States and thus part of their judicial system, with exclusive competence in respect of European patents with unitary effect and European patents granted under the provisions of the EPC". Under paragraph 9, the Preamble recalls that "the obligations of the Contracting Member States under the Treaty on European Union (TEU) and the Treaty on the Functioning of the European Union (TFEU), including the obligation of sincere cooperation as set out in Article 4(3) TEU and the obligation to ensure through the Unified Patent Court

161. Opinion 1/09 of the (full) Court of Justice, 8 March 2011, www.curia.europa.eu, point 73
162. Opinion 1/09 of the (full) Court of Justice, 8 March 2011, www.curia.europa.eu, point 74-76
163. Opinion 1/09 of the (full) Court of Justice, 8 March 2011, www.curia.europa.eu, point 82

the full application of, and respect for, Union law in their respective territories and the judicial protection of an individual's rights under that law".

In the Agreement itself, Article 1 clearly stipulates that the Unified Patent Court shall be a court common to the Contracting Member States and thus subject to the same obligations under Union law as any national court of the Contracting Member States. Article 20 confirms that the Court shall apply Union law in its entirety and shall respect its primacy.

Paragraph 13 of the Preamble recalls that Union law includes the TEU, the TFEU, the Charter of Fundamental Rights of the European Union, the general principles of Union law as developed by the Court of Justice of the European Union, and in particular the right to an effective remedy before a tribunal and a fair and public hearing within a reasonable time by an independent and impartial tribunal, the case law of the Court of Justice of the European Union and secondary Union law. The Court shall always have to respect all these instruments of Union law in its decisions.

2. Preliminary Rulings of the CJEU

The principle of primacy of Union law and its correct application have to be safeguarded by the courts of the Member States and the CJEU.

In its Opinion, the CJEU recalled that Article 267 TFEU (regarding preliminary rulings by the CJEU) aims to ensure that, in all circumstances, Union law has the same effect in all Member States. The preliminary ruling mechanism aims to avoid divergences in the interpretation of European Union law that the national courts have to apply and tends to ensure this application by making available to national judges a means of eliminating difficulties which may be occasioned by the requirement of giving European Union law its full effect within the framework of the judicial systems of the Member States.[164] The system set up by Article 267 TFEU therefore establishes direct cooperation between the Court of Justice and the national courts as part of which the latter are closely involved in the correct application and uniform interpretation of European Union law and also in the protection of individual rights conferred by that legal order.[165]

The CJEU concluded in its Opinion that the envisaged agreement "by conferring on an international court which is outside the institutional and judicial framework of the European Union an exclusive jurisdiction to hear a significant number of actions brought by individuals in the field of the Community patent and to interpret and apply European Union law in that

164. Opinion 1/09 of the (full) Court of Justice, 8 March 2011, www.curia.europa.eu, point 83
165. Opinion 1/09 of the (full) Court of Justice, 8 March 2011, www.curia.europa.eu, point 83

field, would deprive courts of Member States of their powers in relation to the interpretation and application of European Union law and the Court of its powers to reply, by preliminary ruling, to questions referred by those courts and, consequently, would alter the essential character of the powers which the Treaties confer on the institutions of the European Union and on the Member States and which are indispensable to the preservation of the very nature of European Union law."[166] According to the CJEU, the power of the Unified Patent Court to apply and interpret the Unitary Patent Regulation and other EU legal instruments results in depriving the national courts of doing so and of the CJEU ensuring the correct interpretation through preliminary rulings.

In response to the Opinion of the CJEU, the Preamble to the Agreement now considers, under paragraph 8, that the CJEU is to ensure the uniformity of the Union legal order and the primacy of European Union law. The Preamble further stresses under paragraph 10 the parallel between the duty of the national courts and the duty of the Unified Patent Court. As for any national court, the Unified Patent Court must respect and apply Union law and, in collaboration with the CJEU as guardian of Union law, ensure its correct application and uniform interpretation. The Unified Patent Court must in particular cooperate with the CJEU in properly interpreting Union law by relying on the latter›s case law and by requesting preliminary rulings in accordance with Article 267 TFEU.[167]

In the Agreement itself the requests for preliminary rulings are laid down in Article 21. This article provides that as a court common to the Contracting Member States and as part of their judicial system, the Unified Patent Court shall cooperate with the CJEU to ensure the correct application and uniform interpretation of Union law, as any national court, in accordance with Article 267 TFEU in particular.

3. Liability for Infringements of Union Law

Another important remark of the CJEU Opinion was that the submitted draft Agreement could not ensure the liability of the Contracting (Member) States for the non-respect of Union law. This would certainly not be the case if non-EU Member States could participate in the Unified Patent Court.

According to the CJEU, the principle that a Member State is obliged to make good damage caused to individuals as a result of breaches of European Union law for which it is responsible, also applies, under specific conditions, to judicial bodies of a Member State that infringe European Union law.[168] If

166. Opinion 1/09 of the (full) Court of Justice, 8 March 2011, www.curia.europa.eu, point 89
167. §10 of the Preamble to the Agreement
168. Opinion 1/09 of the (full) Court of Justice, 8 March 2011, www.curia.europa.eu, point 86

Union law is infringed, the provisions of Articles 258 TFEU to 260 TFEU provide for the opportunity of bringing a case before the Court to obtain a declaration that the Member State concerned has failed to fulfil its obligations.

Under the draft Agreement which was subject to the CJEU Opinion, a decision of the envisaged patent court which was in breach of Union law could not be attacked by infringement proceedings nor could it give rise to any financial liability on the part of one or more Member States.[169]

To align itself to the CJEU Opinion, the Agreement now contains a liability system for the Contracting Member States in case of infringement of Union law.

Paragraph 11 of the Preamble stipulates that, in general, the Contracting Member States should, in line with the case law of the CJEU on non-contractual liability, be liable for damages caused by infringements of Union law by the Unified Patent Court, including the failure to request preliminary rulings from the CJEU. Further, paragraph 12 adds that infringements of Union law by the Unified Patent Court, including the failure to request preliminary rulings from the CJEU, are directly attributable to the Contracting Member States and infringement proceedings can therefore be brought under Articles 258, 259 and 260 TFEU against any Contracting Member State to ensure the respect of the primacy and proper application of Union law.

Liability in case of a judgment of a national court is easily attributable to a Member State, but the question arose as to what would happen if a court that was common to all Member States, infringes the Union Law. Article 22(1) of the Agreement provides that the Contracting Member States are jointly and severally liable for damage resulting from an infringement of Union law by the Court of Appeal, in accordance with Union law concerning non-contractual liability of Member States for damage caused by their national courts breaching Union law.

To avoid that, in case of damages, the claimant should start proceedings in all Contracting Member States, Article 22(2) works out a procedure to obtain damages for infringement of Union law. An action for such damages shall be brought against the Contracting Member State where the claimant has its residence or principal place of business or, in the absence of residence or principal place of business, its place of business, before the competent authority of that Contracting Member State. Where the claimant does not have its residence, or principal place of business or, in the absence of residence or principal place of business, its place of business in a Contracting Member State, the claimant may bring such an action against the Contracting Member State where the Court of Appeal has its seat (i.e., Luxembourg), before the competent authority

169. Opinion 1/09 of the (full) Court of Justice, 8 March 2011, www.curia.europa.eu, point 88

of that Contracting Member State. This article first determines against which Contracting Member State the action should be brought. Once the (defending) Contracting Member State has been determined, the claimant brings its action before the competent court of that Member State. This means that the national courts of the Contracting Member State against which the action is directed, are competent to decide on the liability.

The competent authority shall apply the *lex fori*, with the exception of its private international law, to all questions not regulated by Union law or by this Agreement. The claimant shall be entitled to obtain the entire amount of damages awarded by the competent authority from the Contracting Member State against which the action was brought.[170]

With the aforementioned procedure, the claimant shall obtain the full amount of damages from one Contracting Member State. Given the joint and several liability of all Contracting Member States for infringement of Union law, the Contracting Member State that has paid damages is entitled to obtain a proportional contribution from the other Contracting Member States.[171] The proportion of the Contracting Member States' contribution shall be calculated in the same way as the initial financial contributions the Contracting Member States need to pay for financing the Court. This means that during the transitional period of seven years, the number of European patents having effect in the territory of that State on the date of entry into force of this Agreement and the number of European patents with respect to which actions of infringement or for revocation have been brought before the national courts of that State in the three years preceding entry into force or ratification of the Agreement, shall be taken into account to determine the contribution.[172] Afterwards, the contribution shall be determined in accordance with the scale for the distribution of annual renewal fees for unitary patents applicable at the time of contribution.[173]

The detailed rules governing the Contracting Member States' contribution in the damages shall be determined by the Administrative Committee.[174]

Finally, Article 23 of the Agreement affirms that actions of the Court are directly attributable to each Contracting Member State individually, including for the purposes of Articles 258, 259 and 260 TFEU, and to all Contracting Member States collectively. Articles 258, 259 and 260 TFEU deal with the infringement procedure the Commission or a Member State can initiate if one or more of the EU Member States fails to fulfil an obligation under the

170. Article 22(2) of the Agreement
171. Article 22(3) of the Agreement
172. Article 37(3) of the Agreement
173. Article 37(4) of the Agreement
174. Article 22(3) of the Agreement

EU Treaties. Consequently, a decision or other action of the Unified Patent Court which would infringe an obligation under the EU Treaties, shall be an infringement of all Participating Member States, for which all Participating Member States can be brought by the Commission or any other EU Member State before the CJEU.

C. LEGAL CAPACITY OF THE COURT

The Court shall have legal personality in each Contracting Member State and shall enjoy the most extensive legal capacity accorded to legal persons under the national law of that State.[175]

The President of the Court of Appeal, who shall be elected in accordance with the Statute, shall be able to represent the Court towards third parties.[176]

The contractual liability of the Court shall be governed by the law applicable to the contract in question in accordance with the Rome I Regulation[177], where applicable, or in accordance with the law of the Member State of the court seized.[178]

The non-contractual liability of the Court in respect of any damage caused by it or its staff in the performance of their duties, to the extent that it is not a civil and commercial matter within the meaning of the Rome II Regulation,[179] shall be governed by the law of the Contracting Member State in which the damage occurred. The court with jurisdiction to settle disputes concerning non-contractual liability shall be a court of the Contracting Member State in which the damage occurred.[180]

175. Article 4(1) of the Agreement
176. Article 4(2) of the Agreement
177. Regulation No. 593/2008 of 17 June 2008 on the law applicable to contractual obligations (Rome I), L177/6, 4 July 2008
178. Article 5(1) of the Agreement
179. Regulation No. 864/2007 of 11 July 2007 on the law applicable to non-contractual obligations (Rome II), L199/40, 31 July 2007
180. Article 5(3) of the Agreement

Chapter II
Structure of the Court

The Unified Patent Court shall have an atypical structure. Therefore, when analysing the functioning of the Court, it is important to first clearly understand the different institutions of the Court. The understanding of this structure should be an important guideline for Member States to determine how they take part in the Unified Patent Court.

The Court shall comprise two levels: the Court of First Instance and the Court of Appeal.

A. COURT OF FIRST INSTANCE

The Court of First Instance shall comprise three categories of division: one central division combined with different local and regional divisions.[181]

Although the terminology ("central") could lead to a different conclusion, it is very important to understand that the central division and the local and regional divisions all act at the same level of jurisdiction. There is no hierarchy between the divisions. All division shall treat patent disputes as a first instance court. Nevertheless, each division has its own competence and in some cases there is exclusive jurisdiction for the central division.

1. Central Division

The main difference between the three divisions is their geographical location. Here again, the name "central" division could be misleading. As a result of a political comprise between Germany, France and the United Kingdom, the European Council of 29 June 2012 decided that the central division shall have three locations. The seat of the central division shall be in Paris, but the central division shall also have sections in London and Munich.

Annex II to the Agreement stipulates the type of cases each geographical section of the central division shall handle. The distribution of cases has been

181. Article 7 of the Agreement

determined according to the eight sections (A to H) of the WIPO International Patent Classification.[182] The London section shall deal with patent disputes in the field of human necessities (A) and chemistry/metallurgy (C). Consequently, London shall play an important role in the pharmaceutical and biotech case law. The Munich section shall be responsible for patent cases in the field of mechanical engineering, lighting, heating, weapons and blasting (F), confirming the great importance Germany historically attaches to mechanical engineering. The Paris seat shall treat all cases in the field of performing operations and transporting (B), textiles and paper (D), fixed constructions (E), physics (G) and electricity (H).

The office of the President of the Court of First Instance shall also be located in Paris. According to Article 13 of the Statute, the President of the Court of First Instance shall be elected by all full-time judges of the Court of First Instance from among their number, for a term of three years. The President may be re-elected twice. The elections of the President shall be by secret ballot. A judge obtaining an absolute majority shall be elected. If no judge obtains an absolute majority, a second ballot shall be held and the judge obtaining the most votes shall be elected. If the office of the President falls vacant before the date of expiry of his or her term, a successor shall be elected for the remainder thereof.

However, in order to facilitate the practical setting up of the Court of First Instance, the first President of the Court of First Instance shall be a national of the Contracting Member State hosting the seat of the central division, which is France.[183] After the initial three-year period, the first President of the Court of First Instance can be re-elected by all full-time judges of the Court of First Instance.

The President of the Court of First Instance shall direct the judicial activities and the administration of the Court of First Instance.[184]

2. Local Division

Each Member State can request to set up a local division of the Court of First Instance.[185] Such a request has to be addressed to the Chairman of the Administrative Committee and indicate the seat of the local division. The decision for setting up a local division has to be taken by the Administrative Committee. The decision shall indicate the number of judges for the division and

182. www.wip.int/classifications/ipc/en
183. Article 14(2) of the Statute
184. Article 14(3) of the Statute
185. Article 7(3) of the Agreement

shall be public.[186] The Administrative Committee shall be composed of one representative per Contracting Member State, each having one vote (*infra*, II.E.1). Decisions are taken with a majority of three-quarters of the Contracting Member States represented and voting.[187]

The Agreement does not include any thresholds for setting up a local division, which may indicate that each Member State (including Member States with only a few patent cases per year) is encouraged to set up a local division.

Upon request of the Contracting Member State, an additional local division can be set up in that Contracting Member State for every one hundred patent cases per calendar year that have been commenced in that Contracting Member State during three successive years prior to or subsequent to the date of entry into force of the Agreement.[188] The number of local divisions in one Contracting Member State may not exceed four. The maximum number of local divisions per Contracting Member State was originally three, but the Competitive Council of 6 December 2011 decided to extend this to four,[189] which primarily favours Germany. Currently, only Germany can be expected to reach more than 300 patent cases per year.

3. Regional Division

A regional division shall be set up for two or more Contracting Member States. The same procedure as for setting up a local division needs to be followed (request to the Chairman of the Administrative Committee and decision of the Administrative Committee).[190] The requesting Contracting Member States shall designate the seat of the division concerned. The regional division may hear cases in multiple locations.

The purpose of regional divisions is to offer Contracting Member States the opportunity to cooperate in patent litigation. Nothing in the Agreement or the Statute prohibits cooperation between non-neighbouring Contracting Member States. Therefore, a regional division between, for example, UK and Sweden would be theoretically possible. It is less clear whether a regional division should cover the whole territory of a Contracting Member State and if a Contracting Member State can take part in several regional divisions.

Since a regional division can hear cases in different locations, it is theoretically perfectly possible that, for example, the Scandinavian countries form a regional division which has three or more locations in each of the

186. Article 18(1) and 18(2) of the Statute
187. Article 12 of the Agreement
188. Article 7(4) of the Agreement
189. Council of the European Union, working document 18239/11, 6 December 2011
190. Article 7(5) of the Agreement

Contracting Member States. In our opinion, the possibility to hear cases in multiple locations makes it possible to work in a regional division with three permanent "sub-divisions" on different locations.

It is unclear if Contracting Member States can participate in a regional division while at the same time having a local division. Nothing in the Agreement or Statute explicitly prohibits such combination.

4. Discontinuance of a Local or Regional Division

The Administrative Committee shall decide to discontinue a local or regional division at the request of the Contracting Member State hosting the local division or a Contracting Member States participating in the regional division. The decision to discontinue a local or regional division shall state the date after which no new cases may be brought before the division and the date on which the division will cease to exist.[191]

As from the date on which a local or regional division ceases to exist, the judges assigned to that local or regional division shall be assigned to the central division, and cases still pending before that local or regional division together with the sub-registry and all of its documentation shall be transferred to the central division.[192]

B. COURT OF APPEAL

The Court of Appeal shall have its seat in one location, Luxembourg.[193]

As for the President of the Court of First Instance, the President of the Court of Appeal shall be elected by all judges of the Court of Appeal for a term of three years, from among their number. The President of the Court of Appeal may be re-elected twice and the elections take place in the same way as for the President of the Court of First Instance.[194]

Unlike the President of the Court of First Instance, the first President of the Court of Appeal is not appointed by the hosting Contracting Member State (Luxembourg).

The President of the Court of Appeal shall direct the judicial activities and the administration of the Court of Appeal and chair the Court of Appeal sitting as a full court.[195]

---

191. Article 18(3) of the Statute
192. Article 18(4) of the Statute
193. Article 9 of the Agreement
194. Article 13(1) of the Statute
195. Article 13(3) of the Statute

C. NO LEGAL REVIEW INSTANCE – PRELIMINARY RULINGS OF THE COURT OF JUSTICE

Unlike several Contracting Member States, the Unified Patent Court system does not provide an instance which carries out a legal review.[196]

However, since the Unified Patent Court shall be considered as a national court under EU law, the CJEU remains the guardian of the correct application and uniform interpretation of EU law. In practice, this means that the Unified Patent Court shall be obliged to rely on the case law of the CJEU in matters of Union law and request preliminary questions in accordance with Article 267 TFEU for matters of Union law.[197]

In practice, the application of Article 267 TFEU shall mean that, if a question regarding the validity and interpretation of Union law is raised before the Court of First Instance (which is to be considered as a court of the Member States), the Court of First Instance may, if it considers that a decision on the question is necessary to enable it to give judgment, request the Court of Justice to give a ruling thereon. When a question is raised in a case pending before the Court of Appeal, the Court of Appeal is obliged to bring the matter before the Court of Justice. Decisions of the CJEU shall be binding on the Unified Patent Court.[198]

The procedures established by the CJEU for referrals for preliminary rulings within the European Union shall apply to the Unified Patent Court.[199]

Whenever the Court of First Instance or the Court of Appeal has decided to refer to the CJEU a question of interpretation of the Treaty on the Functioning of the European Union or of the Treaty on European Union or a question on the validity or interpretation of acts of the institutions of the European Union, it shall stay its proceedings.[200]

D. THE REGISTRY

Since the Unified Patent Court is a supranational court, it cannot rely on the registries of the national courts of the Contracting Member States for its functioning. Therefore, a Registry shall be set up at the seat of the Court of Appeal.

---

196. Like the *Cour de Cassation* in France and Belgium, the *Hoge Raad* in the Netherlands or the *Bundesgerichtshof* in Germany
197. §10 of the Preamble to the Agreement
198. Article 21 of the Agreement
199. Article 38(1) of the Statute
200. Article 62(2) of the Agreement

It shall be managed by a Registrar and shall be public. Sub-registries shall be set up at all divisions of the Court of First Instance.[201]

The purpose of the Registry is to keep records of all cases before the Court. Upon filing, the sub-registry concerned shall notify every case to the Registry.

The Presidium shall appoint the Registrar for a (renewable) term of six years.[202] Two weeks before the date fixed for appointing the Registrar, the President of the Court of Appeal shall inform the Presidium of the applications that have been submitted for the post. Before taking up his or her duties, the Registrar shall swear an oath before the Presidium to perform the duties of the Registrar impartially and conscientiously.

The Registrar may be removed from office only if the Registrar no longer meets the obligations arising from his or her office. Only the Presidium can take such decision after having heard the Registrar. If the office of the Registrar falls vacant before the date of expiry of the term thereof, the Presidium shall appoint a new Registrar for a term of six years.[203]

The Registrar assists the Court, the President of the Court of Appeal, the President of the Court of First Instance and the judges in the performance of their functions. The Registrar shall be responsible for the organisation and activities of the Registry under the authority of the President of the Court of Appeal.

The duties of the Registrar are laid down in Article 18 of the Statute. The Registrar shall not only be responsible for keeping the register which shall include records of all cases before the Court, but also for keeping and administering the list with the Pool of Judges,[204] the list of European patent attorneys authorised to represent parties before the Court[205] and an indicative list of court experts.[206] The Registrar shall keep and publish a list of notifications and withdrawals of opt-outs from the exclusive jurisdiction of the Court by European patent proprietors or applicants[207] and ensure that the information on opt-outs is notified to the European Patent Office. The Registrar shall also publish the decisions of the Court (paying attention to the protection of confidential information) and the annual reports of the Court with statistical data. Up to now there has been very little statistical information within the Contracting Member States regarding patent litigation. Therefore, an annual report of the Court shall be useful to monitor European patent litigation.

201. Article 10 of the Agreement
202. Article 22 of the Statute
203. Article 22(5) of the Statute
204. Article 18 of the Agreement
205. Article 48(3) of the Agreement
206. Article 57(2) of the Agreement
207. Article 83 of the Agreement

Rules governing the Registry shall be adopted by the Presidium. Such rules shall include detailed rules for keeping the register of the Court. The rules on access to documents of the Registry are part of the Rules of Procedure.[208]

The Registry shall also have a Deputy-Registrar responsible for the organisation and activities of sub-registries under the authority of the Registrar and the President of the Court of First Instance.[209] The Deputy-Registrar shall be appointed for a term of six years by the Presidium and may be re-appointed. The duties of the Deputy-Registrar shall in particular include keeping records of all cases before the Court of First Instance and notifying every case before the Court of First Instance to the Registry.[210] The Deputy-Registrar shall also provide administrative and secretarial assistance to the divisions of the Court of First Instance.

E. ADMINISTRATIVE BODIES

In order to ensure the effective implementation and operation of the Unified Patent Court, the Agreement and Statute set up a number of administrative bodies.

1. The Administrative Committee

Each Contracting Member State shall have one representative in the Administrative Committee. The European Commission shall be represented at the meetings of the Administrative Committee as observer.[211]

Each Contracting Member State shall have one vote in the Administrative Committee. The Administrative Committee shall adopt its decisions by a majority of three-quarters of the Contracting Member States represented and voting.[212] The Administrative Committee shall elect a chairperson from among its members for a term of three years. That term shall be renewable.[213]

One of the first decisions of the Administrative Committee shall be the adoption of the Rules of Procedure. Given the fact that the Unified Patent Court is not a part of a national court system, this supranational Court needs its own set of rules of procedure. As can be seen in the second part of this publication, the draft Rules of Procedure are difficult marriage between the

208. Article 24 of the Statute
209. Article 25 of the Statute
210. Article 25(3) of the Statute
211. Article 12(1) of the Agreement
212. Article 12(2) and (3) of the Agreement
213. Article 12(3) of the Agreement

civil law and the common law traditions. The current version of the draft Rules of Procedure shall most certainly have to be further refined in order to be workable.

2. The Budget Committee

As for the Administrative Committee, the Budget Committee shall be composed of one representative of each Contracting Member State, each having one vote.[214] The European Commission is not a member, nor an observer of the Budget Committee.

The main task of the Budget Committee is of course adopting the budget. The budget shall be adopted by the Budget Committee on a proposal from the Presidium.[215]

The Budget Committee shall adopt its own set of rules of procedure and take its decisions by a simple majority of the representatives of the Contracting Member States. However, a majority of three-quarters of the representatives of Contracting Member States shall be required for the adoption of the budget.[216]

The Budget Committee shall elect a chairperson from among its members for a renewable term of three years.[217]

3. The Advisory Committee

The Advisory Committee shall comprise patent judges and practitioners in patent law and patent litigation with the highest recognised competence.[218] They shall be appointed for a renewable term of six years. Each Contracting Member State shall propose a member of the Advisory Committee who fulfils the aforementioned requirements. The members of the Advisory Committee shall be appointed by the Administrative Committee acting by common accord.[219]

The duty of the Advisory Committee is to assist the Administrative Committee in the preparation of the appointment of judges of the Court, make proposals to the Presidium regarding guidelines for the training framework for judges and deliver opinions to the Administrative Committee concerning

214. Article 13(1) and (2) of the Agreement
215. Article 26 of the Statute
216. Article 13(3) and 13(4) of the Agreement
217. Article 13(5) of the Agreement
218. Article 14(2) of the Agreement
219. Article 5 of the Statute

the requirements for qualifications of European patent attorneys to represent parties before the Court.[220]

The composition of the Advisory Committee shall ensure a broad range of relevant expertise and the representation of each of the Contracting Member States. The members of the Advisory Committee shall be completely independent in the performance of their duties and shall not be bound by any instructions.[221] The Advisory Committee shall adopt its own rules of procedure and shall elect a chairperson from among its members for a renewable term of three years.[222]

4. The Presidium

The Presidium is a body which is not set up by the Agreement, but by the Statute. The Presidium shall be composed of the President of the Court of Appeal, who shall act as chairperson, the President of the Court of First Instance, two judges of the Court of Appeal elected from among their number, three judges of the Court of First Instance who are full-time judges of the Court elected from among their number, and the Registrar as a non-voting member.[223] The voting members of the Presidium are all judges. Therefore, the Presidium can be considered as the "managing judges" of the Court.

The Presidium can take valid decisions only when all members are present or duly represented. Decisions shall be taken by a majority of the votes.[224]

The Presidium shall be responsible for the management of the Court and shall in particular draw up proposals for the amendment of the Rules of Procedure and proposals regarding the Financial Regulations of the Court, prepare the annual budget, the annual accounts and the annual report of the Court and submit them to the Budget Committee, establish the guidelines for the training programme for judges and supervise the implementation thereof, take decisions on the appointment and removal of the Registrar and the Deputy-Registrar, lay down the rules governing the Registry including the sub-registries and give an opinion after five years from the entry into force of the Agreement on the reasons for and implications of actions based on European patents that are still brought before national courts.[225]

220. Article 14(1) of the Agreement
221. Article 14(3) of the Agreement
222. Article 14(5) of the Agreement
223. Article 15(1) of the Statute
224. Article 15(5) of the Statute
225. Article 83(5) of the Agreement

F. PATENT MEDIATION AND ARBITRATION CENTRE

Besides a Patent Court, the Agreement also establishes a Patent Mediation and Arbitration Centre (the "Centre"). The Centre shall have its seats in Ljubljana and Lisbon.[226]

The Centre shall provide facilities for mediation and arbitration of patent disputes falling within the scope of the Agreement. The Centre shall establish Mediation and Arbitration Rules and draw up a list of mediators and arbitrators to assist the parties in the settlement of their dispute.[227] To our knowledge, no Mediation and Arbitration Rules are yet drafted or negotiated.

The provision of the Agreement regarding enforcement of decisions and orders shall apply *mutatis mutandis* to any settlement reached through the use of the facilities of the Centre, including through mediation. However, a patent may not be revoked or limited in mediation or arbitration proceedings.[228]

226. Article 16(1) of the Agreement
227. Article 35(3) of the Agreement
228. Article 35(2) of the Agreement

Chapter III

Composition of the Different Divisions of the Court

A. COURT OF FIRST INSTANCE

Any panel of the Court of First Instance shall have a multinational composition, meaning that at least one foreign judge is part of the panel. In principle, each panel shall consist of three judges.[229] Under certain circumstances, a technically qualified judge can be added to the panel.

1. Local Division

The number of patent cases per calendar year shall determine the number of national judges in the panel of a local division.

A local division in a Contracting Member State where, during a period of three successive years prior or subsequent to the entry into force of the Agreement, less than fifty patent cases per calendar year on average have been commenced, shall sit with a composition of one legally qualified judge who is a national of the Contracting Member State hosting the local division concerned and two legally qualified judges who are not nationals of the Contracting Member State concerned and are allocated from a Pool of Judges on a case-by-case basis.[230]

The Pool of Judges shall be composed of all legally qualified judges and technically qualified judges from the Court of First Instance who are full-time or part-time judges of the Court.[231]

Any panel of a local division in a Contracting Member State where, during a period of three successive years prior or subsequent to the entry into force of the Agreement, fifty or more patent cases per calendar year on average have been commenced, shall sit with a composition of two legally qualified judges who are nationals of the Contracting Member State hosting the local

229. Article 8 of the Statute
230. Article 8(2) of the Agreement
231. Article 18 of the Agreement

division concerned and one legally qualified judge who is not a national of the Contracting Member State concerned, allocated from the Pool of Judges. Such third judge shall serve at the local division on a long term basis, where this is necessary for the efficient functioning of divisions with a high workload.[232]

Neither the Agreement, nor the Statute provides any guidance on how the number of patent cases should be calculated to determine the composition of the panels. Does "patent case" mean any case regarding patents brought before a national judge, irrespective of the parties, the claim (interim measures or claims on the merits) or the instance (including appeal and cassation)? Or should the meaning of "patent case" be limited to the whole of proceedings surrounding a particular patent? The verbatim text of the Agreement leads to the first interpretation, so that all proceedings regarding patents may be included in the calculation. This means that if, for example, a patent dispute started with a request by the plaintiff to the judge for inspection of the premises of the defendant, then interim measures were requested by the patent proprietor by summary proceedings, proceedings on the merits were initiated and finally decided by the Court of Appeal, four proceedings are to be taken into account for the calculation of the number of patent cases. Calculating only one patent case in the aforementioned example would mean that only very few Contracting Member States would have a local division with two national judges.

The question remains as to whether in countries in which revocation and infringement claims are split into different proceedings (e.g. Germany), each claim can be calculated as a separate "patent case". If so, then it seems only logical that in other countries which jointly decide upon infringement claims and counterclaims for revocation in one proceeding, such proceedings are calculated as two separate patent cases.

In a local division with 50 or more patent cases, the judge from the Pool of Judges can serve at the local division on a long-term basis, but only when this is necessary for the efficient functioning of the divisions with a high workload. Providing the possibility to serve for a long period in the same local division is praiseworthy, but this may in our opinion not lead to the situation where the third judge remains in service indefinitely. An indefinite (or very long-lasting) service of the third judge could lead to the situation that small local divisions have a permanent rotation of pool judges, making it difficult to establish consistent case law, while large local divisions would always work with the same judges, giving them the opportunity to set out consistent case law, which is considered to be of better quality.

232. Article 8(3) of the Agreement

2. Regional Division

Any panel of a regional division shall sit in a composition of two legally qualified judges chosen from a regional list of judges, who shall be nationals of the Contracting Member States concerned, and one legally qualified judge who shall not be a national of the Contracting Member States concerned and who shall be allocated from the Pool of Judges.[233]

3. Addition of a Technical Judge before Local or Regional Divisions

The local and regional divisions need to request the President of the Court of First Instance to add a technically qualified judge (with qualifications and experience in the field of technology concerned) from the Pool of Judges if in an infringement case a counterclaim for revocation is initiated by the defendant, and the division decides to proceed with both actions.[234]

But in addition to this specific situation, any panel of a local or regional division may at any time, upon request of one of the parties, request the President of the Court of First Instance to allocate from the Pool of Judges an additional technically qualified judge with qualifications and experience in the field of technology concerned. Moreover, any panel of a local or regional division may, after having heard the parties, submit such request on its own initiative, where it deems this appropriate.[235] In cases where such a technically qualified judge is already allocated, no further technically qualified judge may be allocated because of a counterclaim for revocation.

The addition of a technical judge opens up many possibilities for patent specialists. Today, in most Member States, patent attorneys or other patent or technically qualified specialists assist the parties or are appointed by the courts as a court specialist. But it is exceptional that patent specialists are involved in the rulings of the courts and/or can act as a judge in patent matters. Since the Pool of Judges must include at least one technically qualified judge per field of technology[236], many technically qualified judges shall be needed by the Court. Given the languages used in each local or regional division, specific languages (e.g. Scandinavian languages, Dutch or Polish) shall need specific technically qualified judges. According to the Statute, the decision of the Administrative Committee appointing technically qualified judges shall state the field(s) of technology for which a technically qualified judge is appointed.[237] To ensure

233. Article 8(4) of the Agreement
234. Article 33(3)(a) of the Agreement
235. Article 8(5) of the Agreement
236. Article 18(2) of the Agreement
237. Article 3(5) of the Statute

that all fields of technology are covered, it shall be possible to appoint part-time technically qualified judges.[238] As a consequence, many patent specialists (certainly specialists of smaller language territories) shall have the opportunity to be member of the Pool of Judges and act as a judge.

4. Central Division

Any panel of the central division shall sit in a composition of two legally qualified judges who are nationals of different Contracting Member States and one technically qualified judge allocated from the Pool of Judges with qualifications and experience in the field of technology concerned.[239] This means that parties before the central division shall be automatically confronted by a technically qualified judge in all cases.

Only when the central division deals with actions concerning decisions of the European Patent Office in carrying out the new tasks for unitary patents as mentioned in Article 9 of the Unitary Patent Regulation,[240] shall the panel of the central division sit with a composition of three legally qualified judges who are nationals of different Contracting Member States.[241]

5. One or Three Judges?

As mentioned above, any panel of the different divisions of the Court shall sit with three judges, having a multinational composition.[242] Any panel of the Court shall be chaired by a legally qualified judge.[243] However, in accordance with the Rules of Procedure, parties can agree to have their case heard by only one legally qualified judge.[244]

A standing judge for each division to hear urgent cases may be designated in accordance with the Rules of Procedure.[245] Neither the Agreement, nor the Rules of Procedure contain any criterion for urgency, which means that the Court shall have a great deal of discretion to determine whether a case is urgent.

In cases where parties agree to a single judge, or if a standing judge in urgent matters hears a case, that judge shall carry out all functions of a panel.[246]

238. Article 3(6) of the Statute
239. Article 8(6) of the Agreement
240. Article 32(1)(i) of the Agreement
241. Article 8(6) of the Agreement
242. Article 8(1) of the Agreement
243. Article 8(8) of the Agreement
244. Article 8(7) of the Agreement
245. Article 19(3) of the Statute
246. Article 19(4) of the Statute

It seems very unlikely that parties would often agree to have only a single judge decide their case. Furthermore, it is unclear from the Agreement which nationality the single legally qualified judge should have in cases before a local or regional division. Does it have to be a national judge or a judge from the Pool of Judges? If the judge is a national, parties could choose to have only one judge to circumvent interference by judges from other countries (appointed from the Pool of Judges). This would, for example, be interesting to benefit from a specific national jurisprudence of a judge. However, it would be exceptional to have in a specific case all parties benefit from a certain national jurisprudence of a local (or regional) division judge. Therefore, abuse based on the possibility of the parties agreeing on one judge seems unlikely to occur if both parties have to agree to this.

6. Panels

The allocation of judges and the assignment of cases within a division to its panels shall be governed by the Rules of Procedure. One judge on the panel shall be designated as the presiding judge, in accordance with the Rules of Procedure.[247]

The panel may delegate, in accordance with the Rules of Procedure, certain functions to one or more of its judges.[248] In any event, one judge on the panel shall act as Rapporteur, in accordance with the Rules of Procedure.[249]

B. THE COURT OF APPEAL

Any panel of the Court of Appeal shall sit in a multinational composition of five judges. It shall sit with a composition of three legally qualified judges who are nationals of different Contracting Member States and two technically qualified judges with qualifications and experience in the field of technology concerned. Those technically qualified judges shall be assigned to the panel by the President of the Court of Appeal from the Pool of Judges.[250]

However, a panel dealing with actions concerning decisions of the European Patent Office in carrying out the new tasks for unitary patents as mentioned in Article 9 of the Unitary Patent Regulation,[251] shall sit in a

247. Article 19(1) of the Statute
248. Article 19(2) of the Statute
249. Article 19(5) of the Statute
250. Article 9(1) of the Agreement
251. Article 32(1)(i) of the Agreement

composition of three legally qualified judges who are nationals of different Contracting Member States.

Any panel of the Court of Appeal shall be chaired by a legally qualified judge.[252] The allocation of judges and the assignment of cases to panels shall be governed by the Rules of Procedure. One judge on the panel shall be appointed as the presiding judge, in accordance with the Rules of Procedure.[253] The panel may delegate, in accordance with the Rules of Procedure, certain functions to one or more of its judges.[254] One judge on the panel shall act as Rapporteur, in accordance with the Rules of Procedure.[255]

When a case is of exceptional importance, and in particular when the decision may affect the unity and consistency of the case law of the Court, the Court of Appeal may decide, on the basis of a proposal from the presiding judge, to refer the case to the full Court.[256]

The criterion of "exceptional importance" is vague, but originates from the similar criterion in the Statute of the Court of Justice of the European Union.[257] A difference between the competence of the full Court of Appeal of the Unified Patent Court and the CJEU, is that in four articles of the Treaty on the Functioning of the European Union, the full Court of the CJEU has been provided with exclusive jurisdiction in certain specific cases.[258] No such specific exclusive jurisdiction is provided in the Agreement for the full Court of Appeal of the Unified Patent Court.

252. Article 9(3) of the Agreement
253. Article 21(1) of the Statute
254. Article 21(3) of the Statute
255. Article 21(4) of the Statute
256. Article 21(2) of the Statute
257. Article 16 of the Statute of the Court of Justice of the European Union: "Moreover, where it considers that a case before it is of exceptional importance, the Court may decide, after hearing the Advocate-General, to refer the case to the full Court."
258. Articles 228.2, 245, 247 and 286.6 TFEU

Chapter IV
The Judges of the Court

A. REQUIREMENTS

The requirements for legally qualified judges and for technically qualified judges differ.

Legally qualified judges have to possess the qualifications required for appointment to judicial offices in a Contracting Member State.[259] A literal reading of this condition implies that to become a judge in the Court, it is sufficient to have the qualifications in a Contracting Member State to become a judge. This would mean not actually having to be or having been a judge in one of the Member States to be appointed as a judge of the Unified Patent Court.

Article 15 of the Agreement further specifies that judges should ensure the highest standards of competence and have proven experience in the field of patent litigation. Practicing patent judges of course fulfil these conditions, but the wording of Article 15 does not seem to exclude, for example, lawyers who have a proven experience in the field of patent litigation and have acquired the qualifications required for appointment to judicial office in a Contracting Member State (e.g. passed a national judges exam).

Technically qualified judges need to have a university degree and proven expertise in a field of technology.[260] They shall also have proven knowledge of civil law and procedure relevant in patent litigation.

All judges need to have a good command of at least one official language of the European Patent Office.[261] This means that the only obligatory language requirement for judges is a good command of English, French or German. Nevertheless, it is clear that the linguistic skills of the judge shall be taking into account when allocating a judge to a local or regional division.

Article 2 of the Statute specifies that experience with patent litigation may be acquired by training organised under the system of the Unified Patent

259. Article 15(2) of the Agreement
260. Article 15(3) of the Agreement
261. Article 2 of the Statute

Court. The training framework of the Unified Patent Court shall, according to Article 11(4)(a) of the Statute, ensure appropriate training for candidate judges and newly appointed judges of the Court. The facilities of the training framework of the Unified Patent Court shall be situated in Budapest.[262]

B. APPOINTMENT OF JUDGES

The Advisory Committee shall establish a list of the most suitable candidates to be appointed as judges of the Court.[263] Vacancies shall be publicly advertised and shall indicate the relevant eligibility criteria. The Advisory Committee shall give an opinion on candidates' suitability to perform the duties of a judge of the Court. The opinion shall comprise a list of most suitable candidates. The list shall contain at least twice as many candidates as there are vacancies. Where necessary, the Advisory Committee may recommend that, prior to the decision on the appointment, a candidate judge receives training in patent litigation.[264]

On the basis of the list established by the Advisory Committee, the Administrative Committee shall appoint the judges of the Court acting by common accord.[265] When appointing judges, the Administrative Committee shall ensure the best legal and technical expertise and a balanced composition of the Court on as broad a geographical basis as possible among nationals of the Contracting Member States.[266] The requirement of a balanced composition of the Court creates significant opportunities for judges from smaller Member States. Even if the Member State does not have any specialised legally qualified patent judges and/or only a small number of technical specialists, the geographical spread of the judges shall bring about vacancies for the Unified Patent Court.

The Administrative Committee shall appoint as many judges as are needed for the proper functioning of the Court. The Administrative Committee shall initially appoint the necessary number of judges for setting up at least one panel in each of the divisions of the Court of First Instance and at least two panels in the Court of Appeal.[267]

The decision of the Administrative Committee appointing full-time or part-time legally qualified judges and full-time technically qualified judges

262. Article 19(1) of the Agreement
263. Article 16(1) of the Agreement
264. Article 3(2) of the Statute
265. Article 16(2) of the Agreement
266. Article 3(3) of the Statute
267. Article 3(4) of the Statute

shall state the instance of the Court and/or the division of the Court of First Instance for which each judge is appointed and the field(s) of technology for which a technically qualified judge is appointed.[268]

Part-time technically qualified judges shall be appointed as judges of the Court and shall be included in the Pool of Judges on the basis of their specific qualifications and experience. The appointment of these judges to the Court shall ensure that all fields of technology are covered.[269]

Judges shall be appointed for a term of six years, beginning on the date laid down in the instrument of appointment. They may be re-appointed. In the absence of any provision regarding the date, the term shall begin on the date of the instrument of appointment.[270]

C. JUDICIAL INDEPENDENCE AND IMPARTIALITY

Article 17 of the Agreement repeats the general principles of independence and impartiality of judges. The Court, its judges and the Registrar shall enjoy judicial independence. In the performance of their duties, the judges shall not be bound by any instructions. Legally qualified judges, as well as technically qualified judges who are full-time judges of the Court, may not engage in any other occupation, whether gainful or not, unless an exception is granted by the Administrative Committee. Nevertheless, the exercise of the office of judges shall not exclude the exercise of other judicial functions at national level.[271] The combination of a function as a judge within the Unified Patent Court and a national judicial function offers the Contracting Member States the opportunity to let their national patent disputes be decided by the same judges. In a local or regional division of the Unified Patent Court with a limited caseload, this can lead to the judge using his expertise built up at the local or regional division in national disputes.

Before taking up their duties, judges shall, in open court, take an oath to perform their duties impartially and conscientiously and to preserve the secrecy of the deliberations of the Court.[272]

Immediately after taking their oath, judges shall sign a declaration by which they solemnly undertake that, both during and after their term of office, they shall respect the obligations arising therefrom, in particular the duty to

268. Article 3(5) of the Statute
269. Article 3(6) of the Statute
270. Article 4 of the Statute
271. Article 17(3) of the Agreement
272. Article 6 of the Statute

behave with integrity and discretion as regards the acceptance, after they have ceased to hold office, of certain appointments or benefits.[273]

The exercise of the office of technically qualified judges who are part-time judges of the Court shall not exclude the exercise of other functions provided there is no conflict of interest.[274] In case of a conflict of interest, the judge concerned shall not take part in proceedings.

The conflict of interest rules for all types of judges are set out in Article 7 of the Statute. According to Article 7(2) of the Statute, judges may not take part in the proceedings of a case in which they:

(a) have taken part as adviser;
(b) have been a party or have acted for one of the parties;
(c) have been called upon to pronounce as a member of a court, tribunal, board of appeal, arbitration or mediation panel, a commission of inquiry or in any other capacity;
(d) have a personal or financial interest in the case or in relation to one of the parties; or
(e) are related to one of the parties or the representatives of the parties by family ties.

If, for some special reason, a judge considers that he or she should not take part in the judgment or examination of a particular case, that judge shall inform the President of the Court of Appeal accordingly or, in the case of judges of the Court of First Instance, the President of the Court of First Instance. If, for some special reason, the President of the Court of Appeal or, in the case of judges of the Court of First Instance, the President of the Court of First Instance considers that a judge should not sit or make submissions in a particular case, the President of the Court of Appeal or the President of the Court of First Instance shall justify this in writing and notify the judge concerned accordingly.[275]

Any party to an action may object to a judge taking part in the proceedings on any of the grounds listed above or where the judge is suspected, with good reason, of partiality.[276]

Any difficulty arising as to the application of the conflict of interest rules shall be settled by decision of the Presidium, in accordance with the Rules of Procedure. The judge concerned shall be heard but shall not take part in the deliberations.[277]

273. Article 7(1) of the Statute
274. Article 17(4) of the Agreement
275. Article 7(3) of the Statute
276. Article 7(4) of the Statute
277. Article 7(5) of the Statute

D. IMMUNITY OF JUDGES

As for the immunity of judges in the different Contracting Member States, the Statute provides an immunity rule for all judges of the Unified Patent Court. The judges shall be immune from legal proceedings. After they have ceased to hold office, they shall continue to enjoy immunity in respect of acts performed by them in relation to their official capacity.[278]

Only the Presidium may waive the immunity. Where immunity has been waived and criminal proceedings are instituted against a judge, that judge shall be tried, in any of the Contracting Member States, only by the court competent to judge the members of the highest national judiciary.[279]

Without prejudice to the specific provisions of the Statute regarding immunity, the Protocol on the privileges and immunities of the European Union shall apply to the judges of the Court.[280]

E. END OF THE DUTIES OF THE JUDGE

The duties of the judge can end in four ways:[281]

(1) if after expiry of the six-year term, the judge is not re-appointed;
(2) by death;
(3) if the judge resigns;
(4) if the judge is removed from office by the Presidium.

In case of resignation, the letter of resignation of judges of the Court of Appeal shall be addressed to the President of the Court of Appeal or, in the case of judges of the Court of First Instance, to the President of the Court of First Instance, for transmission to the Chairman of the Administrative Committee.[282]

In case of removal from office, a judge is deprived of his or her office or of other benefits in its stead only if the Presidium decides that that judge no longer fulfils the requisite conditions or meets the obligations arising from his or her office. The judge concerned shall be heard but shall not take part in the deliberations of the Presidium.[283] The decision of the Presidium shall be communicated to the Chairman of the Administrative Committee by the Registrar to inform the Administrative Committee of a vacancy.[284]

---

278. Article 8(1) of the Statute
279. Article 8(3) of the Statute
280. Article 8(4) of the Statute
281. Article 9(1) of the Statute
282. Article 9(2) of the Statute
283. Article 10(1) of the Statute
284. Article 10(2) and 10(3) of the Statute

Except in case of removal from the office or death, a judge shall continue to hold office until that judge's successor takes up his or her duties.[285] Any vacancy shall by filled by the appointment of a new judge for the remainder of his or her predecessor's term.[286]

F. POOL OF JUDGES

The Pool of Judges shall be composed of all legally qualified judges and technically qualified judges from the Court of First Instance who are full-time or part-time judges of the Court. The Pool of Judges shall include at least one technically qualified judge per field of technology with the relevant qualifications and experience. Technically qualified judges from the Pool of Judges shall also be available to the Court of Appeal.[287]

The judges from the Pool of Judges shall be allocated to the division concerned by the President of the Court of First Instance. The allocation of judges shall be based on their legal or technical expertise, linguistic skills and relevant experience. The allocation of judges shall guarantee the same high quality of work and the same high level of legal and technical expertise in all panels of the Court of First Instance.[288]

A request addressed to the President of the Court of First Instance by a division to assign a judge from the Pool of Judges shall indicate, in particular, the subject matter of the case, the official language of the European Patent Office used by the judges of the panel, the language of the proceedings and the field of technology required.[289]

The Registrar is responsible for drawing up a list with the names of the judges included in the Pool of Judges. In relation to each judge, the list shall at least indicate the linguistic skills, the field of technology and experience of, as well as the cases previously handled by, that judge.[290] This means that the Unified Patent Court itself shall monitor the experience of the judge by keeping a record of the cases handled.

285. Article 9(3) of the Statute
286. Article 9(4) of the Statute
287. Article 18 of the Agreement
288. Article 18(3) of the Agreement
289. Article 20(2) of the Statute
290. Article 20(1) of the Statute

G. TRAINING FRAMEWORK FOR JUDGES

The Agreement and the Statute pay special attention to the training of judges. It was a clear choice of the legislator to ensure that each division of the Court guarantees a high quality of jurisprudence. Logically, the success of the Unified Patent Court shall mainly depend on the quality of the judgments and the skill of the legally and technically qualified judges. Certainly for smaller Contracting Member States, training of the permanent and part-time judges is very important. According to Article 19(1) of the Agreement, the function of the training framework is to improve and increase available patent litigation expertise and to ensure a broad geographic distribution of such specific knowledge and experience.

The training framework shall in particular focus on internships in national patent courts or divisions of the Court of First Instance hearing a substantial number of patent litigation cases, improvement of linguistic skills, technical aspects of patent law, the dissemination of knowledge and experience in civil procedure for technically qualified judges and the preparation of candidate judges.[291] The internships in national patent courts or divisions with a great number of cases reflects the intention of the Contracting Member States to set up a system in which countries with little experience in patent litigation can learn from countries with a longer tradition of patent litigation. In this respect, it is striking that no internships at the European Patent Office are mentioned in the training framework.

The training framework shall provide for continuous, appropriate and regular training. Regular meetings shall be organised between all judges of the Court in order to discuss developments in patent law and to ensure the consistency of the Court's case law.[292] The Presidium shall adopt Training Regulations ensuring the implementation and overall coherence of the training framework.[293]

The training framework shall provide a platform for the exchange of expertise and a forum for discussion, in particular by organising courses, conferences, seminars, workshops and symposia, cooperating with international organisations and education institutes in the field of intellectual property, and promoting and supporting further vocational training.[294]

An annual work programme and training guidelines shall be drawn up, which shall include for each judge an annual training plan identifying that

291. Article 19(2) of the Agreement
292. Article 19(3) of the Agreement
293. Article 11(1) of the Statute
294. Article 11(2) of the Statute

judge's main training needs in accordance with the Training Regulations.[295] So each judge shall have its own individual training path focused on its own needs.

The training framework shall in addition ensure appropriate training for candidate judges and newly appointed judges of the Court, and support projects aimed at facilitating cooperation between representatives, patent attorneys and the Court.[296]

The facilities for the training framework shall be situated in Budapest.[297]

H. REMUNERATION

The Administrative Committee shall set the remuneration of the judges and of the President of the Court of Appeal, the President of the Court of First Instance, the Registrar, the Deputy-Registrar and the staff.[298]

I. STAFF AND JUDICIAL VACATIONS

The staff of the Unified Patent Court fall under the responsibility of the Registrar, but acts under the authority of the President of the Court of Appeal and the President of the Court of First Instance.[299] The officials and other servants of the Court shall have the task of assisting the President of the Court of Appeal, the President of the Court of First Instance, the judges and the Registrar.

The Administrative Committee shall establish Staff Regulations for the officials and other servants of the Court.[300]

The judicial vacations shall be determined by the President of the Court of Appeal. After consulting the Presidium, the President of the Court of Appeal shall establish the duration of judicial vacations and the rules on observing official holidays. During the period of judicial vacations, the functions of the President of the Court of Appeal and of the President of the Court of First Instance may be exercised by any judge invited by the respective President to that effect. In cases of urgency, the President of the Court of Appeal may convene the judges.[301]

295. Article 11(3) of the Statute
296. Article 11(4) of the Statute
297. Article 19(1) of the Agreement
298. Article 12 of the Statute
299. Article 16(1) of the Statute
300. Article 16(2) of the Statute
301. Article 17(1) and 17(2) of the Statute

In proper circumstances the President of the Court of Appeal or the President of the Court of First Instance can grant leave of absence to judges of the Court of Appeal or judges of the Court of First Instance respectively.[302] This shall likely be the case when judges are ill, injured or when personal emergencies (accidents or deaths involving family members) take place.

302. Article 17(3) of the Statute

Chapter V
Jurisdiction and Competence

A. INTERNATIONAL JURISDICTION

The Agreement states that the international jurisdiction of the Unified Patent Court shall be established in accordance with the Brussels I Regulation, or, where applicable, on the basis of the Lugano Convention on Jurisdiction and the recognition and enforcement of judgments in civil and commercial matters.[303] In the reference to the Brussels I Regulation, the Agreement clearly indicates that this includes any subsequent amendments to this Regulation.

In fact, a recast of the Brussels I Regulation was adopted by the European Council and Parliament on 12 December 2012.[304] Point 11 of the Preamble to the Regulation 1215/2012 now stipulates that "for the purposes of this Regulation, courts or tribunals of the Member States should include courts or tribunals common to several Member States, such as the Benelux Court of Justice when it exercises jurisdiction on matters falling within the scope of this Regulation. Therefore, judgments given by such courts should be recognised and enforced in accordance with this Regulation." Consequently, as a court common to 25 Member States, the Unified Patent Court falls within the scope of the Regulation.

Article 24(4) of the Brussels I Regulation stipulates that, in proceedings concerned with the registration or validity of patents, irrespective of whether the issue is raised by way of an action or as a defence, the courts of the Member State in which the deposit or registration has been applied for, has taken place or is under the terms of an instrument of the Union or an international convention deemed to have taken place have exclusive jurisdiction, regardless of the domicile of the parties. Because the Unified Patent Court is a court common to 25 EU Member States, it shall have exclusive jurisdiction for revocation actions against European patents and unitary patents. Therefore,

303. Article 31 of the Agreement

304. Regulation No. 1215/2012 of the European Parliament and of the Council of 12 December 2012 on jurisdiction and the recognition and enforcement of judgments in civil and commercial matters, *OJ* L 351, 20 December 2012, p. 1

the Unified Patent Court did not explicitly have to be mentioned in Article 22(4) of Regulation 1215/2012.

B. SUBSTANTIVE COMPETENCE OF THE COURT

1. Patents for which the Court is Competent

The Unified Patent Court shall have competence with respect to any:

- unitary patent;
- supplementary protection certificate issued for a product protected by a patent;
- European patent which has not yet lapsed at the date of entry into force of this Agreement, or was granted after that date, without prejudice to the opt-out possibility; and
- European patent application which is pending at the date of entry into force of this Agreement or which is filed after that date, without prejudice to the opt-out possibility.[305]

In principle, the Unified Patent Court shall immediately have competence to take decisions regarding classic European patents, irrespective of whether they are already granted or only granted after the entry into force of the Unified Patent Court. The same goes for classic European patent applications, the Court has competence, whether they are pending at the date of entry into force, or are only filed afterwards.

Nevertheless, during a transitional period, European patent proprietors or applicants shall have the choice to either bring actions before the national courts or before the Unified Patent Court (*infra*). Furthermore, European patent proprietors or applicants can always opt out of the exclusive jurisdiction of the Unified Patent Court before the end of the transitional period. Such choice for national proceedings or opt-out is not available for proprietors of a unitary patent.

2. Actions for which the Court is Competent

Article 32 of the Agreement provides a list of all actions for which the Unified Patent Court has exclusive competence. It concerns the following actions:

305. Article 3 of the Agreement

- actions for actual or threatened infringements of patents and supplementary protection certificates and related defences, including counterclaims concerning licences;
- actions for declarations of non-infringement of patents and supplementary protection certificates;
- actions for provisional and protective measures and injunctions;
- actions for revocation of patents and for declaration of invalidity of supplementary protection certificates;
- counterclaims for revocation of patents and for declaration of invalidity of supplementary protection certificates;
- actions for damages or compensation derived from the provisional protection conferred by a published European patent application;
- actions relating to the use of the invention prior to the granting of the patent or to the right based on prior use of the invention;
- actions for compensation for licences on the basis of Article 8 of the Unitary Patent Regulation;
  Article 8 of the Unitary Patent Regulation enables the proprietor of a unitary patent to file a statement with the EPO that he is prepared to allow any person to use the invention as a licensee in return for appropriate consideration.
- actions concerning decisions of the European Patent Office in carrying out the tasks referred to in Article 9 of the Unitary Patent Regulation.
  Article 9 of the Unitary Patent Regulation provides that the Participating Member States grant a number of tasks to the European Patent Office. These tasks include the administration of requests for unitary effect by proprietors of European patents, the inclusion and administration of a Register for unitary patent protection within the European Patent Register, receiving and registering statements on licensing, withdrawal and licensing commitments undertaken in international standardisation bodies, the publication of the translations during the transitional period, the collection and administration of renewal fees for European patents with unitary effect, the collection and administration of additional fees paid in cases of late payment of renewal fees and the administration of a compensation scheme of translation costs for applicants filing European patent applications in one of the official languages of the Union that is not an official language of the European Patent Office. To provide effective legal protection against the decisions of the European Patent Office in carrying out these tasks, the Unified Patent Court is given exclusive competence for actions that concern such decisions of the European Patent Office.

"Patents" are to be understood as both unitary patents as European patents.[306]

The competence of the Unified Patent Court is very broad. Nevertheless, the national courts of the Contracting Member States remain competent, for example, for compulsory licences, disputes regarding inventorship and disputes regarding Unitary or European patents as objects of property. The national courts remain of course also competent for all actions relating to national patents. Furthermore, during the transitional period, and after the transitional period for all disputes regarding European patents, the national courts shall remain competent to decide all disputes regarding European patents for which the proprietor has opted out from the exclusive competence of the Unified Patent Court.

C. TERRITORIAL COMPETENCE OF THE FIRST INSTANCE DIVISIONS

1. Infringement Actions

Actions for actual or threatened infringement of patents and supplementary protection certificates and all "related defences, including counterclaims concerning licences"[307] can be brought before the following divisions:

- the local division hosted by the Contracting Member State *where the actual or threatened infringement has occurred or may occur*;
- the regional division in which the Contracting Member State *where the actual or threatened infringement has occurred or may occur* participates;
- the local division hosted by the Contracting Member State where the *defendant* or, in the case of multiple defendants, one of the defendants has its *residence*, or *principal place of business,* or in the absence of residence or principal place of business, its *place of business*;
- the regional division in which the Contracting Member State where the *defendant* or, in the case of multiple defendants, one of the defendants has its *residence*, or *principal place of business,* or in the absence of residence or principal place of business, its *place of business,* participates.[308]

When the competence is determined by the residence, principal place of business or place of business of the defendant, an action may be brought against

306. Article 2(g) of the Agreement
307. Article 32(1)(a) of the Agreement
308. Article 33(1)(a) and (b) of the Agreement

multiple defendants only where the defendants have a commercial relationship and where the action relates to the same alleged infringement.[309]

Besides the possibility to bring actions before the local or regional division of the Contracting Member State where the infringement has occurred or may occur, actions against defendants having their residence, or principal place of business or, in the absence of residence or principal place of business, their place of business, *outside* the territory of the Contracting Member States can also be brought before the central division.[310] For example, if the alleged infringing product is imported by a Chinese company into Denmark, an infringement action in which the Chinese company is (co-)defendant can be brought before the Danish local (or regional) division or before the central division.

If the Contracting Member State concerned does not host a local division and does not participate in a regional division, actions shall be brought before the central division.[311]

2. Provisional Protection; Prior Use; Provisional and Protective Measures

Actions for damages or compensation derived from the provisional protection conferred by a published European patent application,[312] actions for provisional and protective measures and injunctions[313] and actions relating to the use of the invention prior to the granting of the patent or to the right based on prior use of the invention,[314] can be brought before the same divisions which are competent for infringement actions.

The competence shall be determined by the place of the actual or threatened infringement or the residence, principal place of business or place of business of the defendant.[315] The rules for defendants outside the territory of the Contracting Member States and multiple defendants equally apply.

Consequently, preliminary injunctions can be granted by any territorially competent local or regional division with effect in the 25 Contracting Member States. Once the local or regional division has granted a preliminary injunction, it remains competent for subsequent actions on the merits.[316] It cannot be ruled out that patent proprietors shall initially search for patentee-friendly

309. Article 33(1)(b) of the Agreement
310. Article 33(4) of the Agreement
311. Article 33(5) of the Agreement
312. Article 32(1)(f) of the Agreement
313. Article 32(1)(c) of the Agreement
314. Article 32(1)(g) of the Agreement
315. Article 33(1) of the Agreement
316. Article 33(2) of the Agreement

local or regional divisions to get a preliminary injunction granted. Protective letters may prevent such a grant.

The actions for provisional protection and provisional protective measures are strongly linked to the infringement, as these are ways for the patent proprietor to protect its rights. Therefore, it is obvious why such actions follow the competence of the infringement action. For actions based on the right of prior use, this is less obvious because the plaintiff can be the party using the invention. This means that in case of actions of prior use based on the competence of residence or (principal) place of business of the defendant, these actions shall be brought before the local or regional division of the patent proprietor and not the division of the alleged infringing party.

3. Actions regarding Compensation for Licences of Unitary Patents

In the absence of a "place of infringement", the actions for compensation for licences on the basis of Article 8 of the Unitary Patent Regulation shall be brought before the local or regional division where the defendant or, in the case of multiple defendants, one of the defendants has its residence, or principal place of business, or in the absence of residence or principal placc of business, its place of business.[317]

Such actions are intended to deal with any compensation discussion between a licensee who has obtained a licence through the new system of Article 8 Unitary Patent Regulation, and the patent proprietor.

4. Conflicts of Jurisdiction

If any of the above-mentioned actions for infringement, provisional and protective measures and injunctions, provisional protection, prior use or compensation for licences, is pending before a division of the Court of First Instance, any other action based on one of the mentioned grounds between the same parties and based on the same patent may not be brought before any other division.

The local or regional division where the first action was initiated has exclusive jurisdiction for all the above-mentioned actions. In case an action between the same parties on the same patent is brought before several different divisions, the division first seized shall be competent for the whole case and

317. Article 33(1), §2 of the Agreement

any division seized later shall declare the action inadmissible in accordance with the Rules of Procedure.[318]

This exclusive jurisdiction has its consequences. If, for example, a patent application proprietor starts an action for damages derived from the provisional protection of patent application based on the residence of the alleged infringing party and the action is still pending at the time the patent is granted, it shall then not be possible for the patent proprietor to start proceedings before the local division of another Contracting Member State in which an infringement takes place. On the other hand, the defendant in an infringement discussion who wants to defend himself by invoking prior use can first start proceedings before the local division of the Contracting Member State in which the alleged infringement takes place (which happens to be the local division of his residence), to avoid the plaintiff first initiating an infringement action in another local division where the infringement also takes place, but which is not the division of the residence of the defendant. The first party who initiates proceedings, receives priority ("first-to-litigate principle").

Another consequence is that preliminary injunctions shall determine the further competence for infringement actions on the merits.

There is one very important exception to the first-to-litigate principle regarding infringement actions. If an infringement action is pending before a regional division and the infringement has occurred in the territories of three or more regional divisions, the regional division concerned shall, at the request of the defendant, refer the case to the central division.[319] This rule was included to ensure that very important (and wide-spread) infringement cases can be dealt with by the central division. However, strangely enough, this rule only applies to cases pending before a regional division. If an infringement action pending before a local division concerns an infringement which occurred in the territories of several local divisions, the defendant cannot request referral to the central division. As a consequence, patent proprietors shall most likely prefer local divisions because then they do not risk a referral to the central division.

5. Counterclaims for Revocation

A counterclaim for revocation[320] may be brought in an infringement case, but it is not certain that the local or regional division shall proceed with both the infringement and revocation action. The divisions shall have several options.

318. Article 33(2) of the Agreement
319. Article 33(2) §2 of the Agreement
320. Article 32(1)(e) of the Agreement

The local or regional division concerned shall, after having heard the parties, have the discretion to either:

- proceed with both the action for infringement and with the counterclaim for revocation and request the President of the Court of First Instance to allocate from the Pool of Judges a technically qualified judge with qualifications and experience in the field of technology concerned;
- refer the counterclaim for revocation for decision to the central division and suspend the action for infringement;
- refer the counterclaim for revocation for decision to the central division and proceed with the action for infringement; or
- with the agreement of the parties, refer the whole case to the central division.[321]

The article on the counterclaim for revocation has been heavily criticised by European patent practitioners. The main reason for this is that it tries to combine the German "bifurcation" system – in which infringement actions and counterclaims for revocation can be separated in different proceedings – and the system of most other Contracting Member States by which counterclaims for revocation and infringement actions are combined in one procedure. The Agreement leaves it to the discretion of the local or regional division concerned to decide whether or not to combine both claims. In our opinion, the way local or regional divisions shall deal with these possibilities will to a large extent depend on the current patent tradition. In a country like Germany, the local or regional division can more easily split up the infringement and the validity question. In other countries with a non-bifurcation tradition, local and regional divisions shall most likely proceed in most cases with both actions.

In many Contracting Member States it is generally accepted that the validity question first needs to be answered before deciding on the infringement question. Therefore, it is to be expected that if the local or regional division of those countries refers the revocation action to the central division, the division shall not proceed with the infringement action but shall suspend proceedings.

However, it seems clear that much discussion before the Court of First Instance shall take place on the referral or not of the revocation action. The Agreement clearly states that the divisions can only decide "*after having heard the parties*". Much preliminary discussion before the Court of First Instance can be expected to be held solely on this matter.

On the other hand, a lot shall depend on the quality of the local or regional divisions. If the local or regional division does not enjoy the confidence of

---

321. Article 33(3) of the Agreement

the parties, parties can agree to refer the whole case to the central division. If local or regional divisions – despite the use of the Pool of Judges – still have a specific "local" or unreliable case law, chances are that major patent cases brought before such divisions shall shift to the central division by choice of the parties.

6. Independent Revocation Actions

Revocation actions[322] are brought before the central division. The central division shall of course only be competent for such actions if no infringement actions are already initiated by the patent proprietor, because if an infringement action is pending before a local or regional division, such a revocation action is in fact a counterclaim for revocation.

If an action for infringement between the same parties relating to the same patent has been brought before a local or a regional division, the revocation actions may only be brought before the same local or regional division.[323] The central division has exclusive competence for "independent" or "initial" revocation actions.

Conversely, if a revocation action is already initiated before the central division, the patent proprietor remains free to initiate an infringement action before the central division or before the division competent for (independent) infringement actions. So, if an action for revocation is pending before the central division, an action for infringement between the same parties relating to the same patent may be brought before any competent local or regional division or before the central division.[324] If the infringement action is brought before a local or regional division, the division concerned shall have the same possibilities to proceed as if a counterclaim for revocation were to be initiated in an infringement proceeding before a local or regional division (*supra*, V.C.7).

7. Non-infringement Actions

The central division is competent for actions for declaration of non-infringement of patents and supplementary protection certificates.[325] Here again, the central division is only competent for such actions if no infringement actions are already initiated by the patent proprietor. If an action for infringement between the same parties relating to the same patent has been brought before

322. Article 33(1)(d)) of the Agreement
323. Article 33(4) of the Agreement
324. Article 33(5) of the Agreement
325. Article 33(4) of the Agreement

a local or a regional division, the actions for declaration of non-infringement may only be brought before the same local or regional division.[326]

An action for declaration of non-infringement pending before the central division shall be stayed once an infringement action between the same parties or between the holder of an exclusive licence and the party requesting a declaration of non-infringement relating to the same patent is brought before a local or regional division within three months of the date on which the action was initiated before the central division.[327]

Consequently, no "bifurcation" possibility is provided for declarations of non-infringement and infringement actions. On the contrary, if a non-infringement action is initiated by the alleged infringing party before the central division, the patent proprietor is given a three-month period to initiate an infringement action before a local or regional division in order to let the infringement question be dealt with by the local or regional division of the place of infringement or the place of residence or (principal) place of business.

8. Actions against Unitary Patent Tasks of the EPO

In Article 9 of the Unitary Patent Regulation the European Patent Office is granted several new tasks with respect to unitary patents. Actions which concern decisions of the European Patent Office in carrying out these tasks can only be brought before the central division.[328]

9. General Exception: Choice of the Parties

Except for actions concerning the decisions of the European Patent Office in carrying out the tasks granted in Article 9 Unitary Patent Regulation, for all other actions the parties can agree to bring them before the division of their choice, including the central division. Consequently, parties can agree to deviate from the rules of competence set out in Article 33 of the Agreement.[329]

Such agreement between the parties can be concluded at the time of initiating proceedings or before, for example, through a jurisdiction clause in an agreement with a licensee.

326. Article 33(4) of the Agreement
327. Article 33(6) of the Agreement
328. Article 33(9) of the Agreement
329. Article 33(7) of the Agreement

10. Relation between EPO Oppositions and Revocation Actions

Revocation actions and counterclaims for revocation can be brought before the Unified Patent Court without the applicant having to file notice of opposition with the European Patent Office.[330]

Conversely, a party must inform the Unified Patent Court of any pending revocation, limitation or opposition proceedings before the European Patent Office, and of any request for accelerated processing before the European Patent Office. The Court may (but is not obliged to) stay its proceedings when a rapid decision may be expected from the European Patent Office.[331]

D. TERRITORIAL SCOPE OF THE DECISIONS OF THE COURT

One of the main goals of the Unified Patent Court is to ensure that parties no longer have to start proceedings in different or all Member States in order to enforce their patent rights in these Member States.

Article 34 of the Agreement provides that decisions of the Court shall cover, in case of classic European patents, the territory of those Contracting Member States for which the European patent has effect. The unitary effect for decisions regarding unitary patents is laid down in Article 3.2 of the Unitary Patent Regulation.

330. Article 33(8)) of the Agreement
331. Article 33(10) of the Agreement

Chapter VI

Sources of Law and Substantive Law

A. SOURCES OF LAW

When hearing a case brought before it, the Court shall base its decisions on:

- Union law, including the Unitary Patent Regulation and the Translation Regulation;
- the Agreement;
- the EPC;
- other international agreements applicable to patents and binding on all the Contracting Member States; and
- national law.[332]

Article 24 of the Agreement stresses that when applying the sources of law, the primacy of Union law has to be respected.

The EPC shall be a predominant instrument for the Court, since – apart from the Biotechnology Directive[333] – the basic requirements for patentability (novelty, inventive step and industrial application), as well as the patentable inventions and the exceptions to patentability, can be found in the EPC. For infringement matters and procedural questions, the two Regulations regarding unitary patent protection and the Agreement itself shall be important.

Because certain clauses of substantive patent law have been deleted from the Unitary Patent Regulation, the importance of national law shall remain. In damage actions, inventorship actions and actions regarding the patents as an object of property, national law shall be the main source of law.

For the new unitary patents, the applicable rules are to be found in different legislation:

- the principle of uniform protection, exhaustion or licences of rights are to be found in the Unitary Patent Regulation;

332. Article 24(1) of the Agreement

333. European Parliament and Council Directive 98/44/EC of 6 July 1988 on the legal protection of biotechnological inventions, *OJ* L 213, 30 July 1998

- the rules regarding direct infringement, indirect infringement, limitations and rights of prior use are to be found in the Agreement;
- the patentability provisions, the scope of protection[334] and the grounds on which a patent may be revoked[335] are to be found in the EPC;
- the rules regarding compulsory licences and the unitary patent as an object of property are to be found in the applicable national law.

To the extent that the Court shall base its decisions on national law, including where relevant the law of non-contracting States (e.g. in case of European patents valid in Member States of the European Patent Organisation which are non-EU Member States), the applicable law shall be determined:

(a) by directly applicable provisions of Union law containing private international law rules, or
(b) in the absence of directly applicable provisions of Union law or where Union law does not apply, by international instruments containing private international law rules; or
(c) in the absence of provisions referred to in points (a) and (b), by national provisions on private international law as determined by the Court.[336]

The law of non-Contracting Member States shall apply when designated by application of the above-mentioned rules. This can particularly be the case in relation to direct infringement, indirect infringement, limitations of the effect, rights based on prior use, burden of proof and reversal of burden of proof, corrective measures in infringement proceedings, award of damages and period of limitation.

B. SUBSTANTIVE PATENT LAW

As explained, for unitary patents the provisions of substantive patent law were first included in the Unitary Patent Regulation, but were then transferred to the Agreement (*supra*, III.G).

Only six articles of substantive patent law are available in the Agreement and relate to direct infringement, indirect infringement, limitations of the effect of a European or unitary patent, prior use, exhaustion of the rights of a European or unitary patent and the effects of supplementary protection certificates. This is a major step forward in European harmonisation because for European patents, Article 64 EPC now provides that a European patent confers on its

334. Article 69 EPC and the Protocol on the Interpretation of Article 69 EPC
335. Article 138 EPC
336. Article 24(2) of the Agreement

proprietor from the date on which the mention of its grant is published in the *European Patent Bulletin*, in each Contracting State in respect of which it is granted, the same rights as would be conferred by a national patent granted in that State. The Agreement harmonises the national laws of 25 EU Member States on these aspects of substantive patent law.

1. Direct Use of the Invention

A patent shall confer on its proprietor the right to prevent any third party not having the proprietor's consent from:

(a) making, offering, placing on the market or using a product which is the subject matter of the patent, or importing or storing the product for those purposes;

(b) using a process which is the subject matter of the patent or, where the third party knows, or should have known, that the use of the process is prohibited without the consent of the patent proprietor, offering the process for use within the territory of the Contracting Member States in which that patent has effect;

(c) offering, placing on the market, using, or importing or storing for those purposes a product obtained directly by a process which is the subject matter of the patent.[337]

2. Indirect Use of the Invention

A European patent or a unitary patent shall confer on its proprietor the right to prevent any third party not having the proprietor's consent from supplying or offering to supply, within the territory of the Contracting Member States in which that patent has effect, any person other than a party entitled to exploit the patented invention, with means, relating to an essential element of that invention, for putting it into effect therein, when the third party knows, or should have known, that those means are suitable and intended for putting that invention into effect.[338]

This shall not apply when the means are staple commercial products, except where the third party induces the person supplied to perform any acts of direct infringement.[339]

There shall remain an indirect infringement even when a third party not having the proprietor's consent supplies or offers to supply to certain persons bound by a limitation with means, relating to an essential element of that

337. Article 25 of the Agreement
338. Article 26(1) of the Agreement
339. Article 26(2) of the Agreement

invention, for putting it into effect therein, when the third party knows, or should have known, that those means are suitable and intended for putting that invention into effect. In this respect, Article 26(3) of the Agreement stipulates that persons performing the acts referred to in Article 27(a)-(e) of the Agreement shall not be considered to be parties entitled to exploit the invention. This shall mean that, for example, a third party which, without the patent proprietor's consent, provides means which are suitable or intended to put the invention into effect, to a person who uses the invention privately and for non-commercial purposes, this still can be considered as an indirect infringement.

3. Limitations

The rights conferred by a European or unitary patent shall not extend to any of the following:[340]

- acts done privately and for non-commercial purposes;
- acts done for experimental purposes relating to the subject matter of the patented invention;
- the use of biological material for the purpose of breeding, or discovering and developing other plant varieties;
- acts allowed pursuant to Article 13(6) of Directive 2001/82/EC[341] or Article 10(6) of Directive 2001/83/EC[342] in respect of any patent covering the product within the meaning of either of those Directives;
- the extemporaneous preparation by a pharmacy, for individual cases, of a medicine in accordance with a medical prescription or acts concerning the medicine so prepared;
- the use of the patented invention on board vessels of countries of the International Union for the Protection of Industrial Property (Paris Union) or members of the World Trade Organisation, other than those Contracting Member States in which that patent has effect, in the body of such vessel, in the machinery, tackle, gear and other accessories, when such vessels temporarily or accidentally enter the waters of a Contracting Member State in which that patent has effect, provided that the invention is used there exclusively for the needs of the vessel;
- the use of the patented invention in the construction or operation of aircraft or land vehicles or other means of transport of countries of the International Union for the Protection of Industrial Property (Paris

340. Article 27 of the Agreement
341. Directive 2001/82/EC of 6 November 2001 on the Community code relating to veterinary medicinal products, *OJ* L 311, 28 November 2001, p. 1, including any subsequent amendments
342. Directive 2001/83/EC of 6 November 2001 on the Community code relating to medicinal products for human use, OJ L 311, 28 November 2001, p. 67, including any subsequent amendments

Union) or members of the World Trade Organisation, other than those Contracting Member States in which that patent has effect, or of accessories to such aircraft or land vehicles, when these temporarily or accidentally enter the territory of a Contracting Member State in which that patent has effect;

- acts specified in Article 27 of the Convention on International Civil Aviation of 7 December 1944, where these acts concern the aircraft of a country party to that Convention other than a Contracting Member State in which that patent has effect;
- the use by a farmer of the product of his harvest for propagation or multiplication by him on his own holding, provided that the plant propagating material was sold or otherwise commercialised to the farmer by or with the consent of the patent proprietor for agricultural use. The extent and the conditions for this use correspond to those under Article 14 of Regulation (EC) No. 2100/94;[343]
- the use by a farmer of protected livestock for an agricultural purpose, provided that the breeding stock or other animal reproductive material were sold or otherwise commercialised to the farmer by or with the consent of the patent proprietor. Such use includes making the animal or other animal reproductive material available for the purposes of pursuing the farmer's agricultural activity, but not the sale thereof within the framework of, or for the purpose of, a commercial reproductive activity;
- acts and the use of the obtained information as allowed under Articles 5 and 6 of Council Directive 2009/24/EC,[344] in particular, by its provisions on decompilation and interoperability; and
- acts allowed pursuant to Article 10 of Directive 98/44/EC.[345]

4. Prior Use

Any person who, if a national patent had been granted in respect of an invention, would have had, in a Contracting Member State, a right based on prior use of that invention or a right of personal possession of that invention, shall enjoy, in that Contracting Member State, the same rights in respect of a European or unitary patent for the same invention.[346]

---

343. Council Regulation No. 2100/94 of 27 July 1994 on Community plant variety rights, *OJ* L 227, 1 September 1994, p. 1, including any subsequent amendments
344. Directive 2009/24/EC of 23 April 2009 on the legal protection of computer programs, *OJ* L 111, 5 May 2009, p. 16, including any subsequent amendments
345. Directive 98/44/EC of 6 July 1998 on the legal protection of biotechnological inventions, *OJ* L 213, 30 July 1998, p. 13, including any subsequent amendments
346. Article 28 of the Agreement

For the rights based on prior use of the invention, Article 28 of the Agreement indirectly refers to national law. Only if a right based on prior use or a right of personal possession would be granted if the user had a national patent instead, the user shall have the same rights for prior use or personal possession of an invention laid down in a unitary patent.

5. Exhaustion of the Rights Conferred by a European Patent

The principle of exhaustion for unitary patents is laid down in Article 6 of the Unitary Patent Regulation. For European patents, Article 29 of the Agreement provides that the rights conferred by a European patent shall not extend to acts concerning a product covered by that patent after that product has been placed on the market in the Union by, or with the consent of, the patent proprietor, unless there are legitimate grounds for the patent proprietor to oppose further commercialisation of the product.

6. Effects of Supplementary Protection Certificates

Article 30 of the Agreement stipulates that a supplementary protection certificate shall confer the same rights as conferred by the patent and shall be subject to the same limitations and the same obligations. In the Agreement, supplementary protection certificates are to be understood as all supplementary protection certificates granted under Regulation No. 469/2009[347] or under Regulation No. 1610/96.[348]

---

347. Regulation (EC) No. 469/2009 of the European Parliament and of the Council of 6 May 2009 concerning the supplementary protection certificate for medicinal products, *OJ* L 152, 16 June 2009, p. 1
348. Regulation (EC) No. 1610/96 of the European Parliament and of the Council of 23 July 1996 concerning the creation of a supplementary certificate for plant protection products, *OJ* L 198, 8 August 1996, p. 30

Chapter VII

Organisation of Proceedings

A. STATUTE AND RULES OF PROCEDURE

The Statute and the Rules of Procedure are two important documents for understanding the organisation, functioning and procedures of the Unified Patent Court. According to the Agreement, the Statute lays down the details of the organisation and functioning of the Court,[349] while the Rules of Procedure lay down the details of the proceedings before the Court.[350]

The Statute is annexed to the Agreement and may be amended by decision of the Administrative Committee, on the basis of a proposal of the Court or a proposal of a Contracting Member State after consultation with the Court. However, such amendments cannot contradict or alter the Agreement.[351] As a matter of principle, the Agreement states that the Statute shall guarantee that the functioning of the Court is organised in the most efficient and cost-effective manner and shall ensure equitable access to justice.[352]

To properly understand the functioning of the Unified Patent Court, one needs to take into account three levels of rules. The general rules and principles are to be found in the Agreement. More detailed rules are included in the Statute and the most detailed and practical rules are provided for in the Rules of Procedure. In the relation between the three documents, the Agreement always prevails. In case of contradiction between the Rules of Procedure and the Statute, the Statute shall prevail.

One of the major problems the Unified Patent Court shall encounter in its formation is that it cannot fall back on general rules of proceedings of the Contracting Member States. In normal circumstances, specialised courts have their own specific rules of proceedings for the subject matter concerned, but for the rest they rely upon the general rules of procedure of the Member States in or for which they operate. As a court common to all Contracting

349. Article 40(1) of the Agreement
350. Article 41(1) of the Agreement
351. Article 40(2) of the Agreement
352. Article 40(3).of the Agreement

Member States, the Unified Patent Court cannot rely on procedural rules of a specific Member State (nor of the European Union) and has to fully establish its own rules of procedure. The advantage of this is that the Court shall not be confronted by conflicts between national procedural rules and its own Rules of Procedure. The disadvantage will be that the Unified Patent Court cannot rely on national rules to complete its own rules or provide interpretation of the Rules of Procedure.

The Rules of Procedure shall comply with the Agreement and the Statute.[353] They shall be adopted by the Administrative Committee on the basis of broad consultations with stakeholders. The prior opinion of the European Commission on the compatibility of the Rules of Procedure with Union law shall be requested.[354] It is expected that such consultations shall start immediately after signing of the Agreement.

The Rules of Procedure may be amended by a decision of the Administrative Committee, on the basis of a proposal from the Court and after consultation with the European Commission. However, such amendments may not contradict or alter the Agreement or the Statute.[355]

For the Rules of Procedure, the Agreement sets out the following principles:

- the Rules of Procedure shall guarantee that the decisions of the Court are of the highest quality and that proceedings are organised in the most efficient and cost-effective manner;
- the Rules of Procedure shall ensure a fair balance between the legitimate interests of all parties;
- the Rules of Procedure shall provide for the required level of discretion of judges without impairing the predictability of proceedings for the parties.[356]

In the second part of this book, the current draft Rules of Procedure are explained by way of flowcharts.

B. PROCEDURAL PRINCIPLES

The Agreement provides a number of procedural principles that should be respected by the Court.

353. Article 41(1) of the Agreement
354. Article 41(2) of the Agreement
355. Article 41(2), §2 of the Agreement
356. Article 41(3) of the Agreement

First of all, the general principles of proportionality and fairness are reaffirmed. The Court shall deal with litigation in ways which are proportionate to the importance and complexity thereof. The Court shall ensure that the rules, procedures and remedies provided for in the Agreement and in the Statute are used in a fair and equitable manner and do not distort competition.[357]

Furthermore, the role of the Court in case management is determined. The Court shall actively manage the cases before it in accordance with the Rules of Procedure without impairing the freedom of the parties to determine the subject matter of, and the supporting evidence for their case.[358]

A very special element regarding the proceedings is the clear choice of the Agreement for as many electronic procedures as possible. The Court shall make best use of electronic procedures, such as the electronic filing of submissions of the parties and stating of evidence in electronic form, as well as video conferencing, in accordance with the Rules of Procedure.[359] For many Contracting Member States the electronic filing of submissions and evidence is totally new. The flexibility of the Court regarding electronic procedures can only be encouraged in further elaborating the functioning of the Court. It is expected that the Court shall make use of document management software to ensure that all procedural documents are electronically available to the parties and the judges, and can be managed by the Court from different locations.

Finally, the proceedings shall be open to the public unless the Court decides to make them confidential, to the extent necessary, in the interest of one of the parties or other affected persons, or in the general interest of justice or public order.[360]

C. PARTIES AND REPRESENTATION

Any natural or legal person, or any body equivalent to a legal person entitled to initiate proceedings in accordance with its national law, shall have the capacity to be a party to the proceedings before the Court.[361] But having the capacity to be a party to the proceedings, does not necessarily entail the ability to start an action before the Court.

In any event the patent proprietor is entitled to bring actions before the Court.[362] Unless the licensing agreement provides otherwise, the holder of an

357. Article 42 of the Agreement
358. Article 43 of the Agreement
359. Article 44 of the Agreement
360. Article 45 of the Agreement
361. Article 46 of the Agreement
362. Article 47(1) of the Agreement

exclusive licence in respect of a patent shall be entitled to bring actions before the Court under the same circumstances as the patent proprietor, provided that the patent proprietor is given prior notice.[363] The holder of a non-exclusive licence shall not be entitled to bring actions before the Court, unless the patent proprietor is given prior notice and in so far as expressly permitted by the licence agreement.[364] In actions brought by a licence holder, the patent proprietor shall be entitled to join the action before the Court.[365] To make sure that as many persons as possible can bring actions before the Court, Article 47(6) of the Agreement provides that any other natural or legal person, or anybody entitled to bring actions in accordance with its national law, who is concerned by a patent, may bring actions in accordance with the Rules of Procedure. This "catch-all" section mainly refers to alleged infringers which can initiate revocation proceedings or declarations for non-infringement.

The validity of a patent cannot be contested in an action for infringement brought by the holder of a licence where the patent proprietor does not take part in the proceedings. The party in an action for infringement wanting to contest the validity of a patent must bring an action against the patent proprietor.[366] Consequently, counterclaims for revocation can only be initiated if the patent proprietor is present in the infringement procedure.

The specific actions against decisions of the European Patent Office in carrying out its new tasks referred to in Article 9 Unitary Patent Regulation, can be brought by any natural or legal person, or anybody entitled to bring actions in accordance with its national law and who is affected by the decision.[367]

Before the Court, parties shall in principle be represented by lawyers. All lawyers authorised to practice before a court of a Contracting Member State can act before the Court.[368]

Besides lawyers, certain patent attorneys may also represent parties. To be able to represent a party before the Court, the patent attorney should first of all be entitled to act as a professional representative before the European Patent Office in accordance with Article 134 EPC. Article 134 EPC requires that the patent attorney appears on a list maintained for this purpose by the European Patent Office. Any natural person who is a national of a Contracting State of the EPC, has his place of business or employment in a Contracting State and has passed the European qualifying examination may be entered on the list of professional representatives. The President of the European Patent

363. Article 47(2) of the Agreement
364. Article 47(3) of the Agreement
365. Article 47(4) of the Agreement
366. Article 47(5) of the Agreement
367. Article 47(7) of the Agreement
368. Article 48(1) of the Agreement

Office may grant exemption from the nationality requirement in special circumstances.[369] Secondly, the European patent attorney should have appropriate qualifications.[370] The requirements for appropriateness shall be established by the Administrative Committee.[371] As an example of proof for appropriate qualifications, the Agreement refers to the European Patent Litigation Certificate.[372] Although education programmes for patent attorneys regarding patent litigation already exist, the Patent Litigation Certificate mentioned in the Agreement is currently not available.[373]

Once the patent attorney has met the requirements, he/she shall be put on the list. The list of European patent attorneys entitled to represent parties before the Court shall be kept by the Registrar.[374]

Representation before the Unified Patent Court has been subject to a heated discussion among the different stakeholders.[375]

The Council of Bars and Law Societies of Europe (CCBE) was of the opinion that disputes involving patents are to be carried out by suitably qualified and properly trained professional lawyers. According to the CCBE, disputes involving patents also involve many other areas of law in which a patent attorney will have no training or experience. The vague concept of a European Union Patent Litigation Certificate would not be a guarantee for the required level of training and the appropriate standards. Moreover, representatives have to be subject to clear, consistent rules of behaviour backed by an effective disciplinary procedure. Because in many EU Member States patent attorneys do not belong to any legal profession, the CCBE was of the opinion that patent attorneys would not bring the same additional guarantees of professional behaviour as provided by bar members.[376]

Following the position paper of the CCBE, the Institute of Professional Representatives before the European Patent Office (EPI) responded with a position paper of 23 June 2010.[377] According to the EPI, European patent attorneys have technical qualifications, are highly experienced in patent matters,

---

369. Article 134.7. EPC
370. Article 48(2) of the Agreement
371. Article 48(3) of the Agreement
372. Article 48(2) of the Agreement
373. E.g. the "*Centre d'études internationales de la propriété intélectuelle*" (CEIPI) of the university of Strasbourg offers a course in patent litigation for patent attorneys (www.ceipi.edu)
374. Article 48(3) of the Agreement
375. For an overview of the different positions we refer to Volker 'Falk' Metzler, "Representation before the Future European and EU Patents Court (EEUPC)", 8 October 2010, www.visaepatentes.com
376. Position paper of the *Conseil des barreaux européens* – Council of Bars and Law Societies of Europe, "Proposal for a European and Community Patents Court – CCBE Position regarding Article 28", 19 February 2009, www.ccbe.eu
377. 216.92.57.242/downloads/Reports/10_33_23062010_representation-before-the-EEUPC.pdf

are regulated by a code of professional conduct, and will have training in the new procedures. The EPI found that the adoption of European patent attorneys as representatives will have significant cost benefits for the parties and provide effective litigation. For rules on professional conduct, the EPI refers to Article 11 of its Regulation on the establishment of an Institute of professional representatives before the European Patent Office and the Regulation on discipline for professional representatives,[378] which prescribe certain rules of professional conduct for European patent attorneys. The Additional Rules of Procedure of the Disciplinary Committee govern a Disciplinary Committee of the EPI and the procedures of the Committee.

It appears that the Contracting Member States wanted to combine in the articles regarding representation the traditions of the different Contracting Member States. In a number of Contracting Member States (e.g. Germany, Austria, Poland and the Netherlands), patent attorneys have traditionally and by law been able to independently represent parties in validity and non-infringement patent cases before national courts. However, in most civil law countries, representation by an attorney-at-law in court proceedings is mandatory.

Before the Unified Patent Court, representation shall be open to European patent attorneys with appropriate qualifications. But if a patent attorney is not authorised to represent parties before the Court (e.g. because of lacking the appropriate qualifications), he or she shall in any event have the right to assist the representative (lawyer or other patent attorney with appropriate qualifications) before the Court. Representatives of the parties may be assisted by patent attorneys. The patent attorneys shall be allowed to speak at hearings of the Court in accordance with the Rules of Procedure.[379]

Article 48(4) of the Agreement installs the attorney-client privilege for communications between a representative and the party or any other person. Representatives of the parties shall enjoy the rights and immunities necessary for the independent exercise of their duties, including the privilege from disclosure in proceedings before the Court in respect of communications between a representative and the party or any other person, under the conditions laid down in the Rules of Procedure, unless such privilege is expressly waived by the party concerned. This is certainly positive because in several Contracting Member States (e.g. Belgium) there are no rules on attorney-client privilege for patent attorneys. Patent attorneys who meet the requirements to be a representative before the Unified Patent Court shall now enjoy this privilege. Furthermore, the privilege shall also extend to "any other person", which implies

378. www.patentepi.com/patentepi/en/Rules-and-Regulations/rules-and-regulations.php
379. Article 48(5) of the Agreement

that communication between a lawyer and a patent attorney who assists the lawyer in a procedure before the Court (without being an official representative of the party concerned) shall also fall within the attorney-client privilege.

Representatives of the parties shall be obliged not to misrepresent cases or facts before the Court either knowingly or with good reasons to know.[380] No explicit sanctions on representatives are provided in the Agreement for misrepresentation of cases or facts.

Article 48(7) of the Agreement states that representation by a lawyer or a patent attorney shall not be required in proceedings against decisions of the European Patent Office in carrying out the tasks referred to in Article 9 Unitary Patent Regulation.[381]

D. LANGUAGE OF THE PROCEEDINGS

1. Court of First Instance

a. Local Divisions

The language of proceedings before any local division shall be an official European Union language which is the official language or one of the official languages of the Contracting Member State hosting the relevant division.[382] Additionally, Contracting Member States may designate one or more of the official languages of the European Patent Office as the language of proceedings of their local division.[383]

For local divisions, the Contracting Member State hosting the local division may choose one or more of its official languages as languages of the proceedings. The Contracting Member State can add to its chosen languages French, German or English (if this is not already an official language of the Contracting Member State).[384]

b. Regional Divisions

The language of proceedings before any regional division shall be an official European Union language which is the official language or one of the official languages of the Contracting Member State hosting the division or the official

380. Article 48(6) of the Agreement
381. Article 32(1)(i) of the Agreement
382. Article 49(1) of the Agreement
383. Article 49(2) of the Agreement
384. Article 14.1 EPC

language(s) designated by the Contracting Member States sharing a regional division.[385] Additionally, Contracting Member States may designate one or more of the official languages of the European Patent Office as the language of proceedings of their regional division.[386]

Contracting Member States that join forces in a regional division can either choose to have the official language(s) of the Member State in which the regional division has its seat, or designate one or more official language(s). This means that two Contracting Member States having two different languages (e.g. Germany and the Netherlands) and wishing to establish a regional division with its seat in one of the two Member States (e.g. Germany), theoretically could choose to have only German (the official language of one of the Contracting Member States sharing a division) and English (one of the official EPO languages) as the official languages of the regional division. Moreover, in a literal reading, Article 49 of the Agreement could even make it possible for a regional division to designate an official EU language which is not one of the official languages of the Contracting Member States sharing a regional division. However, chances are rather small that Contracting Member States that participate in a regional division would give up their own official language(s) for patent proceedings.

c. Central Division

The language of proceedings at the central division shall be the language in which the patent concerned was granted.[387] Since the European Patent Office only has three official languages which can be used to grant a European or unitary patent, proceedings before the central division shall always be in English, French or German.

The central division shall have three locations (Paris, London and Munich). But the place of the seat or section of the central division shall not affect the language regime of the proceedings, meaning that if the language of proceedings of a pharmaceutical patent was German, the London section of the central division shall perform the proceedings in German.

d. General Exception: Agreement on the Use of the Language in which the Patent was Granted

For proceedings before the local and regional divisions, the parties may always agree on the use of the language in which the patent was granted as the

385. Article 49(1) of the Agreement
386. Article 49(2) of the Agreement
387. Article 49(6) of the Agreement

language of proceedings, subject to approval by the competent panel.[388] If the panel does not approve their choice, the parties may request that the case be referred to the central division.[389]

The competent panel itself may, on grounds of convenience and fairness, also decide on the use of the language in which the patent was granted as the language of proceedings, as long as all parties agree.[390]

Article 49(5) of the Agreement deals with the hypothesis that one of the parties requests to use the language in which the patent was granted as the language of the proceedings, but the other party does not agree. Then the decision has to be taken by the President of the Court of First Instance. At the request of one of the parties and after having heard the other parties and the competent panel, the President of the Court of First Instance may, on grounds of fairness and taking into account all relevant circumstances, including the position of parties, in particular the position of the defendant, decide on the use of the language in which the patent was granted as the language of proceedings. In this case, the President of the Court of First Instance shall assess the need for specific translation and interpretation arrangements. Since the office of the President of the Court of First Instance shall be located in Paris, it remains to be seen how this provision shall function in practice. If a local division requests the President to decide in a particular case, the matter shall have to be transferred (electronically) to Paris. Since the President has to "hear" the refusing party and the competent panel, it is unclear whether parties and the panel shall be able to present their arguments electronically or if they have to be heard through video conferencing. Hopefully it will be the first option by which a written (electronic) procedure can be used for these disputes. The terminology "hearing" shall then have to be interpreted broadly to include written statements of the parties. In general, the Court shall have to take care that procedures which are intended to protect defendants are not used by parties to deliberately slow down proceedings and weigh on the effectiveness of the Unified Patent Court. This would have an adverse effect on the intentions of this new court system.

2. Court of Appeal

The language of proceedings before the Court of Appeal shall be the language of proceedings as used before the Court of First Instance.[391] But the parties may also agree on the use of the language in which the patent was granted

388. Article 49(3) of the Agreement
389. Article 49(3) of the Agreement
390. Article 49(4) of the Agreement
391. Article 50(1) of the Agreement

as the language of proceedings.[392] It was the intention of the Participating Member States with Article 50(2) of the Agreement to give the parties the opportunity to change before the Court of Appeal the language used during the first instance proceedings to the language in which the patent was granted.

In exceptional cases and to the extent deemed appropriate, the Court of Appeal may decide on another official language of a Contracting Member State as the language of proceedings for the whole or part of the proceedings, subject to agreement by the parties.[393] Here again, we notice the flexibility of the Agreement with respect to the language of the proceedings. Even if parties wish to change the language for the appeal proceedings in another official language of a Contracting Member State, this is possible.

3. Translation and Interpretation Arrangements

Regarding translations, it should be remembered that Article 4.1 Translation Regulation provides that, in the case of a dispute relating to a unitary patent, the patent proprietor shall provide, at the request and the choice of an alleged infringer, a full translation of the unitary patent into an official language of the Participating Member State in which either the alleged infringement took place or in which the alleged infringer is domiciled.

Article 4.2 Translation Regulation provides that in the course of legal proceedings, a "court competent in the territories of the Participating Member States for disputes concerning European patents with unitary effect" (i.e., the Unified Patent Court) can request a full translation of the patent into the language of the proceedings of that court. Therefore, the Unified Patent Court can at all times oblige the patent proprietor to translate its unitary patent in the language of the proceedings.

On the other hand, any panel of the Court of First Instance and the Court of Appeal may, to the extent deemed appropriate, dispense with translation requirements.[394] If, for example, documents regarding the infringement are drafted in English, while the official language of the proceedings is French, the Court can decide to exempt parties from translating.

At the request of one of the parties, and to the extent deemed appropriate, any division of the Court of First Instance and the Court of Appeal shall provide interpretation facilities to assist the parties concerned at oral proceedings.[395]

Since the proceedings before the central division can only be held in French, German or English, the Agreement provides special protection

392. Article 50(2) of the Agreement
393. Article 50(3) of the Agreement
394. Article 51(1) of the Agreement
395. Article 51(2) of the Agreement

mechanisms for infringement actions dealt with by the central division. In cases where an action for infringement is brought before the central division, a defendant having its residence, principal place of business or place of business in an EU Member State shall have the right to obtain, upon request, translations of relevant documents in the language of the Member State of residence, principal place of business or, in the absence of residence or principal place of business, place of business, in the following circumstances:[396]

- jurisdiction is entrusted to the central division in accordance with Article 33(1) third or fourth subparagraph, i.e., for defendants from outside the territory of the Contracting Member States or if the Contracting Member State does not host a local or regional division, and
- the language of proceedings at the central division is a language which is not an official language of the EU Member State where the defendant has its residence, principal place of business or, in the absence of residence or principal place of business, place of business, and
- the defendant does not have proper knowledge of the language of the proceedings.

E. PROCEEDINGS BEFORE THE COURT

1. Written, Interim and Oral Procedure

The proceedings before the Court shall consist of a written, an interim and an oral procedure, in accordance with the Rules of Procedure. For further detail on these stages of the procedure, we refer to the second part of this book. Article 52(1) of the Agreement provides that all procedures shall be organised in a flexible and balanced manner.

The interim procedure is intended to explore settlement possibilities for the dispute. The interim procedure takes place after the written procedure. If appropriate, the judge acting as Rapporteur, subject to a mandate of the full panel, shall be responsible for convening an interim hearing. That judge shall in particular explore with the parties the possibility for a settlement, including through mediation and/or arbitration by using the facilities of the Patent Mediation and Arbitration Centre.[397]

The oral procedure shall give parties the opportunity to explain properly their arguments. But the Court may, with the agreement of the parties, dispense with the oral hearing.[398] Given the broad tradition in several Contracting

396. Article 51(3) of the Agreement
397. Article 52(1) of the Agreement
398. Article 52(3) of the Agreement

Member States to make use of the oral pleadings, it can be expected that this possibility to dispense with the oral hearing shall not lead to a systematic written procedure.

2. Means of Evidence and Burden of Proof

Article 53 of the Agreement lists the means of giving or obtaining evidence that can be used in proceedings before the Court:

- hearing the parties;
- requests for information;
- production of documents;
- hearing witnesses;
- opinions by experts;
- inspection;
- comparative tests or experiments;
- sworn statements in writing (affidavits).

All the procedures for taking evidence shall be governed by the Rules of Procedure.

Questioning of witnesses and experts shall be under the control of the Court and be limited to what is necessary.[399] It was clearly the intention of the Contracting Member States to limit the use of oral questioning.

The burden of proving facts shall be on the party relying on those facts.[400]

Article 55 of the Agreement installs an important reversal of the burden of proof regarding the relationship between process patents and products. If the subject matter of a patent is a process for obtaining a new product, the identical product when produced without the consent of the patent proprietor shall, in the absence of proof to the contrary, be deemed to have been obtained by the patented process.

The reversal of the burden of proof shall also apply where there is a substantial likelihood that the identical product was made by the patented process and the patent proprietor has been unable, despite reasonable efforts, to determine the process actually used for such identical product.[401]

The presumption can be refuted by the alleged infringing party. But in the adduction of proof to the contrary, the legitimate interests of the defendant in protecting its manufacturing and trade secrets shall be taken into account.[402]

399. Article 52(2) of the Agreement
400. Article 54 of the Agreement
401. Article 55(2) of the Agreement
402. Article 55 of the Agreement

F. POWERS OF THE COURT

1. General Powers

As a general principle, Article 56 of the Agreement provides that the Court may impose such measures, procedures and remedies as are laid down in the Agreement and may make its orders subject to conditions, in accordance with the Rules of Procedure.

The Court shall take due account of the interest of the parties and shall, before making an order, give any party the opportunity to be heard, unless this is incompatible with the effective enforcement of such order.[403] Measures for preserving evidence, as mentioned in Article 7 of the Directive 2004/48 of 29 April 2004 on the Enforcement of Intellectual Property Rights (hereinafter the "Enforcement Directive") and referred to in Article 60 of the Agreement, are an example of an order to which hearing the parties in most cases is incompatible with the enforcement of the order.

All other articles of Chapter IV of the Agreement concern possible orders of the Court. Hereinafter, we have tried to list the orders in a way we feel meets the chronology of a patent case. Titles 2-7 concern orders which could help the Court in gathering evidence and deciding on the merits. The orders treated under Titles 8-14 concern the consequences of a decision on the merits by the Court.

2. Order to Preserve Evidence and to Inspect Premises

Article 60 of the Agreement is very similar to Article 7 of the Enforcement Regulation. Paragraphs 1, 2, 5, 6, 7, 8 and 9 of Article 60 are a quasi-identical rewrite of paragraphs 1-4 of Article 7 of the Enforcement Directive.

Measures to preserve evidence and inspection of premises can be ordered before the commencement of proceedings on the merits.[404]

At the request of an applicant that has presented reasonably available evidence to support the claim that the patent has been infringed or is about to be infringed, the Court may order prompt and effective provisional measures to preserve relevant evidence in respect of the alleged infringement, subject to the protection of confidential information.[405]

Such measures may include the detailed description, with or without the taking of samples, or the physical seizure of the infringing products, and, in

403. Article 56(2) of the Agreement
404. Article 56(1) and (3) of the Agreement
405. Article 60(1) of the Agreement

appropriate cases, the materials and implements used in the production and/or distribution of those products and the documents relating thereto.[406]

Furthermore, the Court may, at the request of the applicant who has presented evidence to support the claim that the patent has been infringed or is about to be infringed, order the inspection of premises. Such inspection of premises shall be conducted by a person appointed by the Court in accordance with the Rules of Procedure.[407] At the inspection of the premises, the applicant itself shall not be present but may be represented by an independent professional practitioner whose name has to be specified in the Court's order.[408]

Although inspection of the premises is not included in the Enforcement Directive, it belongs in most Member States to the core of orders preserving evidence.

Measures shall be ordered, if necessary without the other party having been heard, in particular where any delay is likely to cause irreparable harm to the proprietor of the patent, or where there is a demonstrable risk of evidence being destroyed.[409]

Where measures to preserve evidence or inspect premises are ordered without the other party in the case having been heard, the parties affected shall be given notice, without delay and at the latest immediately after the execution of the measures. A review, including a right to be heard, shall take place upon request of the parties affected with a view to deciding, within a reasonable period after the notification of the measures, whether the measures are to be modified, revoked or confirmed.[410]

The measures to preserve evidence may be subject to the lodging by the applicant of adequate security or an equivalent assurance intended to ensure compensation for any prejudice suffered by the defendant.[411]

The Court shall ensure that the measures to preserve evidence are revoked or otherwise cease to have effect, at the defendant's request, without prejudice to the damages which may be claimed, if the applicant does not bring, within a period not exceeding 31 calendar days or 20 working days, whichever is the longer, action leading to a decision on the merits of the case before the Court.[412]

Where the measures to preserve evidence are revoked, or where they lapse due to any act or omission by the applicant, or where it is subsequently found that there has been no infringement or threat of infringement of the patent,

406. Article 60(2) of the Agreement
407. Article 60(3) of the Agreement
408. Article 60(4) of the Agreement
409. Article 60(5) of the Agreement
410. Article 60(6) of the Agreement
411. Article 60(7) of the Agreement
412. Article 60(8) of the Agreement

the Court may order the applicant, at the defendant's request, to provide the defendant with appropriate compensation for any damage suffered as a result of those measures.[413]

3. Freezing Orders

At the request of an applicant that has presented reasonably available evidence to support the claim that the patent has been infringed or is about to be infringed, the Court may, even before the commencement of proceedings on the merits of the case, order a party not to remove from its jurisdiction any assets located therein, or not to deal in any assets, whether located within its jurisdiction or not.[414]

Article 60(5)-(9) regarding measures for preserving evidence, shall apply by analogy to freezing orders. This means that also for freezing orders the applicant needs to bring an action leading to a decision on the merits, within 31 calendar days or 20 working days, whichever is the longer, to uphold the freezing order, and if the freezing order is revoked, the applicant shall provide appropriate compensation for any damage suffered from the freezing order. The defendant has a right to review.

4. Order for the Protection of Confidential Information

To protect the trade secrets, personal data or other confidential information of a party to the proceedings or of a third party, or to prevent an abuse of evidence, the Court may order that the collection and use of evidence in proceedings before it be restricted or prohibited or that access to such evidence be restricted to specific persons.[415]

Such an order for the protection of confidential information shall be particularly important with respect to measures for preserving evidence and inspection of premises. The Court may order that certain confidential information such as the names of clients and suppliers shall not be included in the description or order that theaccess to this information is limited to specific persons.

5. Provisional and Protective Measures

To stop alleged infringers and prevent the increase of damages for the patent proprietor, the Court can order provisional and protective measures. Article

413. Article 60(9) of the Agreement
414. Article 61(1) of the Agreement
415. Article 58 of the Agreement

62 of the Agreement regarding such measures is similar to Article 9 of the Enforcement Directive.

The Court may, by way of order, grant injunctions against an alleged infringer or against an intermediary whose services are used by the alleged infringer, intended to prevent any imminent infringement, to prohibit, on a provisional basis and subject, where appropriate, to a recurring penalty payment, the continuation of the alleged infringement or to make such continuation subject to the lodging of guarantees intended to ensure the compensation of the right-holder.[416] This section of Article 62 is quasi-identical to Article 9.1 of the Enforcement Directive.

Before ordering such provisional and protective measures, the Court shall weigh up the interests of all parties. The Court shall have the discretion to weigh up the interests of the parties and in particular to take into account the potential harm to either of the parties resulting from the granting or the refusal of the injunction.[417] The weighing up of interest was not mentioned in the Enforcement Directive, but is a condition for provisional or protective measures applied in a number of Contracting Member States.[418] Article 62(2) of the Agreement only mentions the weighing of the interests of the "parties". In life sciences disputes, certain Contracting Member States also take into account the general interest (e.g. public health).

The Court may also order the seizure or delivery up of the products suspected of infringing a patent so as to prevent their entry into, or movement within the channels of commerce. If the applicant demonstrates circumstances likely to endanger the recovery of damages, the Court may order the precautionary seizure of the movable and immovable property of the alleged infringer, including the blocking of the bank accounts and of other assets of the alleged infringer.[419]

For injunctions to prevent the continuation of the infringement and seizures, the Court may require the applicant to provide any reasonable evidence in order to satisfy itself with a sufficient degree of certainty that the applicant is the right-holder and that the applicant's right is being infringed, or that such infringement is imminent.[420]

As for orders to preserve evidence and freezing orders, Article 60(5)-(9) of the Agreement regarding the measures preserving evidence shall apply by analogy to provisional and protective measures.[421]

---

416. Article 62(1) of the Agreement
417. Article 62(2) of the Agreement
418. E.g. in Belgium Article 1369bis/1, §5 of the Procedural Code provides a weighing up of interests, including the general interest
419. Article 62(3) of the Agreement
420. Article 62(4) of the Agreement
421. Article 62(5) of the Agreement

6. Order to Produce Evidence

At the request of a party that has presented reasonably available evidence sufficient to support its claims and has, in substantiating those claims, specified evidence that lies in the control of the opposing party or a third party, the Court may order the opposing party or a third party to present such evidence, subject to the protection of confidential information. Such order shall not result in an obligation of self-incrimination.[422]

At the request of a party, the Court may order, under the same conditions, the communication of banking, financial or commercial documents under the control of the opposing party, subject to the protection of confidential information.[423]

The order to produce evidence is intended to deal with the situation where one party sufficiently demonstrates that the counterparty possesses evidence which has not been submitted. The Court has the power to order the production of such evidence.

7. Court Experts

The Court may at any time appoint court experts in order to provide expertise for specific aspects of the case.[424] This of course does not affect the right of the parties to produce its own expert evidence. It is common in patent cases that parties make use of expert opinions, such as opinions of patent attorneys, professors and researchers. When each party provides expert opinions that come to different conclusions, courts generally appoint a court expert.

The Court shall provide the court expert with all information necessary for the provision of the expert advice. An indicative list of experts shall be drawn up by the Court in accordance with the Rules of Procedure. The indicative list shall be kept by the Registrar.[425] The Agreement does not provide any obligation for the Court to appoint an expert from the list of experts. Furthermore, neither the Agreement nor the Statute contain requirements for court experts. This means that the Court has a very broad discretion to appoint experts. The only limit seems to be any possible conflict of interest.

The court experts shall guarantee independence and impartiality. The rules governing conflicts of interest applicable to judges set out in Article 7 of

422. Article 59(1) of the Agreement
423. Article 59(2) of the Agreement
424. Article 57(1) of the Agreement
425. Article 57(2) of the Agreement

the Statute shall by analogy apply to court experts.[426] Therefore, court experts may not take part in the proceedings of a case in which they:

- have taken part as adviser;
- have been a party or have acted for one of the parties;
- have been called upon to pronounce as a member of a court, tribunal, board of appeal, arbitration or mediation panel, a commission of inquiry or in any other capacity;
- have a personal or financial interest in the case or in relation to one of the parties; or
- are related to one of the parties or the representatives of the parties by family ties.

Any party to an action may object to a judge taking part in the proceedings on any of the listed grounds or where the judge is suspected, with good reason, of partiality.[427]

It is not clear whether Article 7(3) of the Statute can be applied by analogy to court experts. Article 7(3) provides that when a judge considers that he should not take part in the judgment or examination of a particular case, he informs the President of the Court of First Instance (or in appeal cases the President of the Court of Appeal). In our opinion, the intervention of the President of the Court of First Instance is not necessary for court experts considering themselves affected by a conflict of interest. Furthermore, a possible intervention of the President of the Court of First Instance (situated in Paris) risks having an effect on the efficiency of the proceedings.

Expert advice given to the Court by court experts shall be made available to the parties which shall have the possibility to comment on it.[428]

The Agreement does not contain any limitations regarding the mission of the court experts. Generally under national laws court experts are only authorised to pronounce on technical issues, but are not authorised to pronounce on points of law. The Agreement lacks any provisions regarding this subject.

8. Power to Order the Communication of Information

The Court may, in response to a justified and proportionate request of the applicant and in accordance with the Rules of Procedure, order an infringer to inform the applicant of:

- the origin and distribution channels of the infringing products or processes;

426. Article 57(3) of the Agreement
427. Article 5(4) of the Statute
428. Article 57(4) of the Agreement

- the quantities produced, manufactured, delivered, received or ordered, as well as the price obtained for the infringing products; and
- the identity of any third person involved in the production or distribution of the infringing products or in the use of the infringing process.[429]

The Court may, in accordance with the Rules of Procedure, also order any third party who:

(a) was found in the possession of the infringing products on a commercial scale or to be using an infringing process on a commercial scale;
(b) was found to be providing on a commercial scale services used in infringing activities; or
(c) was indicated by the person referred to in (a) or (b) as being involved in the production, manufacture or distribution of the infringing products or processes or in the provision of the services,

to provide the applicant with the aforementioned information.[430]

A previous version of Article 67[431] provided that the communication of information could be ordered against an "alleged infringer". This opened up the possibility to order the communication of such information before the infringement was established. The current Article is clear that this order can only be granted once the infringement question has been answered by the Court.

The communication of this information gives the patent proprietor the opportunity to not only pursue the known infringer, but also the manufacturer, distributor, seller, service provider or any other third party involved in the infringement and/or in infringing the patent.

9. Permanent Injunctions in Case of Infringement

Where a decision is taken finding an infringement of a patent, the Court may grant an injunction against the infringer aimed at prohibiting the continuation of the infringement. The Court may also grant such an injunction against an intermediary whose services are being used by a third party to infringe a patent.[432] Article 63 of the Agreement is aligned with Article 11 of the Enforcement Directive.

429. Article 67(1) of the Agreement
430. Article 67(2) of the Agreement
431. Council working document 14268/12 of 27 September 2012, Draft Agreement on a Unified Patent Court and draft Statute – consolidated text, Article 39
432. Article 63(1) of the Agreement

Article 11 of the Enforcement Directive provides that non-compliance with an injunction shall, where appropriate, be subject to a recurring penalty payment, with a view to ensuring compliance. Normally penalty payments are to be paid by the infringing party to the plaintiff. However, Article 63 of the Agreement stipulates that, where appropriate, non-compliance with the injunction shall be subject to a periodic penalty payment that is payable to the Court. Does this mean that the Court shall gain income from penalty payments? Or should the Court pass on the penalty payment to the plaintiff(s)?

Article 82(4) of the Agreement repeats that if a party does not comply with the terms of an order of the Court, that party may be sanctioned with a periodic penalty payment which is payable to the Court. But by stipulating that the penalty payment is "without prejudice to the party's right to claim damages or security", this Article could provide an argument for the Court to pass the penalty payment to the plaintiff.[433]

10. Corrective Measures in Infringement Proceedings

Without prejudice to any damages due to the injured party by reason of the infringement, and without compensation of any sort, the Court may order, at the request of the applicant, that appropriate measures be taken with regard to products found to be infringing a patent and, in appropriate cases, with regard to materials and implements principally used in the creation or manufacture of those products.[434] Article 64(1) of the Agreement is quasi-identical to Article 10.1 of the Enforcement Directive. But the measures enumerated by Article 64(2) are broader than the measures listed in Article 10.2 of the Enforcement Directive. Article 10.2 of the Enforcement Directive merely provides recall from the channels of commerce, definitive removal from the channels of commerce or destruction.

Corrective measures that can be ordered by the Court are:

- a declaration of infringement;
- recalling the products from the channels of commerce;
- depriving the product of its infringing property;
- definitively removing the products from the channels of commerce; or
- the destruction of the products and/or of the materials and implements concerned.[435]

Identical to Article 10.2 of the Enforcement Directive, Article 64(2) of the Agreement stipulates that the Court shall order that those measures be carried

433. Article 82(4) of the Agreement
434. Article 64(1) of the Agreement
435. Article 64(2) of the Agreement

out at the expense of the infringer, unless particular reasons are invoked for not doing so.

In considering a request for corrective measures, the Court shall take into account the need for proportionality between the seriousness of the infringement and the remedies to be ordered, the willingness of the infringer to convert the materials into a non-infringing state, as well as the interests of third parties.[436] The willingness of the infringer to convert the materials into a non-infringing state is not mentioned in Article 10.3 of the Enforcement Directive and was specifically included in the Agreement. Apparently, the Contracting Member States were of the opinion that corrective measures such as destruction and recall can be avoided if the infringing party corrects the infringement itself.

Contrary to orders for protective and provisional measures, the interests of third parties are explicitly mentioned in Article 64(4) of the Agreement as an element that can be taken into account for ordering corrective measures.

11. Decision on the Validity of a Patent

The Court shall decide on the validity of a patent on the basis of an action for revocation or a counterclaim for revocation.[437]

The Court may revoke a classic European patent or a unitary patent, either entirely or partly, only on the grounds referred to in Articles 138(1) and 139(2) EPC. These grounds are:

- the subject matter of the patent is not patentable under Articles 52 to 57 EPC: these Articles concern patentable inventions, exceptions to patentability, novelty, non-prejudicial disclosures, inventive step and industrial application;
- the patent does not disclose the invention in a manner sufficiently clear and complete for it to be carried out by a person skilled in the art;
- the subject matter of the patent extends beyond the content of the application as filed or, if the patent was granted on a divisional application or on a new application filed under Article 61 EPC[438] (European patent applications filed by non-entitled persons), beyond the content of the earlier application as filed;

436. Article 64(4) of the Agreement
437. Article 65(1) of the Agreement
438. Article 61 EPC states: "If by a final decision it is adjudged that a person other than the applicant is entitled to the grant of the European patent, that person may, in accordance with the Implementing Regulations:
   (a) prosecute the European patent application as his own application in place of the applicant;
   (b) file a new European patent application in respect of the same invention; or
   (c) request that the European patent application be refused."

- the protection conferred by the patent has been extended;
- the proprietor of the European patent is not entitled under Article 60, paragraph 1 EPC;[439]
- if a national patent application and a national patent in a Contracting State has a prior right effect over a European patent designating that Contracting State.[440]

Certain Contracting Member States have proceedings to transfer the ownership of a patent (application) in case of filings by non-entitled persons. Belgium, for example, has a specific procedure to transfer the ownership of a patent if the invention concerned was unlawfully relieved from the inventor or its successor in title or if a patent application was filed by setting aside a legal or contractual obligation.[441] An action to transfer the ownership of a patent is not included in the actions that can be brought before the Unified Patent Court.[442] Under the Agreement, the only possible reaction to filings by non-entitled persons is a claim for revocation of the patent.

In accordance with Article 138, paragraph 3 EPC the proprietor of a patent shall have the right to limit the patent by amending the claims in proceedings before the Court. The patent as thus limited shall form the basis for the proceedings.

If the grounds for revocation affect the patent only in part, the patent shall be limited by a corresponding amendment of the claims and revoked in part.[443]

To the extent that a patent has been revoked, it shall be deemed not to have had, from the outset the effects specified in Articles 64 and 67 EPC.[444] Article 64 EPC stipulates that a patent confers on its proprietor from the date on which the mention of its grant is published in the *European Patent Bulletin*, in each Contracting State in respect of which it is granted, the same rights as would be conferred by a national patent granted in that State. Article 67 EPC deals with the rights conferred by a European patent application after publication.

Where the Court, in a final decision, revokes a patent, either entirely or partly, it shall send a copy of the decision to the European Patent Office and,

---

439. Article 60, §1 EPC stipulates: "The right to a European patent shall belong to the inventor or his successor in title. If the inventor is an employee, the right to a European patent shall be determined in accordance with the law of the State in which the employee is mainly employed; if the State in which the employee is mainly employed cannot be determined, the law to be applied shall be that of the State in which the employer has the place of business to which the employee is attached."
440. Article 139(2) EPC
441. Article 9 of the Belgian Patent Act of 28 March 1984
442. Article 32(1) of the Agreement
443. Article 65(3) of the Agreement
444. Article 65(4) of the Agreement

with respect to a European patent, to the national patent office of any Contracting Member State concerned.[445]

12. Powers of the Court Concerning Decisions of the European Patent Office

In actions concerning decisions of the European Patent Office in carrying out the tasks referred to in Article 9 Unitary Patent Regulation, the Court may exercise any power entrusted to the European Patent Office by Article 9 Unitary Patent Regulation, including the rectification of the Register for unitary patent protection.[446]

The tasks of Article 9 of the Unitary Patent Regulation concern the administration of requests for unitary effect by proprietors of European patents, the inclusion and administration of a Register for unitary patent protection within the European Patent Register, receiving and registering statements on licensing, withdrawal and licensing commitments undertaken in international standardisation bodies, the publication of the translations during the transitional period, the collection and administration of renewal fees for European patents with unitary effect, the collection and administration of additional fees paid in cases of late payment of renewal fees and the administration of a compensation scheme of translation costs for applicants filing European patent applications in one of the official languages of the Union that is not an official language of the European Patent Office. If the European Patent Office fails to carry out one of these specific tasks correctly, the Court can put itself in the place of the European Patent Office and carry out the task itself or order the EPO to fulfil its task correctly.

For actions against decisions of the European Patent Office regarding unitary patents, the parties shall bear their own costs.[447] This is an exception to the general arrangement regarding costs, set out in Article 69 of the Agreement.

13. Award of Damages

a. Determination of the Damages

The article on the award of damages is again based on the Enforcement Directive.

Article 68 of the Agreement is to a large extent identical to Article 13 of the Enforcement Directive. The only difference is that Article 68(2) of the

---

445. Article 65(5) of the Agreement
446. Article 65(1) of the Agreement
447. Article 66(2) of the Agreement

Agreement gives clear guidance to the aim and limits of damages. The injured party shall, to the extent possible, be placed in the position it would have been in if no infringement had taken place. The infringer shall not benefit from the infringement, but damages may not be punitive.[448] This section confirms the civil law tradition of damage determination. Both parties should be placed as far as possible in the same position as would have occurred in the absence of an infringement. To reach that goal, the Court can take away all elements by which the infringer benefited from the infringement, but in doing so the Court cannot go any further than the theoretical position in which both parties would have been if no infringement had taken place. The common law concept of punitive damages is clearly rejected by the Contracting Member States.

Furthermore, the Agreement and the Enforcement Directive clearly distinguish between the infringer who knowingly, or with reasonable grounds to know, has infringed the patent and the infringer who did not know, or did not have reasonable grounds to know he was infringing a patent.

The Court shall, at the request of the injured party, order the infringer who knowingly, or with reasonable grounds to know, engaged in a patent infringing activity, to pay the injured party damages appropriate to the harm actually suffered by that party as a result of the infringement.[449]

When the Court sets the damages:

(a) it shall take into account all appropriate aspects, such as the negative economic consequences, including lost profits, which the injured party has suffered, any unfair profits made by the infringer and, in appropriate cases, elements other than economic factors, such as the moral prejudice caused to the injured party by the infringement; or
(b) as an alternative to (a), it may, in appropriate cases, set the damages as a lump sum on the basis of elements such as at least the amount of the royalties or fees which would have been due if the infringer had requested authorisation to use the patent in question.[450]

Where the infringer did not knowingly, or with reasonable grounds to know, engage in the infringing activity, the Court may order the recovery of profits or the payment of compensation.[451]

In order to assess whether the infringer knowingly infringed the patent, special attention should be given to Article 4.4 of the Translation Regulation. This Article provides that in the case of a dispute concerning a claim for damages, the court hearing the dispute shall take into consideration that the alleged

448. Article 68(2) of the Agreement
449. Article 68(1) of the Agreement
450. Article 68(3) of the Agreement
451. Article 68(4) of the Agreement

infringer (in particular where the alleged infringer is a small and medium-sized enterprise, a natural person, a non-profit organisation, a university or a public research organisation) may have acted without knowing or having reasonable grounds to know that it was infringing the patent before having been provided by the patent proprietor with a full translation of the unitary patent into an official language of the Participating Member State in which either the alleged infringement took place or in which the alleged infringer is domiciled.

b. Period of Limitation

For all forms of financial compensation, the Agreement contains a period of limitation. Actions relating to all forms of financial compensation may not be brought more than five years after the date on which the applicant became aware, or had reasonable grounds to become aware, of the latest fact justifying the action.[452] The reference to "all forms of financial compensation" makes it clear that the period of limitation also applies to claims regarding legal costs and expenses for corrective measures.

The injured party can only go back five years for damages. The limitation to five years is meant to avoid patent proprietors from first tolerating an infringement until the lapse of the 20-year term of a patent (or longer in case of a supplementary protection certificate) and then at the end claim damages for the full 20 years. The period of limitation encourages patent proprietors to bring action against infringement within a reasonable period of time.

14. Legal Costs

Reasonable and proportionate legal costs and other expenses incurred by the successful party shall, as a general rule, be borne by the unsuccessful party, unless equity requires otherwise, up to a ceiling set in accordance with the Rules of Procedure.[453]

Although this is identical to Article 14 of the Enforcement Directive, the principle that the successful party pays is not implemented in all Contracting Member States in the same way. In Belgium, for example, a system of lump sum compensations for attorney fees and costs has been put into place. The lump sum compensation principle is laid down in the Procedural Code[454] and a Royal Decree determines the actual sums that can be granted by the judge.[455]

452. Article 72(1) of the Agreement
453. Article 69(1) of the Agreement
454. Article 1022 of the Belgian Procedural Code
455. Royal Decree of 26 October 2007 regarding the determination of the tariff of the procedural compensation meant in article 1022 of the Procedural Code and the determination of the date of

Where a party succeeds only in part, or in exceptional circumstances, the Court may order that costs be apportioned equitably or that the parties bear their own costs.[456] A party should bear any unnecessary costs it has caused the Court or another party.[457]

At the request of the defendant, the Court may order the applicant to provide adequate security for the legal costs and other expenses incurred by the defendant which the applicant may be liable to bear, in particular in the case of orders to produce evidence,[458] orders to preserve evidence and to inspect premises,[459] freezing orders[460] and provisional and protective measures.[461]

G. COURT FEES AND LEGAL AID

Parties to proceedings before the Court shall pay court fees.[462]

These Court fees shall be fixed by the Administrative Committee. They shall consist of a fixed fee, combined with a value-based fee above a pre-defined ceiling. Article 36(3) of the Agreement stipulates that the Court fees shall be fixed at such a level as to ensure a balance between the principle of fair access to justice, in particular for small and medium-sized enterprises, micro-entities, natural persons, non-profit organisations, universities and public research organisations, and an adequate contribution of the parties for the costs incurred by the Court, recognising the economic benefits to the parties involved, and the objective of providing the Court with self-balanced finances. The level of the Court fees shall be reviewed periodically by the Administrative Committee. Targeted support measures for small and medium-sized enterprises and micro entities may be considered.[463]

The level of Court fees has been subject to extensive political discussions between the Contracting Member States. Therefore, the following section regarding Court fees was included in the draft declaration of the Contracting Member States concerning the preparations for the coming into operation of the UPC agreement:

---

entry into force of the articles 1 to 13 of the Law of 21 April 2007 regarding the recovery of fees and costs connected to legal advice by a lawyer, *Belgian Official Gazette,* 9 November 2007

456. Article 69(2) of the Agreement
457. Article 69(3) of the Agreement
458. Article 59 of the Agreement
459. Article 60 of the Agreement
460. Article 61 of the Agreement
461. Article 62 of the Agreement
462. Article 70(1) of the Agreement
463. Article 36(3) of the Agreement

> "The Signatory States consider that the fee system of the Unified Patent Court should be straightforward and predictable for the users. Accordingly, the Unified Patent Court should apply a mixed system of fixed and value-based fees. The Court should be accessible for parties with limited resources. Thus the court fees should be set at an appropriate level. Whilst all users of the Unified Patent Court should contribute to its financing, users having more significant economic interests should provide a reasonable and proportionate contribution to the functioning of the Court, on the basis of an additional value-based fee, proportionate to the economic value of the case at stake in the specific procedure, applicable above a predefined ceiling. The fee system should provide adequate and specific tools to ensure proper access for small and medium-sized enterprises, micro entities, natural persons, non-profit organisations, universities and public research organisations to the Unified Patent Court, especially in relation to cases of high economic value."[464]

Court fees shall be paid in advance, unless the Rules of Procedure provide otherwise. Any party which has not paid a prescribed court fee may be excluded from further participation in the proceedings.[465]

For natural persons, the Agreement provides the possibility for legal aid. Legal persons are excluded from legal aid. A party who is a natural person and who is unable to meet the costs of the proceedings, either wholly or in part, may at any time apply for legal aid.[466] The conditions for granting of legal aid shall be laid down in the Rules of Procedure. On a proposal from the Court, the Administrative Committee shall set the level of, and rules on, bearing the costs of legal aid.[467]

In specific cases, the Court shall decide whether legal aid should be granted in full or in part, or whether it should be refused, in accordance with the Rules of Procedure.[468]

464. Updated draft declaration of the contracting Member States concerning the preparations for the coming into operation of the UPC agreement, 14 November 2012, Council Document 16221/12, section 8
465. Article 70(2) of the Agreement
466. Article 70(1) of the Agreement
467. Article 71(3) of the Agreement
468. Article 71(2) of the Agreement

H. APPEAL PROCEEDINGS

1. Appeal

The decisions on the merits of the Court of First Instance, as well as all orders the Court of First Instance may decide upon during the course of proceedings, can be appealed.

An appeal against a decision of the Court of First Instance may be brought before the Court of Appeal by any party which has been unsuccessful, in whole or in part, in its submissions, within two months of the date of the notification of the decision.[469]

While the appeal term for decisions of the Court is quite long, the appeal term for specific orders is only 15 calendar days. An appeal against an order of the Court of First Instance may be brought before the Court of Appeal by any party which has been unsuccessful, in whole or in part, in its submissions:

(a) for the orders that decide to use, with the agreement of the parties, the language in which the patent was granted as the language of proceedings,[470] orders to produce evidence,[471] orders to preserve evidence and to inspect premises,[472] freezing orders,[473] orders for provisional and protective measures[474] and orders to communicate information,[475] within 15 calendar days of the notification of the order to the applicant;
For these orders, the appeal term starts at the date of notification since certain measures can be ordered without the other party being heard.

(b) for orders other than the orders referred to in point (a):
   (i) together with the decision, or
   (ii) where the Court grants leave to appeal, within 15 days of the notification of the Court's decision to that effect.[476]

"Leave to appeal" is a common law concept which has been introduced in the Unified Patent Court system, but can be seen as a permission to appeal. If, for example, an order for the appointment of a Court expert or for the protection of confidential information is rendered by the Court before the whole case is

469. Article 73(1) of the Agreement
470. Article 49(5) of the Agreement
471. Article 59 of the Agreement
472. Article 60 of the Agreement
473. Article 61 of the Agreement
474. Article 62 of the Agreement
475. Article 67 of the Agreement
476. Article 73(2) of the Agreement

decided, to appeal such an order, the permission of the Court itself is needed. Such permission is called a “leave to appeal”.

The appeal against a decision or an order of the Court of First Instance may be based on points of law and matters of fact.[477]

For new facts and new evidence that is only presented for the first time in appeal, the Agreement provides a threshold. New facts and new evidence may only be introduced in accordance with the Rules of Procedure and where the submission thereof by the party concerned could not reasonably have been expected during proceedings before the Court of First Instance.[478]

2. Effects of an Appeal

Only decisions on actions or counterclaims for revocation and on actions regarding decisions of the European Patent Office in carrying out the tasks referred to in Article 9 of the Unitary Patent Regulation shall always have suspensive effect.[479]

For all other actions, an appeal shall not have suspensive effect unless the Court of Appeal decides otherwise at the motivated request of one of the parties. The Rules of Procedure shall guarantee that such a decision is taken without delay.[480] The non-suspensive effect of decisions in infringement cases are new for a number of Contracting Member States.

If a defendant brings a counterclaim for revocation in an infringement case and the Court eventually decides that the patent is valid and infringed, the plaintiff shall be entitled to demand from the defendant to cease the patent infringement, even if the defendant has appealed the decision regarding the validity of the patent.

An appeal against an order that decides to use, at the request of one of the parties, the language in which the patent was granted as the language of proceedings,[481] an order to produce evidence,[482] an order to preserve evidence and to inspect premises,[483] a freezing order,[484] an order for provisional and protective measures[485] or an order to communicate information,[486] shall not prevent the continuation of the main proceedings. However, the Court of First

477. Article 73(3) of the Agreement
478. Article 73(4) of the Agreement
479. Article 74(2) of the Agreement
480. Article 74(1) of the Agreement
481. Article 49(5) of the Agreement
482. Article 59 of the Agreement
483. Article 60 of the Agreement
484. Article 61 of the Agreement
485. Article 62 of the Agreement
486. Article 67 of the Agreement

Instance shall not give a decision in the main proceedings before the decision of the Court of Appeal concerning an appealed order has been given.[487]

3. Decision on Appeal and Referral Back

If an appeal is well-founded, the Court of Appeal shall revoke the decision of the Court of First Instance and give a final decision. The Court of Appeal may in exceptional cases, and in accordance with the Rules of Procedure, refer the case back to the Court of First Instance for decision.[488]

It is unclear in which cases a referral back to the Court of First Instance shall be necessary. The Agreement refers to "exceptional cases", but no guidance is given regarding the nature of such exceptionality.

Where a case is referred back to the Court of First Instance, the Court of First Instance shall be bound by the decision of the Court of Appeal on points of law.[489]

I. DECISIONS

1. Basis for Decisions

The Court shall decide in accordance with the requests submitted by the parties and shall not award more than is requested.[490] This general procedural principle has as consequence that the Court is bound for its decision by the matters presented by the parties. The judges of the Court cannot refuse to decide upon the submitted requests, but may on the other hand go no further than such submitted requests.

Decisions on the merits may only be based on grounds, facts and evidence submitted by the parties or introduced into the procedure by an order of the Court and on which the parties have had an opportunity to present their comments.[491]

The Court shall evaluate evidence freely and independently.[492]

487. Article 74(3) of the Agreement
488. Article 75(1) of the Agreement
489. Article 75(2) of the Agreement
490. Article 76(1) of the Agreement
491. Article 76(2) of the Agreement
492. Article 76(3) of the Agreement

2. Formal Requirements of Decisions

Decisions and orders of the Court shall be reasoned and shall be given in writing in accordance with the Rules of Procedure.[493] Decisions and orders of the Court shall be delivered in the language of proceedings.[494]

Decisions of the Court shall contain the names of the judges deciding the case.[495]

Decisions shall be signed by the judges deciding the case and by the Registrar for decisions of the Court of Appeal. For decisions of the Court of First Instance, the Deputy-Registrar and the deciding judges shall sign. The decisions shall be read in open court.[496]

3. Decisions and Dissenting Opinions

a. Decision-Making Process

Decisions and orders of the Court shall be taken by a majority of the panel.[497] Normally, a panel shall be composed of three judges (*supra*, III.A.1), but if a technically qualified judge is added in case of a counterclaim for revocation, there shall be an even number of judges. When a panel sits in composition of an even number of judges, decisions of the Court shall be taken by a majority of the panel.[498] In case of equal vote, the vote of the presiding judge shall prevail.[499]

In the event of one of the judges on a panel being prevented from attending, a judge from another panel may be called upon to sit in accordance with the Rules of Procedure.[500]

In cases where the Court of Appeal shall take a decision sitting as a full court (*supra*, III.B), such decision shall be valid only if it is taken by at least three-quarters of the judges comprising the full court.[501]

The deliberations of the Court shall be and shall remain secret.[502]

---

493. Article 77(1) of the Agreement
494. Article 77(2) of the Agreement
495. Article 35(4) of the Statute
496. Article 35(5) of the Statute
497. Article 78 of the Agreement
498. Article 35(1) of the Statute
499. Article 78(1) of the Agreement and Article 35(1) of the Statute
500. Article 35(2) of the Statute
501. Article 35(3) of the Statute
502. Article 34 of the Statute

b. Dissenting Opinions

Following the common law tradition, any judge on the panel may, in exceptional circumstances, express a dissenting opinion separately from the decision of the Court.[503] A dissenting opinion expressed separately by a judge on a panel shall be reasoned, given in writing and shall be signed by the judge expressing this opinion.[504]

c. Decisions by Default

The Statute also provides the possibility for decisions by default, under certain circumstances. At the request of a party to an action, a decision by default may be given in accordance with the Rules of Procedure, where the other party, after having been served with a document instituting proceedings or with an equivalent document, fails to file written submissions in defence or fails to appear at the oral hearing.[505]

An objection against a decision by default may be lodged within one month of it being notified to the party against which the default decision has been given. The objection shall not have the effect of staying enforcement of the decision by default unless the Court dccides otherwise.[506]

4. Settlement Decisions

The parties may, at any time in the course of proceedings, conclude their case by way of settlement, which shall be confirmed by a decision of the Court.[507] Article 79 of the Agreement provides that a patent may not be revoked or limited by way of settlement.

This does not mean that parties cannot agree on the limitation of a patent, but in such a case, the patent proprietor who agrees to limit its patent, should do so by a unilateral limitation notified to the respective national offices of the Member States in which a European patent is validated or to the EPO in case of a unitary patent, not by a settlement confirmed by a decision of the Court.[508]

503. Article 78(2) of the Agreement
504. Article 36 of the Statute
505. Article 37(1) of the Statute
506. Article 37(2) of the Statute
507. Article 79 of the Agreement
508. Article 9.1(b) of the Unitary Patent Regulation

5. Publication of Decisions

Article 80 of the Agreement provides that the Court may order, at the request of the applicant and at the expense of the infringer, appropriate measures for the dissemination of information concerning the Court's decision, including displaying the decision and publishing it in full or in part in public media.

Although this Article is included in Chapter VI of the Agreement, which deals with decisions of the Court, it gives the Court the power to order publication measures. Publication measures are in fact a remedy for the plaintiff in patent cases, and would therefore have been better included in Chapter IV of the Agreement ("Powers of the Court"). The wording of Article 54 is identical to Article 15 of the Enforcement Directive.

6. Rehearing

The Unified Patent Court system does not include a "Cassation" or "Supreme Court" instance controlling the correct application of the law. But the Agreement does provide a possibility for rehearing, which could be considered as an exceptional (third) instance after the normal appeal term has lapsed or after an appeal decision. A request for rehearing after a final decision of the Court may exceptionally be granted by the Court of Appeal in the following circumstances:

- on discovery of a fact by the party requesting the rehearing, which is of such a nature as to be a decisive factor and which, when the decision was given, was unknown to the party requesting the rehearing; such a request may only be granted on the basis of an act which was held, by a final decision of a national court, to constitute a criminal offence; or
- in the event of a fundamental procedural defect, in particular when a defendant who did not appear before the Court was not served with the document initiating the proceedings or an equivalent document in sufficient time and in such a way as to enable him to arrange for the defence.[509]

The term for a request for rehearing is ten years from the date of the decision but not later than two months from the date of the discovery of the new fact or of the procedural defect. Such a request shall not have suspensive effect unless the Court of Appeal decides otherwise.[510]

509. Article 81(1) of the Agreement
510. Article 81(2) of the Agreement

If the request for a rehearing is well-founded, the Court of Appeal shall set aside, in whole or in part, the decision under review and re-open the proceedings for a new trial and decision, in accordance with the Rules of Procedure.[511] Persons using patents which are the subject matter of a decision under review and who act in good faith should be allowed to continue using such patents.[512] The question remains as to how the further use of a patent shall be taken into account for the calculation of damages, if the re-hearing results in a final decision of infringement. Can an alleged infringer who was successful in an infringement procedure that was reheard afterwards be held liable for acts committed after the first final (non-infringement) decision of the Court and before the final (infringement) decision resulting from the rehearing?

7. Enforcement of Decisions and Orders

Decisions and orders of the Court shall be enforceable in any Contracting Member State. An order for the enforcement of a decision shall be appended to the decision by the Court.[513]

Where appropriate, the enforcement of a decision may be subject to the provision of security or an equivalent assurance to ensure compensation for any damage suffered, in particular in the case of injunctions.[514]

Enforcement procedures shall be governed by the law of the Contracting Member State where the enforcement takes place. Any decision of the Court shall be enforced under the same conditions as a decision given in the Contracting Member State where the enforcement takes place.[515]

511. Article 81(3) of the Agreement
512. Article 81(4) of the Agreement
513. Article 82(1) of the Agreement
514. Article 82(2) of the Agreement
515. Article 82(3) of the Agreement

Chapter VIII
Court Finances

A. BUDGET OF THE COURT

The budget of the Court shall be financed by the Court's own financial revenues and, at least in the transitional period of seven years after the date of entry into force (*infra*), as necessary, by contributions from the Contracting Member States. The budget shall be balanced.[516]

The Court's own financial revenues shall comprise court fees and other revenues.[517] It is unclear which "other revenues" the Court would obtain. If the Court could withhold the penalty payments paid in case of non-respect of orders or injunctions,[518] this could be a potential revenue for the Court (*supra*, VI.F.9).

If the Court is unable to balance its budget out of its own resources, the Contracting Member States shall remit to it special financial contributions.[519]

The training framework for judges[520] and the operating costs of the Patent Arbitration and Mediation Centre[521] shall be financed by the budget of the Court.

B. FINANCING OF THE COURT

The operating costs of the Court shall be covered by the budget of the Court, in accordance with the Statute.

On the date of entry into force of the Agreement, the Contracting Member States shall provide the initial financial contributions necessary for the setting up of the Court.[522]

---

516. Article 36(1) of the Agreement
517. Article 36(2) of the Agreement
518. Article 63(2) of the Agreement
519. Article 36(4) of the Agreement
520. Article 38 of the Agreement
521. Article 39 of the Agreement
522. Article 37(2) of the Agreement

The basis for the calculations of the financial contributions of the Contracting Member States was subject to extensive political discussions in the European Competitiveness Council. Finally, the Competitiveness Council of 5 December 2011 agreed that, during the initial transitional period (first seven years) the financial contributions should be based on the number of European patents in force and the number of European patents litigated in the Member State concerned.[523]

Therefore, Article 37(3) of the Agreement provides that, during the initial transitional period of seven years, starting from the date of the entry into force of this Agreement, the contribution by each Contracting Member State having *ratified or acceded to the Agreement before the entry into force* thereof shall be calculated on the basis of the number of European patents having effect in the territory of that State on the date of entry into force of this Agreement and the number of European patents with respect to which actions for infringement or for revocation have been brought before the national courts of that State in the year preceding entry into force of this Agreement.

During the same initial transitional period of seven years, for Member States which *ratify or accede to this Agreement after the entry into force* thereof, the contributions shall be calculated on the basis of the number of European patents having effect in the territory of the ratifying or acceding Member State on the date of the ratification or accession and the number of European patents with respect to which actions for infringement or for revocation have been brought before the national courts of the ratifying or acceding Member State in the year preceding the ratification or accession.

After the transitional period, it is expected that the Court shall be self-financing. If this is not the case and exceptional contributions by the Contracting Member States become necessary, they shall be determined in accordance with the scale for the distribution of annual renewal fees for unitary patents applicable at the time the contribution becomes necessary.[524]

Besides the purely financial contributions of Contracting Member States, the Unified Patent Court also needs facilities and administrative support. Contracting Member States setting up a local division shall provide the facilities necessary for that purpose. Contracting Member States sharing a regional division shall provide jointly the facilities necessary for that purpose. And the Contracting Member States hosting the central division, its sections or the Court of Appeal (France, UK, Germany and Luxembourg), shall provide the facilities necessary for that purpose.[525]

---

523. Council of the European Union, Draft Agreement on the creation of a Unified Patent Court, Presidency – compromise text, Council working document 18239/11 of 6 December 2011, p. 2
524. Article 37(4) of the Agreement
525. Article 37(1) of the Agreement

During the initial transitional period of seven years, the Contracting Member States concerned shall provide administrative support staff, without prejudice to the Statute of that staff. The addition of "without prejudice to the Statute of that staff" refers to the fact that the Administrative Committee (and not the Contracting Member States) shall establish the Staff Regulations of officials and other servants of the Court.[526]

C. OPERATING THE BUDGET

The budget shall be adopted by the Budget Committee on a proposal from the Presidium.[527] The Presidium shall submit the draft budget of the Court to the Budget Committee no later than the date prescribed in the Financial Regulations.[528]

The budget shall be drawn up in accordance with the generally accepted accounting principles laid down in the Financial Regulations. These Financial Regulations shall be adopted by the Administrative Committee and shall include arrangements relating to the establishment and implementation of the budget and for the rendering and auditing of accounts, the method and procedure whereby the payments and contributions, including the initial financial contributions of the Contracting Member States, are to be made available to the Court, the rules concerning the responsibilities of authorising and accounting officers[529] and the arrangements for their supervision, and the generally accepted accounting principles on which the budget and the annual financial statements are to be based.[530] The Financial Regulations shall be amended by the Administrative Committee on proposal of the Court.

The Registrar shall be responsible for the implementation of the budget in accordance with the Financial Regulations.[531] The Registrar shall annually make a statement on the accounts of the preceding financial year relating to the implementation of the budget which shall be approved by the Presidium.[532]

The accounting period shall commence on 1 January and end on 31 December.[533] If, at the beginning of the accounting period, the budget has not been adopted by the Budget Committee, the Court can make use of a provisional

526. Article 16(2) of the Agreement
527. Article 26 of the Statute
528. Article 30 of the Statute
529. In the draft version of the Statute it was not clear if this would be the officers of the Court or of each division of the Court.
530. Article 33 of the Statute
531. Article 26(3) of the Statute
532. Article 26(4) of the Statute
533. Article 29 of the Statute

budget divided into provisional twelfths. Then expenditure may be effected on a monthly basis per heading or other division of the budget, in accordance with the Financial Regulations, up to one-twelfth of the budget appropriations for the preceding accounting period, provided that the appropriations thus made available to the Presidium do not exceed one-twelfth of those provided for in the draft budget.[534] The Budget Committee may authorise expenditure in excess of one-twelfth of the budget appropriations for the preceding accounting period.[535]

In a normal budget, the expenditure entered in the budget shall be authorised for the duration of one accounting period unless the Financial Regulations provide otherwise.[536] In accordance with the Financial Regulations, any appropriations, other than those relating to staff costs, which are unexpended at the end of the accounting period may be carried forward, but not beyond the end of the following accounting period.[537] Appropriations shall be set out under different headings according to type and purpose of the expenditure, and subdivided, to the extent necessary, in accordance with the Financial Regulations.[538]

Within the budget, the Presidium may, in accordance with the Financial Regulations, transfer funds between the various headings or subheadings.[539]

The budget of the Court may include appropriations for unforeseeable expenditure. The employment of these appropriations by the Court shall be subject to the prior approval of the Budget Committee.[540]

The annual financial statements of the Court shall be examined by independent auditors. The auditors shall be appointed and if necessary dismissed by the Budget Committee.[541] The audit, which shall be based on professional auditing standards and shall take place, if necessary, in situ, shall ascertain that the budget has been implemented in a lawful and proper manner and that the financial administration of the Court has been conducted in accordance with the principles of economy and sound financial management. The auditors shall draw up a report after the end of each accounting period containing a signed audit opinion.[542] The Presidium shall submit to the Budget Committee the annual financial statements of the Court and the annual budget imple-

534. Article 31(1) of the Statute
535. Article 31(2) of the Statute
536. Article 27(1) of the Statute
537. Article 27(2) of the Statute
538. Article 27(3) of the Statute
539. Article 26(2) of the Statute
540. Article 28 of the Statute
541. Article 32(1) of the Statute
542. Article 32(2) of the Statute

mentation statement for the preceding accounting period, together with the auditors' report.[543]

The Budget Committee shall approve the annual accounts together with the auditors' report and shall discharge the Presidium in respect of the implementation of the budget.[544]

543. Article 32(3) of the Statute
544. Article 32(4) of the Statute

Chapter IX
Implementation and Operation of the Agreement

A. TRANSITIONAL REGIME

Upon entry into force, the Unified Patent Court system shall immediately apply to unitary patents. This is logical since the main intention of the Unitary Patent Regulation is to provide a title with equal effect in all participating EU Member States. To be of consequence, the proprietor of a unitary patent should be able to enforce its patent in all territories at the same time.

The situation is different for classic European patents. At the time proprietors of European patents obtained their title, the Unified Patent Court was not yet in place. It is possible that proprietors of European patents which would have known that the Unified Patent Court system applied to their patent would have decided not to apply for a European patent, but instead could have chosen for national protection of their invention. Therefore, the Agreement contains a transitional period in which European patent proprietors can still bring action before national courts. The Competitiveness Council of 5 December 2011 decided that the transitional period in which actions for European patents can still be brought before national courts, should be fixed at seven years, with the possibility of prolongation for a maximum of up to a further seven years. During the transitional period of seven years after the date of entry into force of the Agreement, an action for infringement or for revocation of a European patent or an action for infringement or for declaration of invalidity of a supplementary protection certificate issued for a product protected by a European patent may still be brought before national courts or other competent national authorities.[545] Consequently, during the transitional period, parties shall have the choice to either start infringement or revocation proceedings at a national court or at the Unified Patent Court.

But it shall also be possible for European patent proprietors to avoid the exclusive jurisdiction of the Unified Patent Court after the end of the

545. Article 83(1) of the Agreement

transitional period. Unless an action has already been brought before the Unified Patent Court, a proprietor of or an applicant for a European patent granted or applied for prior to the end of the transitional period, as well as a holder of a supplementary protection certificate issued for a product protected by a European patent, shall have the possibility to opt out of the exclusive competence of the Court. To this end they shall notify their opt-out to the Registry at the latest one month before expiry of the transitional period. The opt-out shall take effect upon its entry into the Register.[546]

The opt-out possibility was a result of political compromise, undermining to some extent the whole purpose of a transitional period. Normally a transitional period is meant to provide a smooth transition to a new system. Here, it is possible for European patents to completely avoid the jurisdiction of the Unified Patent Court during the full life cycle of a patent.

However, such an opt-out can always be withdrawn if no proceedings have been started. In this respect, Article 83(4) of the Agreement stipulates that unless an action has already been brought before a national court, proprietors of or applicants for European patents or holders of supplementary protection certificates issued for a product protected by a European patent, which have made use of the opt-out shall be entitled to withdraw their opt-out at any moment. In this event they shall notify thc Rcgistry accordingly. The withdrawal of the opt-out shall take effect upon its entry into the Registry.[547]

An action pending before a national court at the end of the transitional period shall not be affected by the expiry of this period.[548]

Five years after the entry into force of the Agreement, the Administrative Committee shall carry out a broad consultation with the users of the patent system and a survey on the number of European patents and supplementary protection certificates issued for products protected by European patents with respect to which actions for infringement or for revocation or declaration of invalidity are still brought before the national courts, the reasons for this and the implications thereof. On the basis of this consultation and an opinion of the Court, the Administrative Committee may decide to prolong the transitional period by up to seven years.[549]

If the transitional period is prolonged, patent proprietors shall still be able to go to national courts for the enforcement of a European patent and defendants shall be able to revoke European patents before national courts during a period of 14 years. As a transitional period, this is very long and equals almost three-quarters of the total duration of a patent. Taking into account that

546. Article 83(3) of the Agreement
547. Article 83(4) of the Agreement
548. Article 83(2) of the Agreement
549. Article 83(5) of the Agreement

the grant of a European patent takes several years, it is theoretically possible that some European patents granted at the same time as the date of signing of the Agreement, shall have lapsed before the end of the prolonged transitional period.

B. RATIFICATION AND ENTRY INTO FORCE

1. Signature, Ratification and Accession

The Agreement is in fact a treaty between (initially) 25 Member States of the European Union. Because of the legal status of the Court (*supra*, I.B), only EU Member States can accede to the Agreement.

The Agreement shall be subject to ratification in accordance with the respective constitutional requirements of the EU Member States. Instruments of ratification shall be deposited with the General Secretariat of the Council of the European Union (the Depositary).[550]

Each Member State having signed the Agreement shall notify the European Commission of its ratification of the Agreement at the time of the deposit of its ratification instrument,[551] as prescribed by Article 18.3 of the Unitary Patent Regulation. The Commission shall publish in the *Official Journal* of the European Union the date of entry into force of the Agreement and a list of the Member States that have ratified the Agreement at the date of its entry into force. The Commission shall thereafter regularly update the list of the Participating Member States which have ratified the Agreement and shall publish such updated list in the *Official Journal* of the European Union.[552]

The Agreement shall be open to accession by any EU Member State. Instruments of accession shall be deposited with the Depositary.[553]

The Depositary shall draw up certified true copies of the Agreement and shall transmit them to the governments of all signatory or acceding Member States.[554] The Depositary shall notify the governments of the signatory or acceding Member States of:

- any signature;
- the deposit of any instrument of ratification or accession;
- the date of entry into force of this Agreement.[555]

550. Article 84(2) of the Agreement
551. Article 84(3) of the Agreement
552. Article 18.3 Unitary Patent Regulation
553. Article 84(4) of the Agreement
554. Article 85(1) of the Agreement
555. Article 85(2) of the Agreement

The Depositary shall also register the Agreement with the Secretariat of the United Nations.[556]

2. Revision

The Agreement shall be of unlimited duration,[557] but possibility for revision is included in Article 87.

Either seven years after the entry into force of this Agreement or once 2000 infringement cases have been decided by the Court, whichever is the later point in time, and if necessary at regular intervals thereafter, a broad consultation with the users of the patent system shall be carried out by the Administrative Committee on the functioning, efficiency and cost-effectiveness of the Court and on the trust and confidence of users of the patent system in the quality of the Court's decisions. On the basis of this consultation and an opinion of the Court, the Administrative Committee may decide to revise the Agreement with a view to improving the functioning of the Court.[558] The Administrative Committee may also amend this Agreement to bring it into line with an international treaty relating to patents or Union law.[559]

Some Member States have argued in the European Council that a review of the Agreement should require unanimity in the Administrative Committee. Other Member States feared that unanimity may render a necessary review too difficult. The Competitiveness Council of 5 December 2011 decided as a compromise to maintain the three-quarters majority in the Administrative Committee for review of the Agreement, but to give Member States the possibility to reject a review on the basis of their relevant internal decision making procedures.[560] For this reason, a decision of the Administrative Committee for revision shall not take effect if a Contracting Member State declares, within twelve months of the date of the decision, on the basis of its relevant internal decision-making procedures, that it does not wish to be bound by the decision. In this case, a Review Conference of the Contracting Member States shall be convened.[561]

556. Article 85(3) of the Agreement
557. Article 86 of the Agreement
558. Article 87(1) of the Agreement
559. Article 87(2) of the Agreement
560. Council of the European Union, Draft Agreement on the creation of a Unified Patent Court, Presidency – compromise text, Council working document 18239/11 of 6 December 2011, p. 4
561. Article 87(3) of the Agreement

3. Authentic Languages of the Agreement

The Agreement shall be drawn up in a single original in the English, French and German languages, each text being equally authentic.[562] After signature of the originals, the Agreement shall be translated in all other official languages of the Contracting Member States.

The texts of the Agreement that are drawn up in official languages of Contracting Member States other than English, French and German shall, if they have been approved by the Administrative Committee, be considered as official texts. In the event of divergences between the various texts, the texts of the authentic English, French and German originals shall prevail.[563]

Nothing is provided to solve any divergences between the English, French and German texts.

4. Entry into Force

There was a general agreement between the Contracting Member States that the Agreement should enter into force once a minimum number of Member States have ratified the Agreement. In previous versions nine Member States were proposed.[564] But the Competitiveness Council of 5 December 2011 finally decided to fix the number at 13 Member States.[565]

Article 89 of the Agreement provides that the Agreement shall enter into force on 1 January 2014 or on the first day of the fourth month after the deposit of the thirteenth instrument of ratification or accession, including the three EU Member States in which the highest number of European patents had effect in the year preceding the year in which the signature of the Agreement takes place or on the first day of the fourth month after the date of entry into force of the amendments to Regulation (EC) 44/200113 of 22 December 2000 on jurisdiction and the recognition and enforcement of judgments in civil and commercial matters, concerning its relationship with this Agreement, whichever is the latest.

The three EU Member States in which the highest number of European patents had effect are currently Germany, France and the United Kingdom.

---

562. Article 88(1) of the Agreement
563. Article 88(2) of the Agreement
564. Council of the European Union, Draft Agreement on the creation of a Unified Patent Court – revised presidency text, Council working document 16741/11 of 11 November 2011
565. Council of the European Union, Draft Agreement on the creation of a Unified Patent Court – Presidency compromise text, Council working document 18239/11 of 6 December 2011, p. 4

Any ratification or accession after the entry into force of this Agreement shall take effect on the first day of the fourth month after the deposit of the instrument of ratification or accession.[566]

5. Minutes of the Signing

The EU Council has prepared draft minutes of the signing of the Agreement. These minutes contain a declaration of the signing Member States (the "Signatory States") regarding the coming into operation of the Unified Patent Court. In this declaration, the Signatory States intend to set up without any delay a Preparatory Committee which will be composed of their representatives. The Preparatory Committee shall prepare the practical arrangements and set out a roadmap for the early establishment and coming into operation of the Unified Patent Court. It may establish subgroups as appropriate and make use of teams of experts.

According to the declaration, the Signatory States are determined to ensure that the Unified Patent Court achieves a high degree of efficiency and delivers expeditious and high quality decisions from the outset. With this in mind they think it necessary that all practical arrangements for the proper functioning of the Unified Patent Court are already in place or are duly prepared before the entry into force of the Agreement.

The declaration sees the following important tasks for the Preparatory Committee:

- organise without delay training of future judges;
  The Signatory States see the organisation of training for future judges from Member States where there is currently little experience with patent litigation as the most urgent task. To this end, the Contracting Member States who have specialised courts dealing with a significant number of patent cases shall offer appropriate training possibilities, in particular internships, for candidate judges from other Member States without delay. The Preparatory Committee shall draw up an appropriate training plan, covering all relevant areas of law including competition law, and provide support for the organisational arrangements.
- prepare Rules of Procedure for the Unified Patent Court;
  In the draft declaration, the Signatory States recall the importance of appropriate Rules of Procedure for the Unified Patent Court and of their uniform application, which are vital to guarantee that the decisions of the Court are of the highest quality and that proceedings are organised in the most efficient and cost-effective manner. They affirm

566. Article 89(2) of the Agreement

their willingness to draw up a complete and detailed set of Rules of Procedure before the entry into force of the Agreement.

The Preparatory Committee shall complete a first draft of Rules of Procedure on the basis of input from expert judges, lawyers and industry representatives within three months. This draft should be the basis of a broad consultation with stakeholders before it is finalised with a view to reaching agreement on it well before the end of the ratification procedures.

The adoption of the Rules of Procedure by the Administrative Committee should be preceded by a consultation with the European Commission on their compatibility with Union Law.

- prepare the budget of the Unified Patent Court for the first financial year;
- make proposals for appropriate facilities for the divisions of the Court of First Instance and the Court of Appeal;

  In the declaration, the Signatory States emphasise that, for the proper functioning of the Unified Patent Court, it is important that from the outset it has appropriate facilities at its disposal. The Signatory States intending to host a local, regional or the central division of the Court of First Instance or the Court of Appeal affirm their intention to have the appropriate facilities in terms of premises, furniture, office and IT equipment and administrative support staff in place before the entry into force of the Agreement.

  The Preparatory Committee shall serve as an interlocutor for the host Signatory States and shall provide the necessary support for the organisational arrangements.
- prepare the setting-up of the Administrative Committee and the adoption of its Rules of Procedure;
- prepare the setting-up of the Budget Committee;
- prepare the election of the members of the Advisory Committee;
- prepare the election of judges;
- recruit administrative staff.

THE (DRAFT) RULES OF PROCEDURE OF THE UNIFIED PATENT COURT

Object

This study is aimed at unravelling the proposed draft Rules of Procedure of the UPC and as such allowing a comprehensive overview of the different procedural stages.

The subsequent stages of the proceedings are represented in flowcharts. Should such representation not add value to unravel a rule, or combination of rules, this rule, part or combination thereof, will be explained in plain words.

A supplementary part is provided for language issues throughout the subsequent stages of the proceedings.

A further aim of this study is that it can be used by stakeholders as a working tool to criticise, to point out shortcomings, to ameliorate, to elaborate upon the Rules of Procedure.

Introduction

Part III of the Agreement introduces the principles of Unified Patent Court procedural law:

- Under *Chapter I* the following principles are stated: Proportionality and Fairness (Art. 42), Case Management (Art. 43), Electronic Procedures (Art. 44), Public Proceedings (Art. 45), Legal Capacity (R. 46), Parties (Art. 47) and Representation (Art. 48).
- *Chapter II* sets out the general arrangements regarding the language of proceedings. They are separately detailed under the Supplementary part of this study.
- *Chapter III* deals in general terms with the proceedings before the Court: Written, Interim and Oral Procedures (Art. 52); Means of Evidence (Art. 53); Burden of Proof (R. 54) and Reversal of Burden of Proof (Art. 55).
- *Chapter IV* deals with the powers of the Court: General Powers of the Court (R. 56), Court Experts (R. 57), Protection of Confidential Information (R. 58), Order to Produce Evidence (Art. 59), Order to Preserve Evidence and to Inspect Property (Art. 60), Freezing Orders (Art. 61), Provisional and Protective Measures (Art. 62), Permanent Injunctions (Art. 63), Corrective Measures in Infringement Proceedings (Art. 64), Decisions on the Validity of a Patent (Art. 65), Powers of the UPC concerning Decisions of the EPO (Art. 66), Powers to Order the Communication of Information (Art. 67), Award of Damages (R. 68), Legal Costs (Art. 69), Court Fees (Art. 70), Legal Aid (Art. 71), and Period of Limitation (Art. 72).
- *Chapter V* deals with the Appeal Proceedings (Art. 73), its Effects (Art. 74) and Decision on Appeal and Referral Back (Art. 75).
- *Chapter VI* goes into decisions, and more specifically: Basis for Decisions and Right to be Heard (Art. 76), Formal Requirements (Art. 77), Decisions of the Court and Dissenting Opinions (Art. 78), Settlement (Art. 79), Publication of Decisions (Art. 80), Rehearing (Art. 81) and Enforcement of Decisions and Orders (Art. 82).

Article 41 states that the Rules of Procedure will lay down the details of the proceedings before the Court. The Rules of Procedure need to comply with the Agreement and the Statute. This principle is reiterated in the Rules of Procedure itself, where Rule 1 stipulates that in the event of a conflict between the provisions of the Agreement or Statute and those of the Rules of Procedure, the provisions of the Agreement or Statute will prevail.

The Rules of Procedure should guarantee that Court decisions are of the highest quality and proceedings should be organised in the most efficient and cost-effective manner. A fair balance should be ensured between the legitimate interests of all parties. They need to provide for the required level of discretion for the judges without impairing predictability of proceedings for the parties (Art. 41(3)).

Upon the signature of the Agreement, the Contracting Member States will start the necessary preparations for the ratification of the Agreement to ensure its entry into force without delay. Together with these efforts the Contracting Member States should set up a *Preparatory Committee* in charge of preparing the practical arrangements for the early establishment and coming into operation of the UPC.[1] However, the delay in signing the Agreement has in turn delayed the setting up of the *Preparatory Committee*.

To avoid further delay, a small *Drafting Committee*[2] of expert judges and lawyers was appointed to take the work forward. The aim of the *Drafting Committee* is to assist the *Preparatory Committee* (when appointed) to complete the draft Rules of Procedure within three months of the signature of the Agreement.

It will be the *Administrative Committee*[3] which shall adopt the Rules of Procedure (Art. 12(4)).

This part of the book is based on the 14th draft Rules of Procedure as received on 31 January 2013. It is possible that minor changes are introduced to the (draft) Rules of Procedure between the receipt of the final draft and the actual distribution of the Rules by the European Commission.

1. This Committee should start working a few months after the signing of the Agreement (when writing this study scheduled in February 2013). The coming into operation is scheduled in April 2014.
2. Members of the Drafting Committee: Mr. K. Mooney (UK), Mr. C. Floyd (UK), Mr. K. Grabinski (GE), Mr. W; Tilmann (GE), Mrs. Pérard. (FR) and Mr. Véron (FR) and Mr. W. Hoyng (NL).
3. The Administrative Committee is composed of one representative of each Contracting Member State (Art. 12(1)).

Preamble

The Preamble to the Rules of Procedure refers to the Articles dealing with *proportionality*, *flexibility*, *fairness* and *equity* regarding its application and interpretation (cf. Art. 41(3), Art. 42(1) and (2) and Art. 52(1)). In accordance with these principles, the Court should apply and interpret the Rules of Procedure in a way that ensures decisions of the highest quality.

Proceedings should be conducted in such a way that normally allows the final oral hearing on the issues of infringement and validity at first instance to take place within a year. Decisions on the costs and/or damages may take place at the same time or *as soon as practicable* thereafter.

Case management should be organised in such a way that the aimed-for objectives are met. A burden is placed on the parties to set out their full case as early as possible in the proceedings.

The Court should endeavour to ensure consistent application and interpretation of the Rules of Procedure. Due consideration should be given to this objective in any decision concerning leave to appeal against procedural orders.

Application and Interpretation

After reiterating the general principle in Rule 1.1 regarding a possible conflict between the provisions of the Agreement and/or the Statute on the one hand and these of Rules of Procedure on the other hand, Rule 1.2 states that where the Rules of Procedure provide for the Court to perform any act other than an act exclusively reserved for a panel of the Court, the President of the Court of First Instance or the President of the Court of Appeal, that act may be performed by:

(a) the presiding judge or the J-R of the panel to which the case has been assigned,
(b) a single legally qualified judge where the case has been assigned to a single judge,
(c) the standing judge designated pursuant to Rule 445.

The expressions "patent" and "proprietor" include whenever appropriate, respectively, a *supplementary protection certificate* as defined in Article 2(h) and granted in respect of the *patent* and the *proprietor* of such certificate (R. 2). References in the Rules of Procedure to the language in which the patent was granted mean that language, and not the language in which a supplementary certificate in respect of the patent was granted.

Where the Rules of Procedure refer to the Registry and provide for the Registry to perform any act, that reference shall include the relevant sub-registry and that act may be performed by a member of staff of the Registry or relevant sub-registry (R. 3).

Written pleadings and documents need to be lodged at the Registry in electronic form, making use of the official forms available on-line[4] (R. 4).

Rule 5 sets out the procedure regarding the lodging of an Application to opt out and withdrawal of an opt out (with reference to Art. 83(3))[5] regarding any patent or application which can be represented graphically as follows:

---

4. For all separate procedural documents on-line guidance is (will be) provided in the form of standardised documents. That such a document is present is not repeated throughout this study. Generally, such on-line guidance is present regarding any written action to be taken by a party.
5. In conformity with Article 83(3), a proprietor of an application for a European patent granted or applied for prior to the end of the transitional period of seven years after the date of entry into

Flowchart: Application to opt out (R. 5)

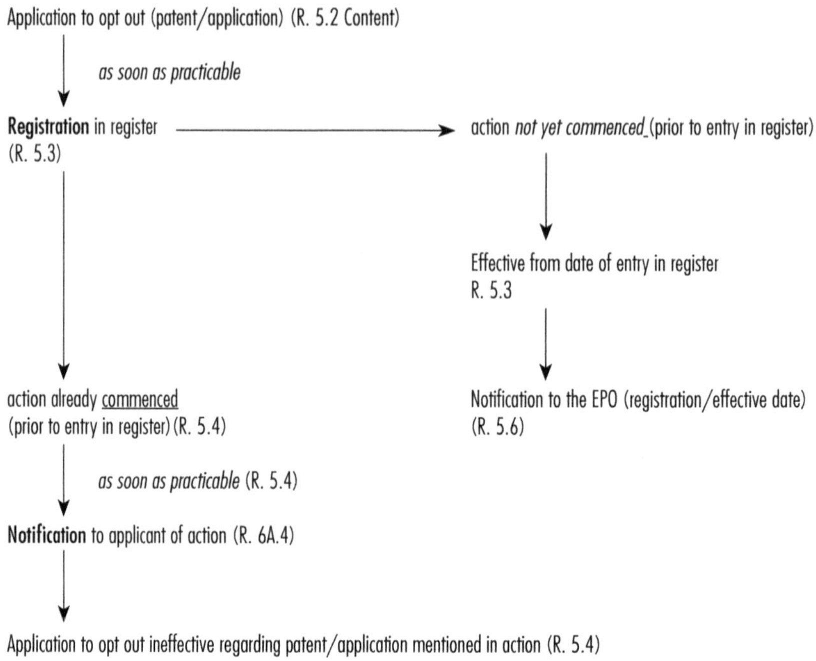

Flowchart: Application to withdraw opt out (R. 5)

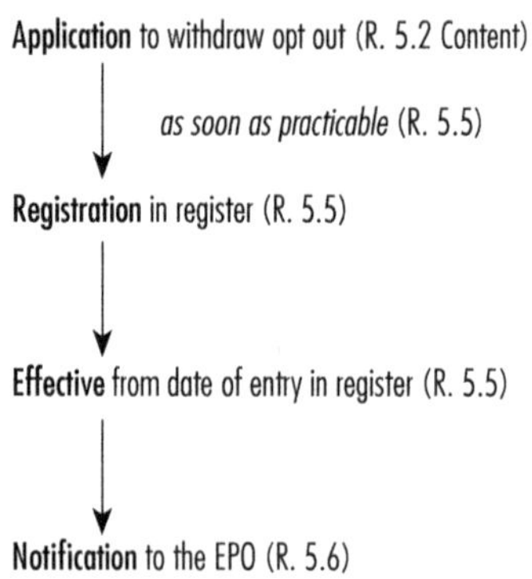

---

force of the Agreement or a prolonged period (as set in conformity with Article 83(5)), has the possibility to opt out from the exclusive competence of the Court unless an action has already been brought before the Court.

Rule 6 sets out the principles regarding the service and supply of orders, decisions, written pleadings and other documents by the Registry.

As a general principle, the Registry needs to serve *as soon as practicable* orders and decisions of the Court on the parties and written pleadings of a party to the other party. If applicable, the Registry informs the parties of the opportunity to reply or to take any other appropriate step in the proceedings and of any time period for so doing (R. 6.1). Further, the Registry needs to supply *as soon as practicable* to the parties copies of documents referred to in and lodged with pleadings and written evidence (R. 6.2). Where the postal or electronic address for service provided by a party pursuant to the Rules of Procedure has changed, that party shall give notice in writing to the Registry and to every other party as soon as such change has taken place (R. 6.3).

When setting the term within which an action should be taken by the Registry/Court the term "*as soon as practicable*" is frequently used. It seems no precise time limits have been set in order to avoid liability of the Registry/Court if a time limit is not adhered to.

Written pleadings and other documents, including written evidence, need to be lodged in the language of the proceedings, unless the Court or these Rules otherwise provide (R. 7).

A party should be represented in accordance with Article 48 unless otherwise provided by the Rules (Rule 88.5 and Rule 378.5) (R. 8.1). For the purpose of all proceedings, where the Rules provide that a party should perform an act (or that any act should be performed upon a party) that act shall be considered to be performed by or upon the representative of the party (R. 8.2).

Rule 9 lists the powers of the Court whereby under Rule 9.1 the Court may, at any stage of the proceedings, of its own motion or on reasoned request by a party, order a party to take any step, answer any question or provide any clarification or evidence, within time periods to be specified. Rule 9.2 states that the Court may disregard any step, fact, evidence or argument which a party has not submitted in due time. With the exception of time periods for lodging a Statement of appeal (R. 224.1) and the Statement of grounds of appeal (R. 224.1), the Court may (on a reasoned request by a party) extend, even retrospectively, a time period referred to in the Rules of Procedure or imposed by the Court. The Court may also on a reasoned request by a party shorten any such time period (R. 9.3).

PART 1
PROCEDURES BEFORE THE COURT OF FIRST INSTANCE (R. 10 – R. 157)

Stages of the Proceeding (*Inter Partes* Proceedings)

1. BIRD'S EYE VIEW

When stating the stages of the proceedings (*inter partes*) the Rules of Procedure make a distinction between the following actions to be brought before the Court of First Instance (see also Art. 32(1)(a)-(j)):

- infringement action
- revocation action
- action for declaration of non-infringement
- actions within Article 33(5)-(6)
- action for compensation for licences on the basis of Article 8 of Regulation (EU) No. 1257/2012 implementing enhanced cooperation in the area of the creation of unitary patent protection
- action against decisions of the EPO in carrying out the tasks referred to in Article 9 of Regulation (EU) No. 1257/2012 implementing enhanced cooperation in the area of the creation of unitary patent protection

The following distinctive stages of proceedings are identified (R. 10):

- a written procedure – the written procedure comprises generally:
  - statement of claim
  - statement of defence
  - reply to statement of defence
  - rejoinder to reply
- an interim procedure, which may include an interim conference with the parties;
- an oral procedure, which includes an oral hearing of the parties, except if both parties do not wish to be present at the oral hearing;

and where necessary

- a procedure for the award of damages; and/or
- procedures for cost orders.

The exceptional action is the "Action for Compensation for licences on the basis of Art. 8 of the Regulation (EU) No. 1257/2012 implementing enhanced cooperation in the area of the creation of unitary patent protection" (R. 80). The specific stages are set out when examining this action.

In any of the above stages, the Court, more specifically the J-R, may propose that the parties make use of the facilities of the Patent Mediation and Arbitration Centre in order to settle or to explore a settlement of the dispute (R. 11.1). Such exploration of the possibilities of a settlement is one of the aims of the interim conference detailed hereafter (cf. R. 104(d)). The terms of such settlement may be confirmed on the request of a party by order of the Court (R. 11.2). No documents, opinions, proposals, concession, suggestions, and so on may be relied on as evidence by the Court or the parties in proceedings before the Court or any other court (R. 11.3), unless it was agreed by parties that such matter was made on an "open basis" and freely disclosable to the Court or any other court.

Flowchart: Bird's eye view

1. Principle (R. 10)

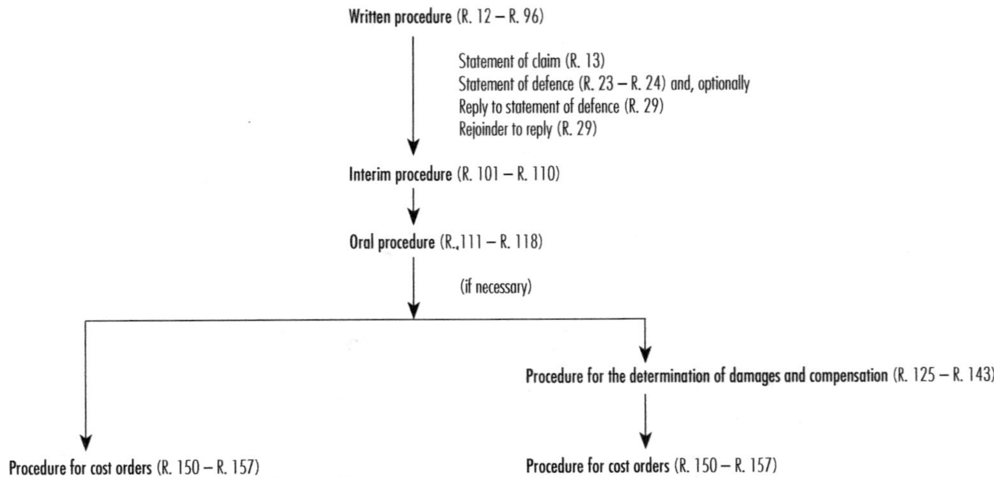

2. Exception (R. 80): "Action for Compensation for licences on the basis of Art. 8 of the Regulation (EU) No. 1257/2012 implementing enhanced cooperation in the area of the creation of unitary patent protection"

3. Settlement (R. 11) (R. 365)

2. SIMILAR PROCEDURAL ELEMENTS THROUGHOUT THE PROCEEDINGS

A. Examination as to Formal Requirements

Before examining the separate stages of the proceedings, more specifically the *written* stage which is the most elaborate, it should be noted that the examination as to the formal requirements, as usually performed by the Registry, is standardised in different actions.

Reference is made to Rules 16–17 (for the introductory Statement of claim) and Rules 27 (for the Statement of defence) (if appropriate using the indication *mutatis mutandis*).

A similar application relates to the *designation of the J-R* (as mentioned in R. 18) following the formal examination by the Registry of the introductory statements and the *further schedule* (as mentioned in R. 28) upon the formal examination of the subsequent defence statements.

The similar application can be identified in the following different actions (within the written stage):

Infringement action
- Statement of claim (R. 16 – R. 17)
- Statement of defence (either including a Counterclaim for revocation or not) (R. 27)

Revocation action
- Statement for revocation (R. 16 – R. 18)
- Defence to revocation (R. 27 – R. 28)

Action for declaration of non-infringement
- Statement for the declaration of non-infringement (R. 16 – R. 18)
- Defence to Statement for the declaration of non-infringement (R. 27 – R. 28)

Actions within Art. 33(5) and (6)
- R. 70.2 *juncto* R. 16 – R. 17
- R. 71.2 *juncto* R. 16 – R. 17

Flowchart: Formal examination statements (R. 16/R. 17) and designation of J-R (R. 18)

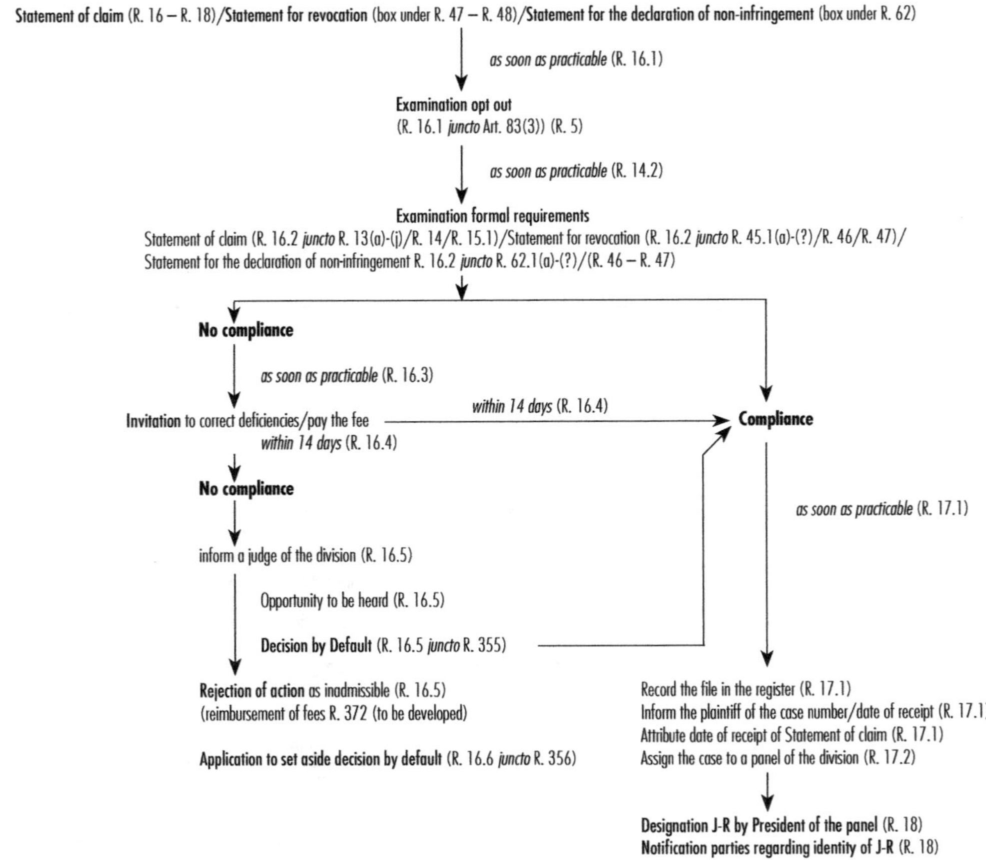

Flowchart: Formal examination defences (R. 25/R. 26)

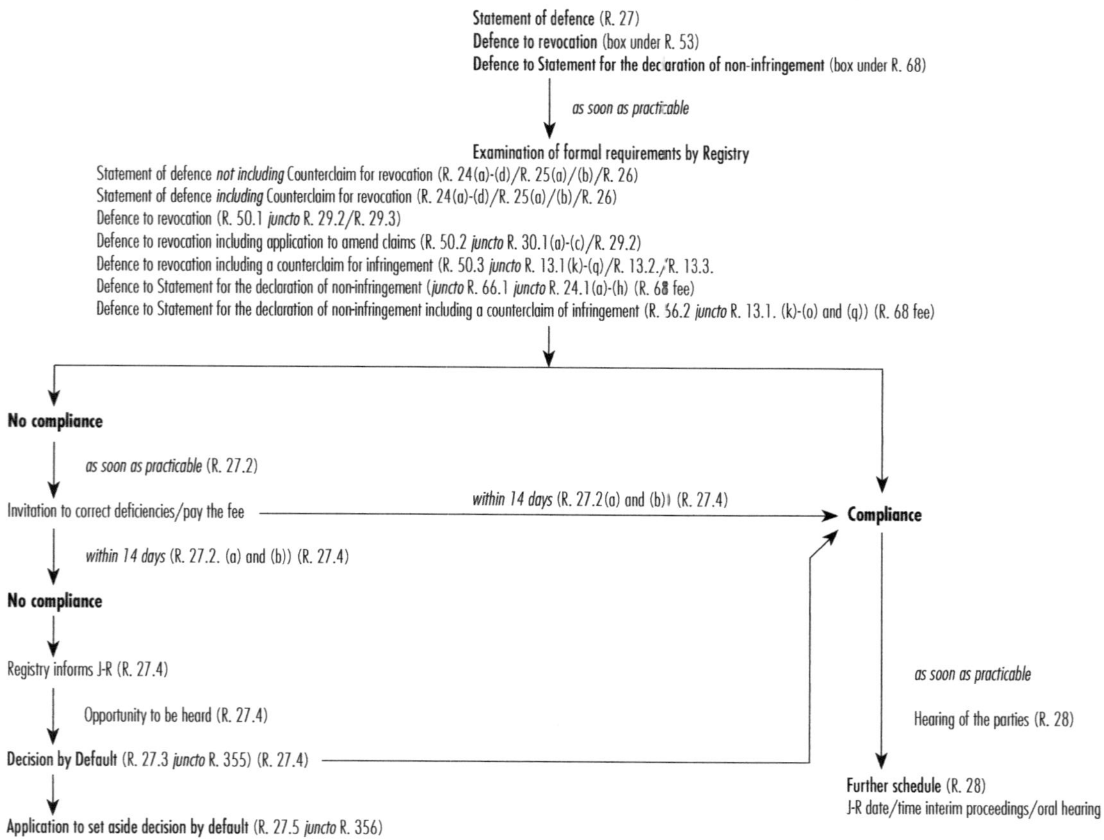

B. Preliminary Objection

The second similar procedural element relates to the *Preliminary objections* as stipulated in Rules 19 to 21 in following actions:

- infringement action (R. 19 – R. 21)
- revocation action (R. 48 and the box under R. 48 (with reference to R. 19 – R. 21))
- action for declaration of non-infringement (box under R. 62) (with reference to R. 19 – R. 21)

The Preliminary objection is directed towards (R. 19.1):

- the jurisdiction and competence of the Court
- the competence of the division indicated by the plaintiff
- the language of the Statement concerned.

If no Preliminary objection is lodged, this is regarded as a submission to jurisdiction/competence of the Court and Division (R. 19.6).

Flowchart: Preliminary objection (R. 17 – R. 19)

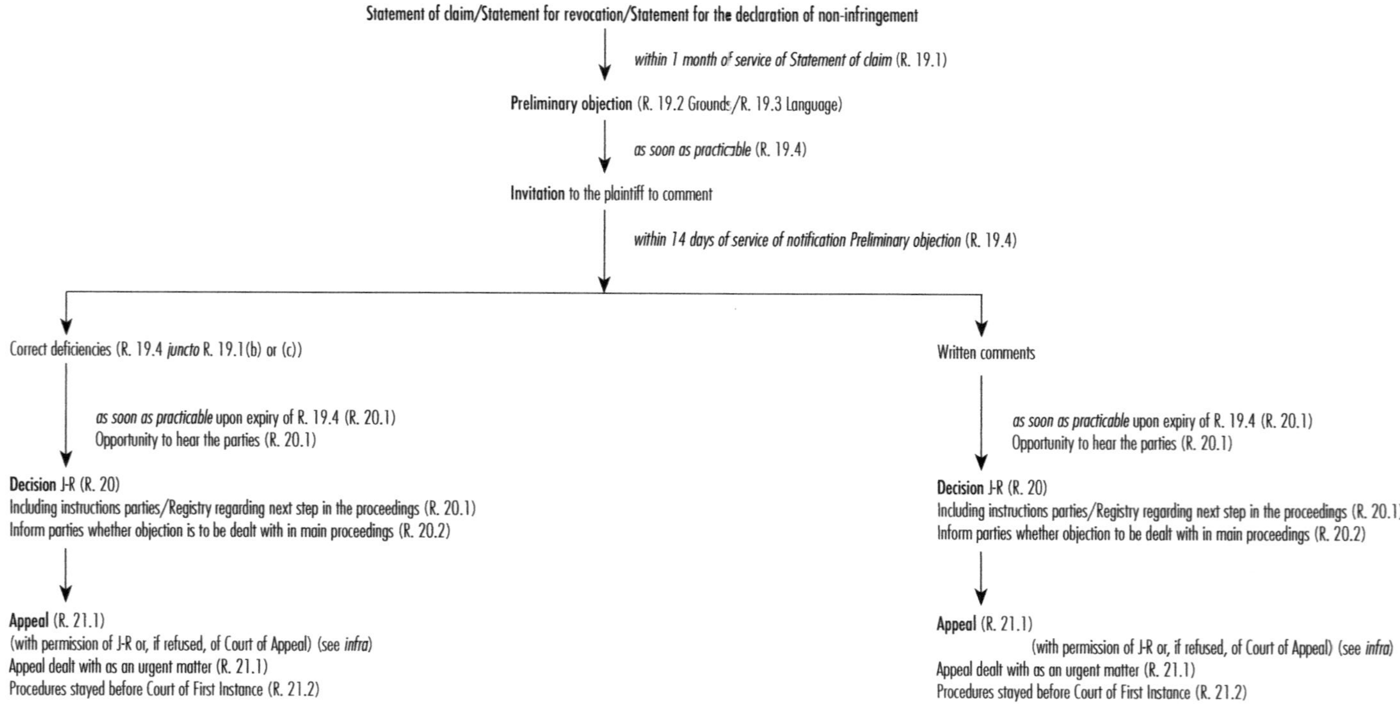

Chapter 1
Written Procedure (R. 12 – R. 96)

1. INFRINGEMENT ACTION (R. 12 – R. 42)

(See flowchart overleaf)

Flowchart: Infringement Action (R. 12 – R. 42)

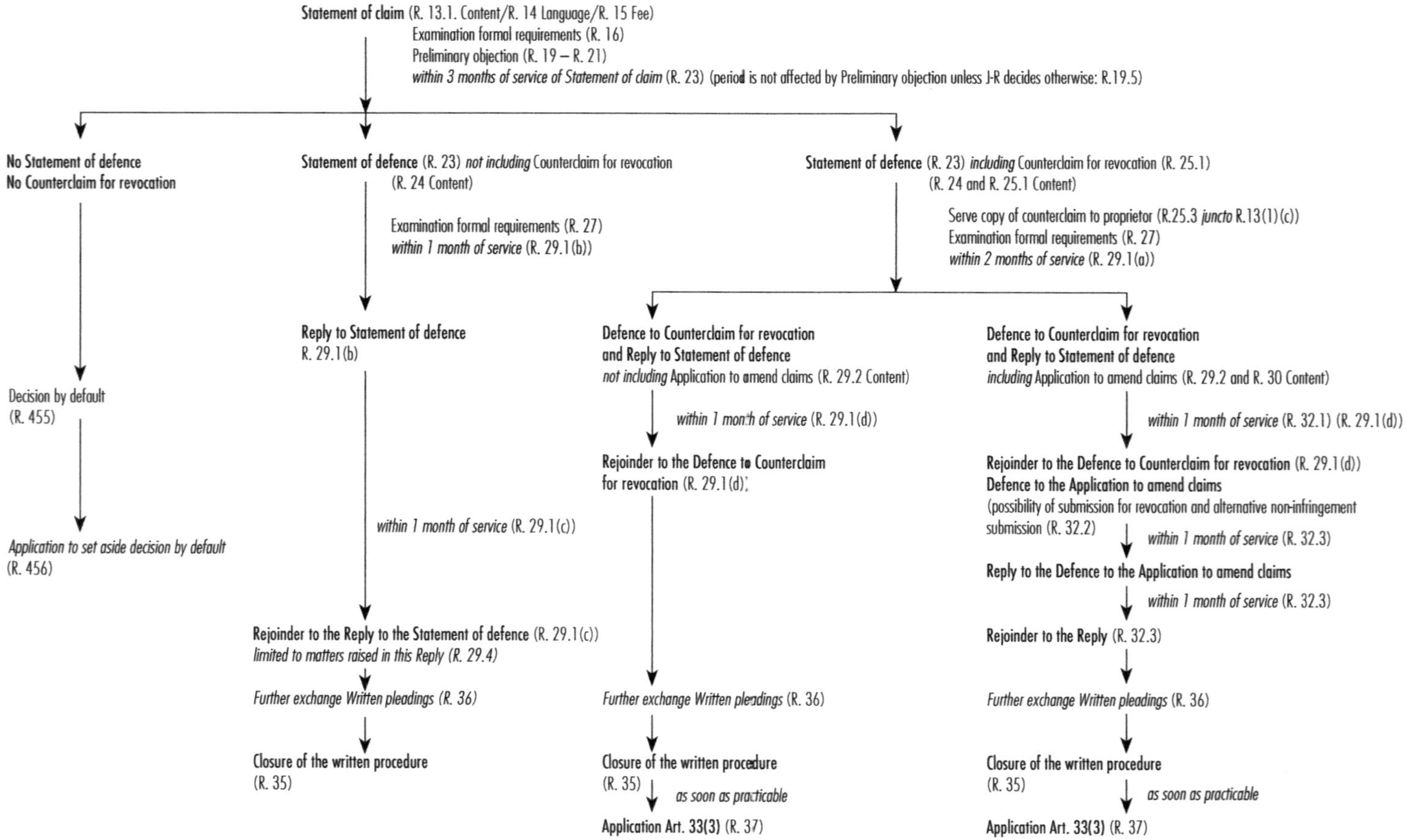

Before going into the application for a revocation action, the following specific elements regarding the infringement action should be noted:

Value-based fee for the infringement action. The *value-based fee* is stipulated throughout the Rules of Procedure for different actions: Rule 22, Rule 31, Rule 57, Rule 58, Rule 69, Rule 104(i) and Rule 133. The principle will not be repeated throughout this study. Reference is made to Part 6 (R. 370.2 and R. 371.4).

Under this R. 20 the following procedure is mentioned: The value of infringement action shall be determined by the J-R where the value of the dispute is assessed by one or both parties as exceeding € XXXXX by way of order during the interim procedure (R. 22.1). Where the value exceeds € XXXXX, the plaintiff shall pay a value-based fee for the infringement action, in accordance with Part 6. In the above-mentioned rules, a similar procedure is followed.

Rule 33 – Application for allocating a technically qualified judge. A party to the proceedings may lodge an application for allocating a technically qualified judge to the panel which needs to contain an indication of the relevant field of technology (R. 33.1). Such application should be lodged as early as possible in the written procedure. An application lodged after the closure of the written procedure will only be granted if justified in view of changed circumstances, such as new submissions presented by the other party and allowed by the Court (R. 33.2). If the requirements have been complied with, the President of the Court of First Instance needs to allocate a technically qualified judge to the panel, after consulting the J-R (R. 33.3).

Rule 34 – Request by the J-R for allocating a technically qualified judge. The J-R himself may at any time during the written procedure, after consulting the presiding judge and the parties, request the President of the Court of First Instance to allocate a technically qualified judge to the panel (R. 34.1). Where a technically qualified judge is allocated to the panel, the J-R may at any time consult the technically qualified judge (R. 34.2).

Rule 35 – Application of Art. 33(3). The application of mentioned article is graphically represented hereafter. For convenience, Article 33(3) is cited hereunder:

> A counterclaim for revocation as referred to in Article 32(1)(e) may be brought in the case of an action for infringement as referred to in

Article 32(1)(a). The local or regional division concerned shall, after having heard the parties, have the discretion either to:

(a) proceed with both the infringement action and with the counterclaim for revocation and request the President of the Court of First Instance to allocate from the Pool of Judges in accordance with Article 18.3 a technically qualified judge with qualifications and experience in the field of technology concerned;

(b) refer the counterclaim for decision to the central division and suspend or proceed with the infringement proceedings; or

(c) with agreement of the parties, refer the case for decision to the central division.

Flowchart: Application of Article 33(3) (R. 37)

Counterclaim for revocation referred to the central division under Article 33(3)(b) (R. 38 – R. 40)
Case referred to the central division under Article 33(3)(c) and 33(3)(b) (R. 41 – R. 42)

Statement of defence including Counterclaim for revocation

↓

Closure of written procedure (R. 35)

↓ *as soon as practicable upon closure of written procedure* (R. 37.1)
After hearing the parties (Art. 33(3))

Decision of the panel regarding application Art. 33(3) (R. 37.1)

↓

Panel proceeds (R. 37.2)
In accordance with Art. 33(3)(a)

↓

Local/regional division
(Infringement/revocation)
Request J-R to allocate technically qualified judge (R. 37.2)

Referral of counterclaim to central division
Proceed with infringement proceedings
In accordance with Art. 33(3)(b)

↓

Local/regional division
(Infringement)

↓

- Possibility to stay the proceedings pending final decision in the revocation procedure (R. 37.3)
- Shall stay the proceedings when high likelihood that the relevant claims will be held invalid (R. 37.3)

Central division
(Revocation)

↓

Accelerated proceedings where:
- an application for provisional measures has been lodged (R. 40(a))
- the local/regional division has referred counterclaim for revocation to central division (R. 40(b))

R. 38(a) *juncto* R. 17.2: case is assigned to a panel except if the parties request to bring the case before a single judge (R. 39a(a))
R. 38(b) *juncto* R. 18: assignation of J-R
R. 38(c): J-R sets date and time for interim conference or confirms date under R. 26
R. 39: language of the proceedings

Referral of the case as a whole to central division
In accordance with Art. 33(3)(c)

↓

Central division
(Infringement/revocation)

↓

Accelerated proceedings where
- an application for provisional measure has been lodged (R. 40(a))

R. 42(a) *juncto* R. 17.2: case is assigned to a panel except if the parties request to bring the case before a single judge.
R. 42(b) *juncto* R. 18: assignation of J-R
R. 42(c)-(d) language of the proceedings
R. 42(e): direction given by J-R regarding further pleadings and terms
R. 42(f): J-R sets date and time for interim conference or confirms date under R. 28

2. REVOCATION ACTION (R. 43 – R. 58)

Flowchart: Revocation action (R. 43 – R. 58)

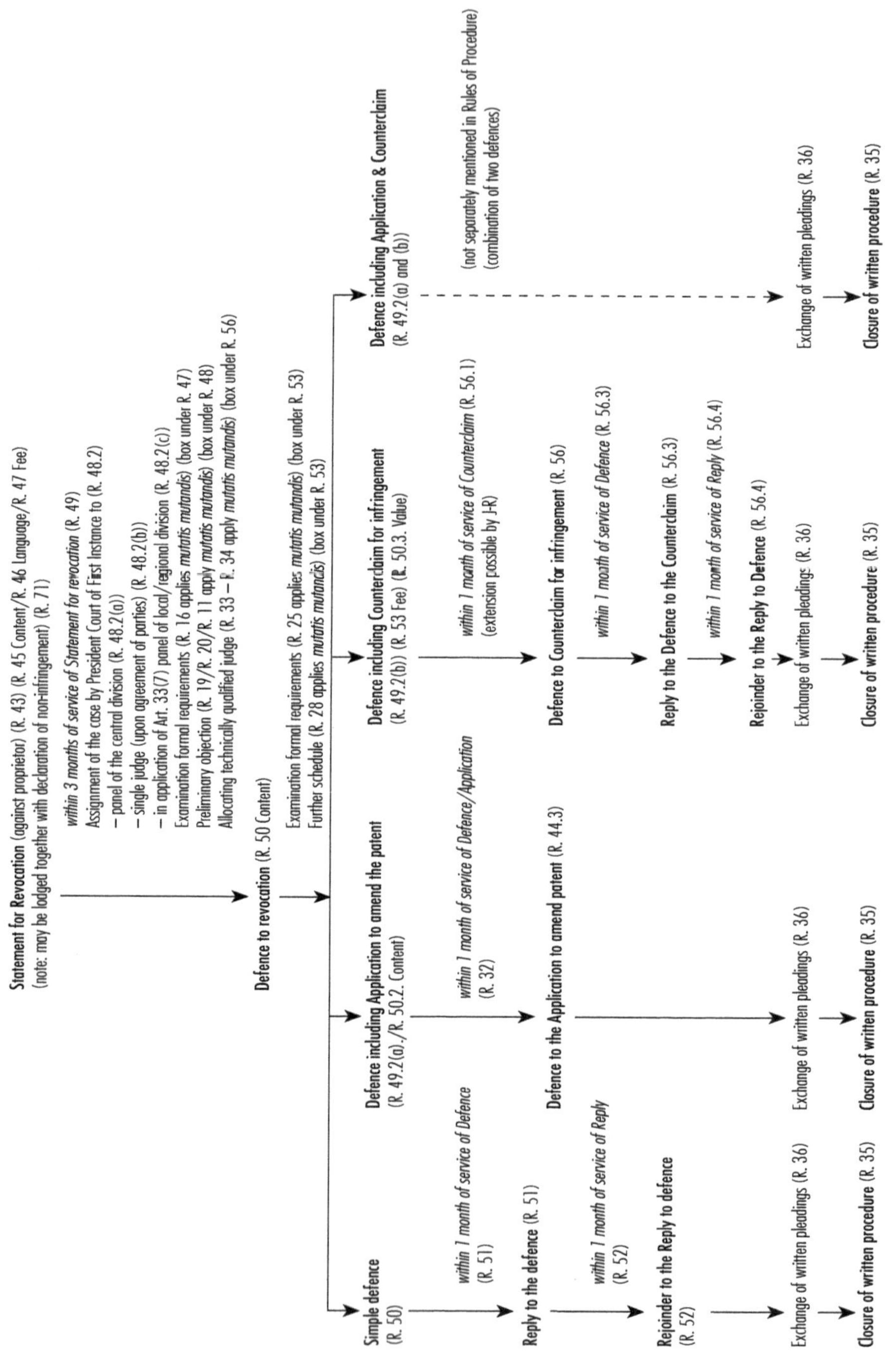

3. ACTION FOR DECLARATION OF NON-INFRINGEMENT (R. 60 – R. 69)

The Court can declare that the performance of a specific act does not, or a proposed act would not, constitute an infringement of a patent.

Such declaration can be made in proceedings between the person doing or proposing to do the act and the patent proprietor or licensee entitled to commence infringement proceedings pursuant to Article 47 (R. 60.1):

- if the patent proprietor or such licensee has asserted that the act is an infringement, or
- if no such assertion has been made by the patent proprietor or licensee
  (a) that person has applied in writing to the proprietor or licensee for a written acknowledgment to the effect of the declaration claimed, and has provided him with full particulars in writing of the act in question and
  (b) the proprietor or licensee has refused or failed to give any such acknowledgment within one month.

The action for declaration shall be directed against the proprietor of the patent or the licensee who has asserted an infringement or refused or failed to give an acknowledgement pursuant to Rule 60.1(b) (R. 60.2).

Flowchart: Action for Declaration of non-infringement (R. 60 – R. 69)

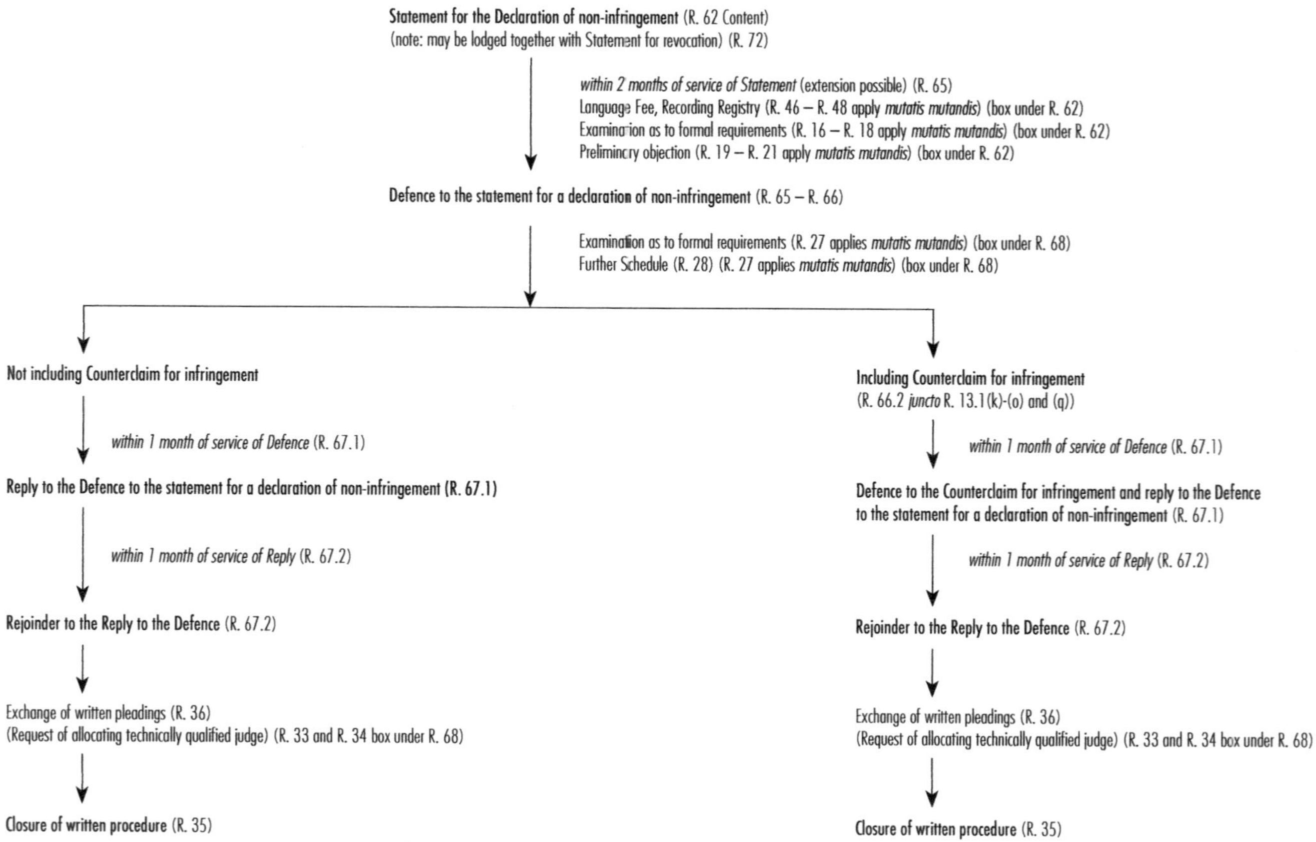

4. ACTIONS WITHIN ARTICLE 33(5) AND ARTICLE 33(6) (R. 70 – 72)

For convenience purposes the concerned article of the Agreement is cited hereafter:

> **Article 33: Competence of the divisions of the Court of First Instance**
>
> …
>
> (5) If an action for revocation as referred to in Article 32(1)(d)) is pending before the central division, an action for infringement as referred to in Article 32(1)(a) between the same parties relating to the same patent may be brought before any division in accordance with paragraph 1 of this Article or before the central division. The local or regional division concerned shall have the discretion to proceed in accordance with paragraph 2 of this Article.
>
> (6) An action for declaration of non-infringement as referred to in Article 32(1)(b) pending before the central division shall be stayed once an infringement action as referred to in Article 32(1)(a) between the same parties or between the holder of an exclusive licence and the party requesting a declaration of non-infringement relating to the same patent is brought before a local or regional division within three months of the date on which the action was initiated before the central division.

Flowchart: Actions within Article 33(5) and Article 33(6) (R. 70 – R. 72)

Plaintiff: **Statement of revocation** (Art. 33(5)) (R. 45)
before central division (R. 70.1)
(possibility: together with action for declaration for non-infringement (R. 72))

↓

Defendant: **Infringement action** before local/regional division (R. 70.1)

↓ *as soon as practicable* (R. 70.2 *juncto* R. 16 and R. 17)

Examination formal requirements (R. 70.2)

↓ *as soon as practicable* (R. 70.2)

Notification of President Court of First Instance (R. 70.2)

↓

(unless otherwise agreed by parties)
Hearing of the revocation action by central division (R. 48.2). Stay of all proceedings pending a decision of the panel hearing the action for infringement pursuant Art. 33(3) and R. 37 (R. 70.3)

The panel hearing the action for infringement shall, when exercising its discretion under Art. 33(3), take into consideration how far the revocation action in the central division was advanced prior to the stay referred to in Rule 70.3 (R. 70.4)

Where the panel hearing the action for infringement decides to proceed in accordance with Art. 33(3)(a), R. 33 to R. 36 apply *mutatis mutandis* to the action for infringement. (R. 70.5)

Where the panel hearing the action for infringement decides to proceed in accordance with Art. 33(3)(b) or (c), R. 37.3, R. 38 – R. 40 or R. 41 apply *mutatis mutandis* (R. 70.6).

Plaintiff: **Declaration of non-infringement** (Art. 33(6)) (R. 62)
before central division (R. 71.1)
(possibility: together with action for revocation (R. 72))

↓

Defendant: **Infringement action** before local/regional division (R. 71.1)

↓ *as soon as practicable* (R. 71.2 *juncto* R. 16 and R. 17)

Examination formal requirements (R. 71.2)

↓ *as soon as practicable* (R. 71.2)

Notification of President Court of First Instance (R. 71.2)

↓

Dcte
attributed to the action for infringement **within 3 months** of date attributed to the action for declaration of non-infringement (R. 71.3)

↓

Stay
of all further proceedings by the panel of the central division in the action for a declaration (R. 71.3)

Date
attributed to the action for infringement is **outside the 3-month** period of date attributed to the action for declaration of non-infringement (R. 71.3)

↓

No stay
but consultation between respective presiding judges (central and the local or regional division) to agree on the future progress of proceedings including the possibility of a stay of one action pursuant to Rule 295.1(h) (R. 71.3)

5. ACTIONS ON COMPENSATION FOR LICENCES ON THE BASIS OF ARTICLE 8 OF REGULATION (EU) NO. 1257/2012 IMPLEMENTING ENHANCED COOPERATION IN THE AREA OF THE CREATION OF UNITARY PATENT PROTECTION (R. 80)

Article 8 of the Regulation enables the proprietor of a European patent with unitary effect to file a statement with the EPO that he is prepared to allow any person to use the invention as a licensee in return for appropriate compensation (contractual licence).

The Court has exclusive jurisdiction in respect of actions for compensation for licences on the basis of Article 8 of the Regulation (Art. 32.1(h)).

The application for appropriate compensation (Art. 32(1)(f)) under R. 80.1 should contain:

(a) particulars in accordance with Rule 13 (a)-(d);
(b) information on the filing of the statement as referred to in Article 8(1) of the Regulation;
(c) the licence agreement referred to in Article 8(2) of the Regulation.

A reference is made to Rules 135 to 140 to be applied *mutatis mutandis* (regarding proceedings related to the applications for the determination of damages) (R. 80.2).

6. ACTIONS AGAINST A DECISION BY THE EPO WITH REGARD TO ARTICLE 9 OF REGULATION (EU) NO. 1257/2012 IMPLEMENTING ENHANCED COOPERATION IN THE AREA OF THE CREATION OF UNITARY PATENT PROTECTION (R. 85 – R. 96)

Article 9 of the Regulation lays down the tasks, within the meaning of Article 143 EPC, which the Participating Member States entrust to the EPO. The EPO shall carry out these tasks in conformity with its internal rules. The EPO shall administer requests for unitary effect, include and administer in the European Patent Register entries relating to European patents with unitary effect, receive and register statements on licensing, ensure the publication of the translations required during the transitional period, collect and administer the renewal fees (as well as additional fees), the distribution of a part of the collected renewal fees to the Participating Member States and administer a compensation scheme of translation costs for applicants filing European patent applications in one of the official languages of the Union that is not an official language of the EPO.

The Participating Member States shall ensure that requests by the patent proprietor for unitary effect are submitted in the language of the proceedings as defined in Article 14(3) of the EPC no later than one month after the grant is published in the *European Patent Bulletin.* The Participating Member States shall also ensure that the unitary effect is indicated in the Register for unitary patent protection, where the relevant conditions are fulfilled. The EPO shall be informed of limitations and revocations of European patents with unitary effect.

The Court has exclusive jurisdiction in respect of actions concerning decisions of the EPO in carrying out the tasks referred to in Article 9 of the Regulation (Article 32).

Flowchart: Actions against a decision by the EPO with regard to Art. 9 Regulation (EU) No. 1257/2012 implementing enhanced cooperation in the area of the creation of unitary patent protection (R. 85)

Written procedure
(possibility of interlocutory review)
R. 85(a)

↓

Interim procedure
(possibility of interim conference)
R. 85(b)

↓

Oral procedure
(on request of plaintiff or at the instance of the Court may include oral hearing)
R. 85(c)

An action against a decision of the Office has suspensive effect (R. 86).

Flowchart: Actions against a decision by the EPO with regard to Art. 9 Regulation (EU) No. 1257/2012 implementing enhanced cooperation in the area of the creation of unitary patent protection (I) (R. 85)

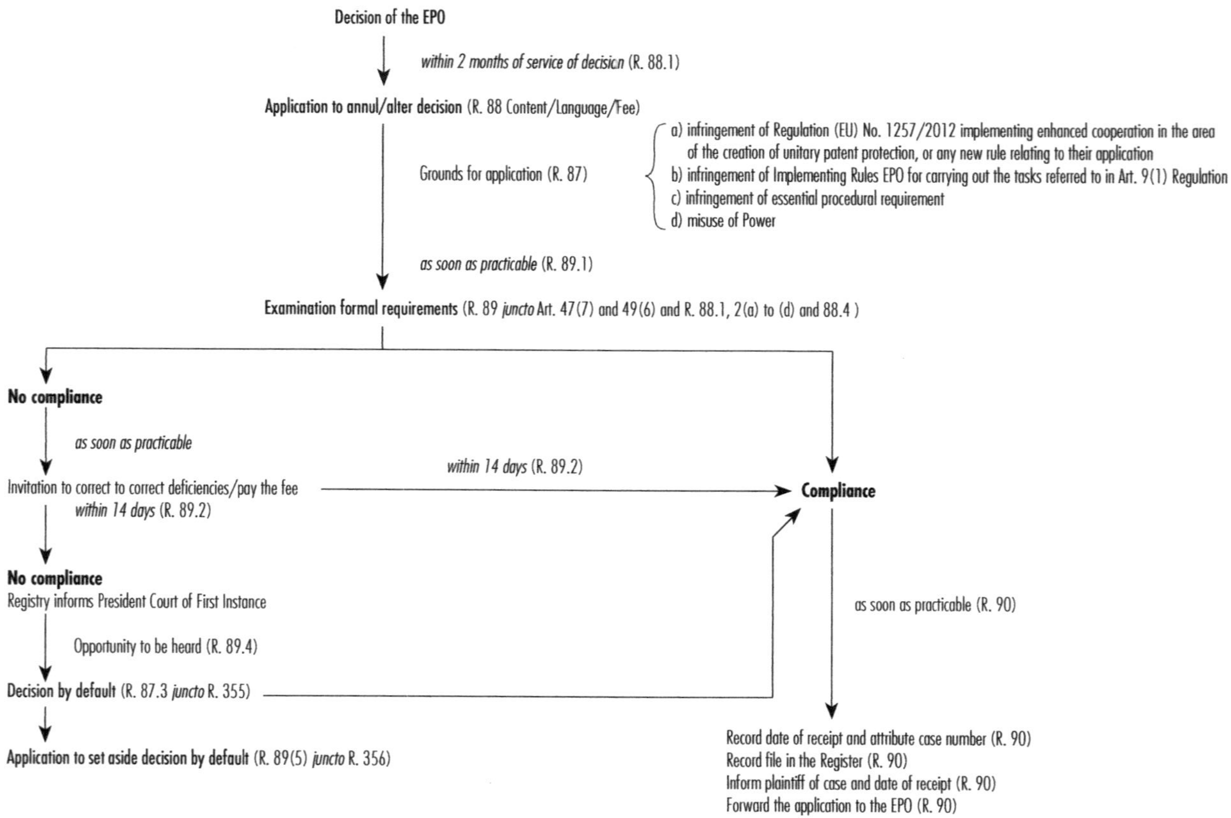

Flowchart: Actions against a decision by the EPO with regard to Art. 9 Regulation (EU) No. 1257/2012 implementing enhanced cooperation in the area of the creation of unitary patent protection (II) (R. 85)

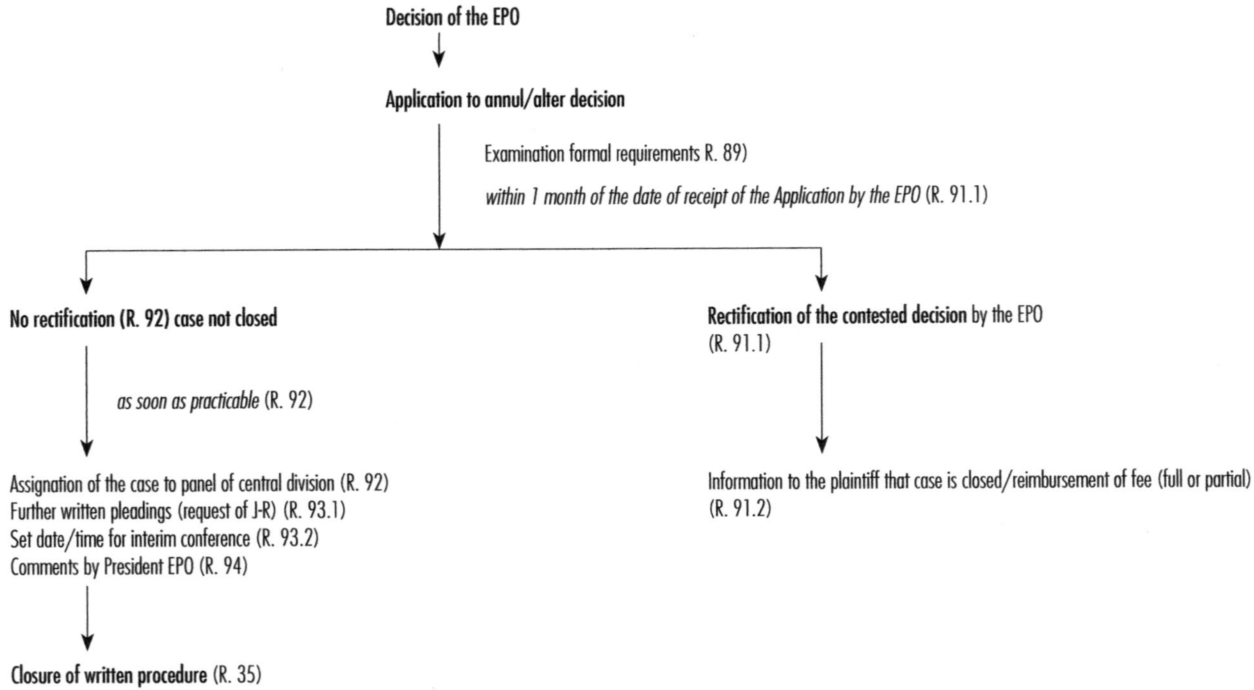

During the interim procedure, the J-R invites the plaintiff to indicate whether he wishes an oral hearing to be convened. The J-R may convene an oral hearing at his own instance (R. 95 *juncto* R. 111 – R. 118). Should an oral hearing not be convened, the panel need to decide in accordance with Rule 117 (Absence of both parties from the oral hearing) (R. 96).

Chapter 2

Interim Procedure (R. 101 – R. 110)

As a case of case management and during the interim procedure, the J-R makes all necessary preparations for the oral hearing. He may in particular, where necessary, hold an interim conference with the parties and this on more than one occasion (R. 101.1). The J-R has the obligation to ensure a fair, orderly and efficient interim procedures (R. 101.2), though should complete the interim procedure within 3 months of the closure of the written procedure (R. 101.3).

The J-R may refer any matter to the panel for decision and the panel may of its own motion review any decision or order of the J-R or the conduct of the interim procedure (R. 102.1). A party may request that a decision or order of the J-R be referred to the panel for an early review (cf. R. 333) (R. 102.2). Pending such review, the decision or order of the J-R is effective.

Flowchart: Interim procedure (R. 101 – R. 110)

Preparation for the interim conference (R. 103)

↓

- Clarifications
- Answers
- Production of evidence
- Lodging of documents
- (General aim R. 104)

Interim conference

↓

- Telephone or video conference (R. 105.1)
- In court (approval of J-R) (R. 105.2)
- In any language mastered by the parties representatives (R. 105.3)
- Recorded (audio/video) if held in Court (R. 106.1) except if J-R orders otherwise (R. 106.2)

Preparation of the oral hearing (on the date set interim conference) (R. 108-110)

↓

- 2 months notice unless parties agree to a shorter time period (R. 108)
- 1 month before oral hearing request for simultaneous interpretation (R. 109.1) decision by J-R (R. 109.2)
- J-R decides simultaneous interpretation on own motion (R. 109.3)
- 2 weeks before oral hearing request to engage interpreter on own expense (R. 109.4)

Closure of the interim procedure in view of oral hearing (R. 110)

↓

- As soon as the J-R considers that the state of preparation of the file is adequate, he needs to inform the presiding judge and the parties that the interim procedure is closed in view of the oral hearing (R. 110.1)

Oral hearing

Chapter 3

Oral Procedure (R. 111 – R. 118)

Being responsible for case management, the presiding judge will (R. 111):

(a) have all authority to ensure a fair, orderly and efficient oral procedure and

(b) ensure that the case is ready for decision on the merits at the end of the oral hearing.

The oral hearing is held before the panel and directed by the presiding judge (R. 112.1). The hearing will consist of (R. 112.1):

(a) the hearing of the parties' oral submissions,

(b) if ordered during the interim procedure, the hearing of witnesses and experts under the control of the presiding judge.

The presiding judge and the judges of the panel may provide a preliminary introduction to the case and put questions to the parties, to the parties' representatives and to any witness or expert (R. 112.3). Parties may put questions to the witness (under control of the presiding judge) (R. 112.4). The witness may give his evidence in a language other than the language of the proceeding (R. 112.5).

The presiding judge needs to endeavour to complete the oral hearing within one day. The presiding judge may set time limits for parties' oral submissions in advance of the oral hearing (R. 113.1). An oral testimony is limited to issues identified by the J-R or the presiding judge as having to be decided on the basis of oral evidence (R. 113.2) and may be limited if the panel is sufficiently informed (R. 113.3).

In exceptional cases, the Court may, after hearing the parties' oral submissions, decide to adjourn proceedings and call for further evidence (R. 114).

The oral hearing and any separate hearing of witnesses is open to the public unless the Court decides to make a hearing, to the extent necessary, confidential in the interests of one or both parties or third parties, or in the general interests of justice or public order (R. 115). The hearing is (audio/video) recorded.

Flowchart: Oral procedure (R. 111 – R. 117)

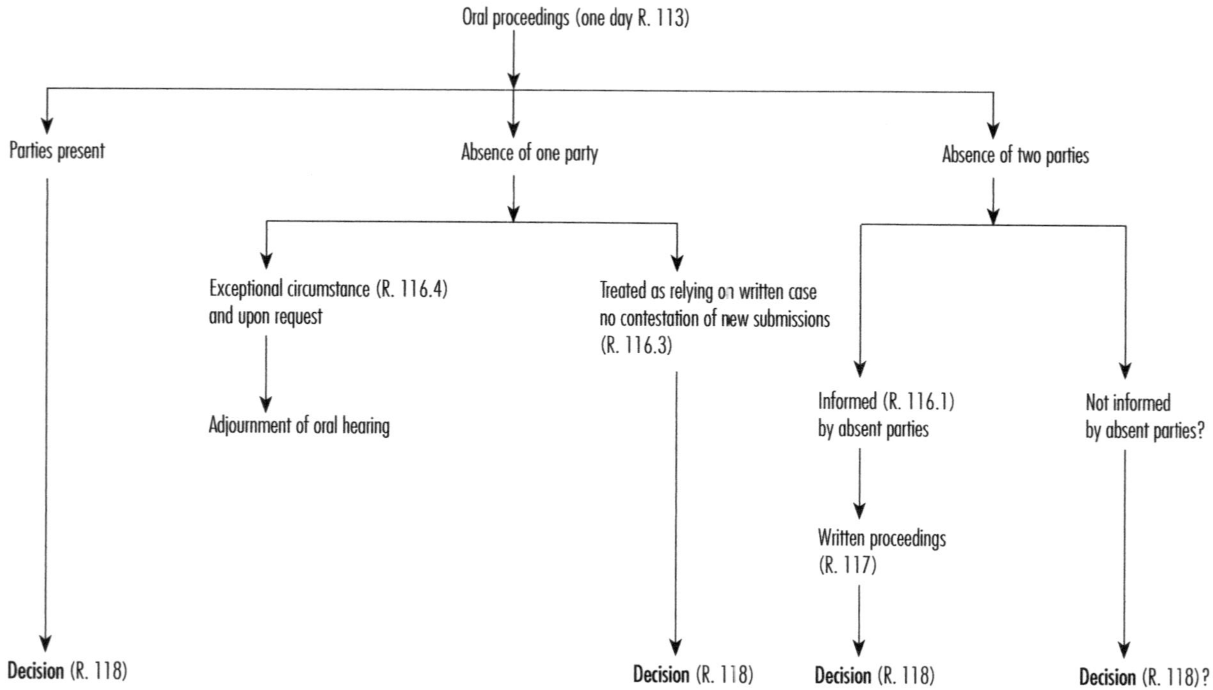

1. THE DECISION ON THE MERITS (R. 118)

In addition to the orders and measures referred to in Article 63 (permanent injunction), Article 64 (corrective measures in infringement proceedings), Article 66 (Powers concerning decisions of the European Patent Office), Article 67 (power to order the communication of information) and Article 80 (Publication of decisions), the Court can, if requested, order the payment of damages and compensation according to Articles 69 and 32(1)(f). The amount of the damages and the compensation are stated in the order or determined in separate proceedings (R. 125 – R. 143).

The Court can subject any order or measure to a security to be given by the successful party to the unsuccessful party as determined by the Court (R. 118.1 *juncto* R. 352).

At the request of the party liable to the orders and measures provided for in Rule 118.1, the Court can order damages and/or compensation to be paid to the injured party instead of applying the orders and measures if that person acted unintentionally and without negligence, if execution of the orders and measures in question would cause such party disproportionate harm and if damages and/or compensation to the injured party appears to the Court to be reasonably satisfactory (R. 118.2).

Should a revocation action be pending before the central division, then the local or regional division (R. 118.3):

(a) may render its decision on the merits of the infringement claim, including its orders, under the condition subsequent pursuant to Art. 56(1) that the patent(s) is (are) not held to be wholly or partially invalid by the final decision in the revocation procedure or a final decision of the EPO or under any other term or condition, or,

(b) may suspend the infringement proceedings pending a final decision in the revocation procedure or a final decision of the EPO and suspend the infringement proceedings if it is of the view that there is a high likelihood that the relevant claims of the patent(s) will be held to be invalid on any ground by the final decision in the revocation procedure or of the EPO.

Where, in the decision on the merits of a direct action or a counterclaim for revocation, the patent(s) is (are) found to be entirely or partially invalid, the Court revokes the patent(s) entirely or partially according to Art. 65 (decision on the validity of a patent) (R. 118.4).

Where the Court has made orders in accordance with Rule 118.3(a), any party may apply to the local or regional division within two months following a final decision of the central division or the Court of Appeal or the EPO, as the case may be, for orders consequential on such final decision (R. 354.4) (R. 118.5).

The Court shall decide in principle on the obligation to bear the legal costs in accordance with Article 69 (R. 118.6).

The Court gives the decision on the merits *as soon as possible* after the closure of the oral hearing. The Court endeavours to issue the decision on the merits in writing within six weeks of the oral hearing (R. 118.7). In exceptional cases, the Court may give its decision immediately after the closure of the oral hearing and provide its reasons at a subsequent date (R. 118.8).

The orders of the Court referred to above are enforceable on the defendant only after the plaintiff has notified the Court which part of the orders he intends to enforce and the said notice has been served on the defendant by the Registry (R. 118.9).

Chapter 4

Procedures for the Determination of Damages and Compensation (R. 125 – R. 143)

1. APPLICATION FOR THE DETERMINATION OF DAMAGES

(See flowcharts overleaf)

Flowchart: Application for the determination of damages (I)

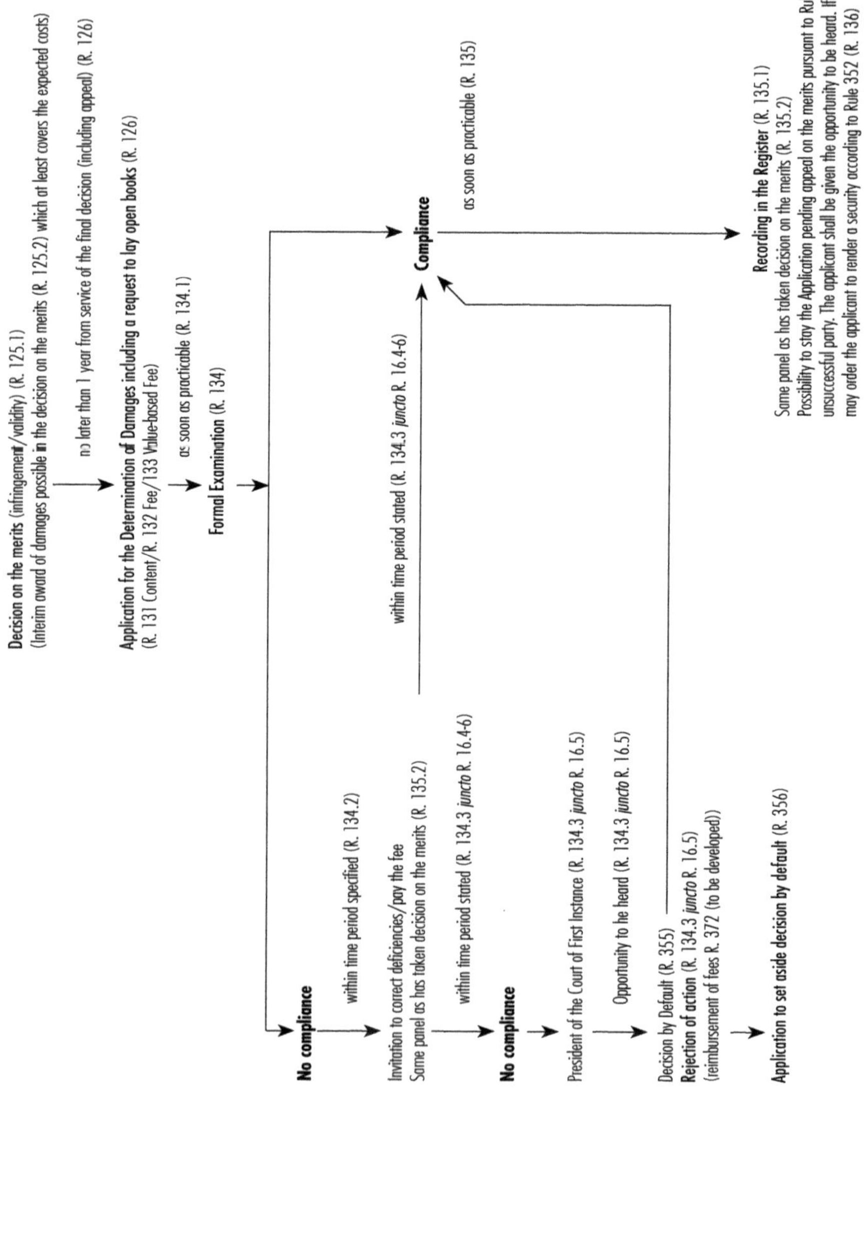

Flowchart: Application for the determination of damages (II)

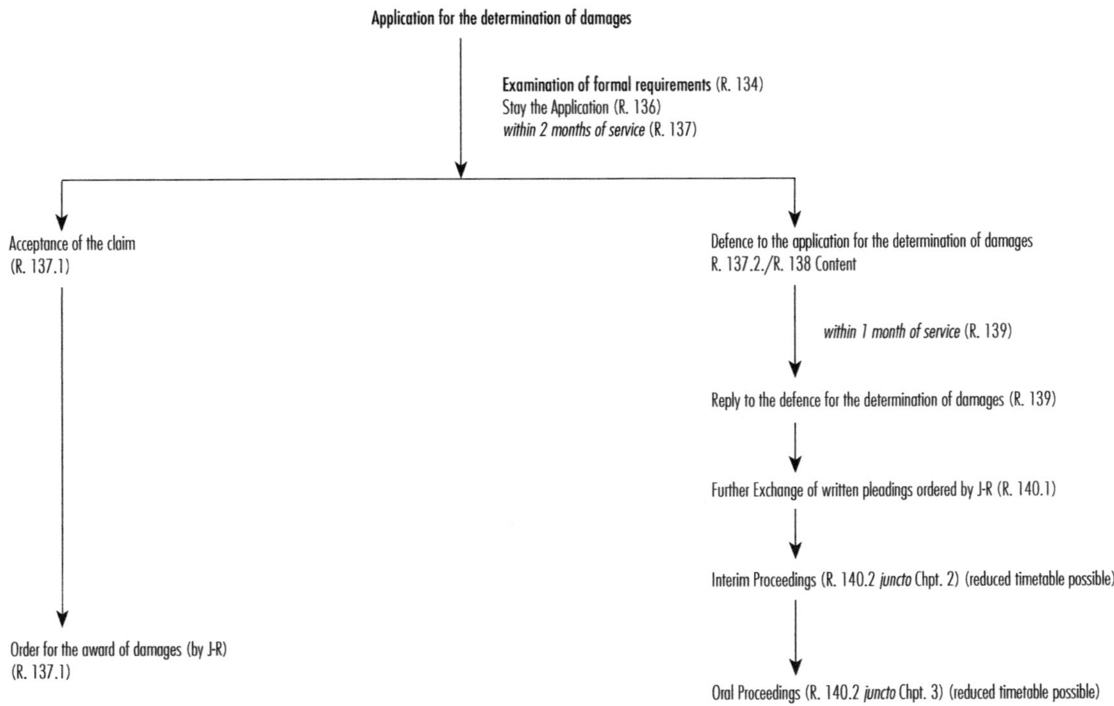

2. REQUEST TO LAY OPEN BOOKS

Flowchart: Request to lay open books

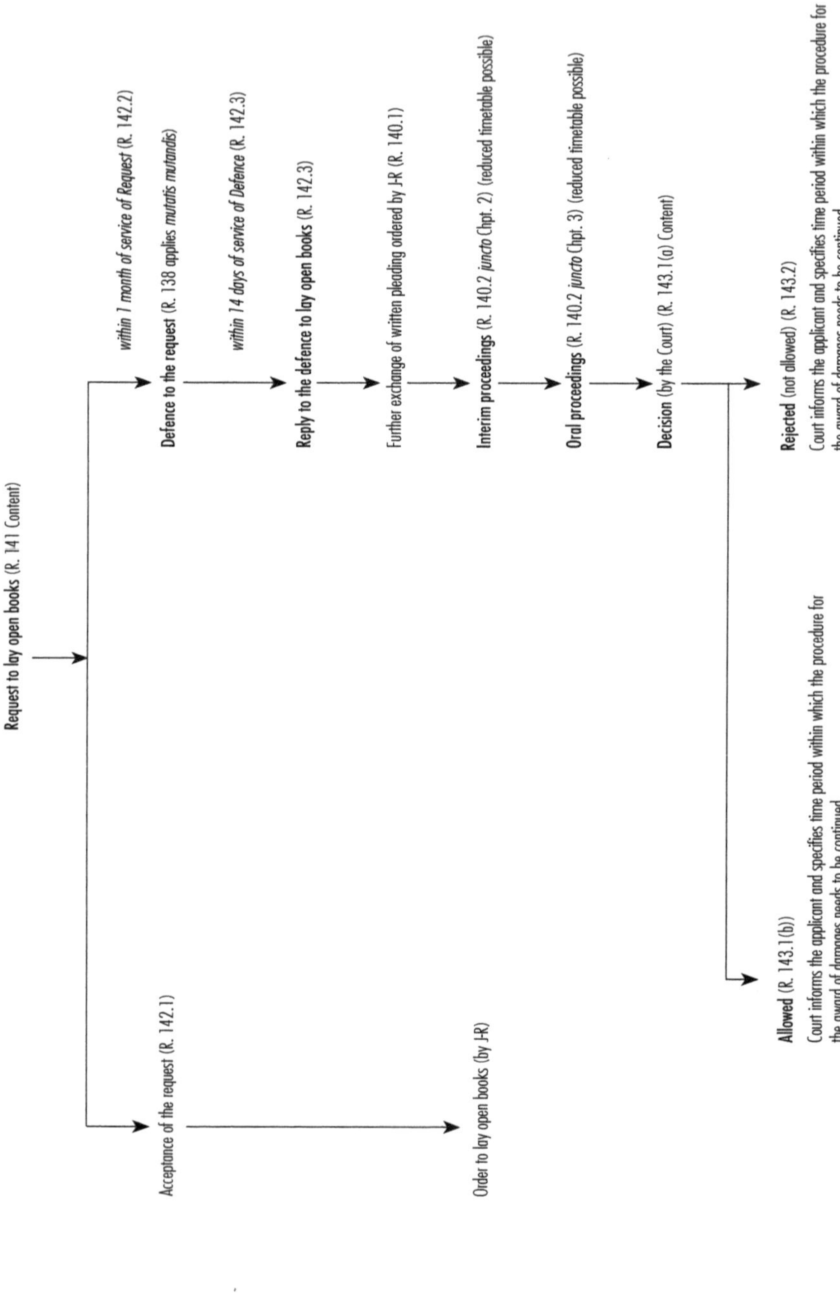

Chapter 5

Procedure for Cost Orders (R. 150 – R. 157)

Rule 150 – Separate proceedings for cost orders. A cost order may be the subject of separate proceedings following a decision on the merits and, if applicable, a decision for the determination of damages (R. 150.1). The Court may order an interim award of costs to the successful party in the decision on the merits or in a decision for the determination of damages, subject to any conditions that the Court may decide (R. 150.2).

Flowchart: Procedure for cost orders (R. 150 – R. 157)

Decision on the merits (infringement/validity)
Decision for the determination of damages
Interim award of costs possible in decision on the merits (R. 150.2)

↓ *within 1 month of service of the Decision* (R. 151)

Application for Cost Order (R. 151 Content)

↓
- R. 152: representation costs
- R. 153: costs of experts
- R. 154: costs of witnesses
- R. 155: costs of interpreters and translators

Further procedure

↓
Written evidence by applicant on the request of the J-R (R. 156.1)
Comment in writing by unsuccessful party (R. 156.1)

Decision (by J-R) (R. 156.2 *juncto* Art. 69(1)-(3))

↓

Appeal (with leave by the Court of Appeal) (R. 157 *juncto* R. 220.2)

PART 2
EVIDENCE (R. 170 – R. 202)

Rule 170 – Means of evidence and means of obtaining evidence

Flowchart: Means of evidence and means of obtaining evidence (R. 170)

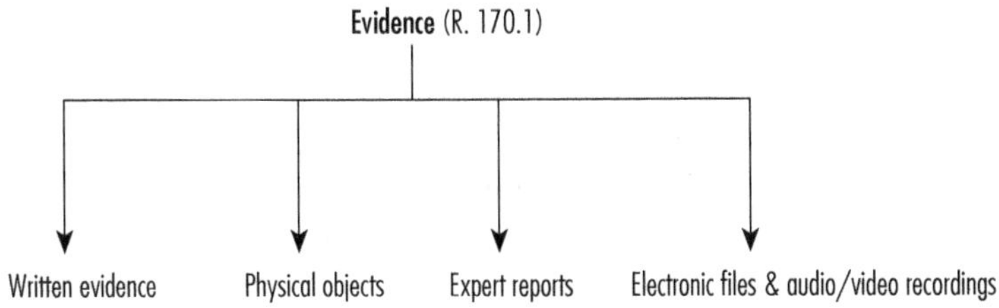

Means of obtaining evidence (R. 170.2)

- hearing of parties (R. 170.2(a))
- summoning, hearing and questioning of witnesses (R. 170.2(b))
- appointing and hearing experts (R. 170.2(c))
- order to produce evidence (R. 170.2(d))
- order to inspect place of physical object (R. 170.2(e))
- order to preserve evidence (R. 170.2(f))

Rule 171 – Offering of evidence. A party making a statement of fact that is contested or likely to be contested by the other party has to indicate the means of evidence to prove it. In case of failure to indicate the means of evidence regarding a contested fact, the Court takes such failure into account when deciding the issue in question (R. 171.1). A statement of fact which is not specifically contested by any party is held to be true (R. 171.2).

Rule 172 – Duty to produce evidence. Evidence available to a party regarding a statement of fact that is contested or likely to be contested by the other party must be produced by the party making that statement of fact (R. 172.1). At any time the Court may order a party making a statement of fact to produce evidence that lies in the control of that party. If the party fails to produce the evidence, the Court takes failure into account when deciding on the issue in question (R. 172.2).

Chapter 1

Witnesses and Experts of the Parties (R. 175 – R. 181)

Flowchart: Witnesses (R. 175 – R. 181)

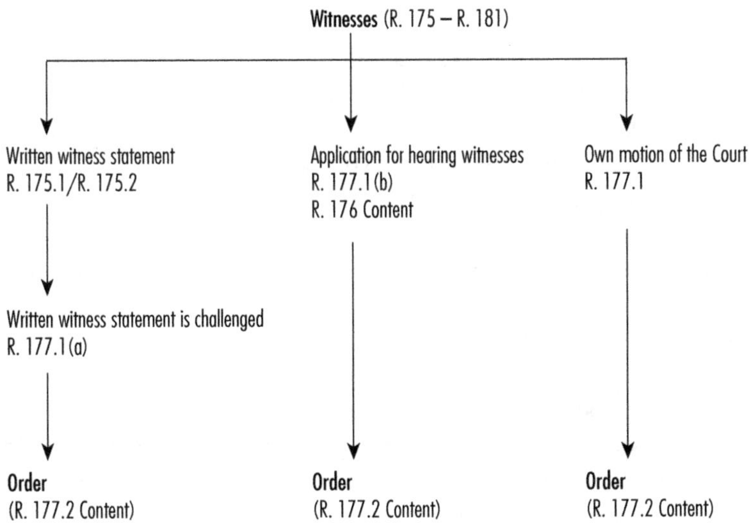

Rule 178 – Hearing of the witness. This rule details the declaration to be made by the witness (R. 178.1). The hearing of a witness who has signed a written witness statement shall begin with the confirmation of the evidence given therein. The witness may elaborate on the evidence contained in his written witness statement (R. 178.3). Thereafter the judges may put questions to the witness (R. 178.4). Then, under the control of the presiding judge, the representatives of the parties may put questions to the witness. The presiding judge may decide that a certain question is not admissible and does not need to be answered by the witness (R. 178.5). The Court may allow a witness to give evidence through electronic means, such as video conference (R. 178.6). If the Court consents, the witness may give evidence in a language other than the language of proceedings (R. 178.7).

Rule 179 – Duties of the witnesses. The duties of the witnesses are listed in this rule and comprise an obligation to attend the oral hearing (R. 179.1), to give evidence (R.179.2) and to make a declaration as mentioned in Rule 178.1. Should the witness not abide to these duties the Court may impose upon him a pecuniary sanction not exceeding [EUR***] and may order that a further summons be served at the witness's own expense (R. 179.2). Further the Court may send a Letter Rogatory to the competent national court pursuant to Rule 202. Rule 178.3 states that nobody may be obliged to sign a written witness statement or to give evidence at an oral hearing if he/she is a spouse, partner equal to a spouse under applicable national law, descendant, sibling or parent of a party. A witness may also refuse to answer questions if answering them would violate a professional privilege or other duty of confidentiality imposed by the national law applicable to the witness or expose him or his spouse, partner equal to a spouse under applicable national law, descendant, sibling or parent to criminal prosecution under applicable national law. Should false evidence be given the Court may decide to report to the competent authorities of the Contracting Member States whose courts have criminal jurisdiction in case of the giving of false evidence on the part of a witness (R. 179.4).

Rule 180 – Reimbursement of expenses of the witnesses. A witness shall be entitled to reimbursement of (a) expenses for travelling and stay and (b) loss of income caused by his attending a hearing in person (R. 180.1). After the witness has carried out his duties and upon his request, the Registry shall make a payment to the witness towards the expenses incurred (R. 180.1).

Where a party has lodged an Application for the hearing of a witness in person, the Court shall make the summoning of the witness conditional upon the deposit of a sum sufficient to cover the expenses referred to above (R. 180.2).

Where the Court orders of its own motion that a witness be heard in person, the funds necessary shall be provided by the Court (R. 180.3).

Rule 181 – Experts of the parties. A party has the possibility to provide expert evidence that it considers necessary and this subject to the orders of the Court referred to in Rule 104(e) and Rule 113.2(b) (R. 181).

Chapter 2

Court Experts (R. 185 – R. 188)

Flowchart: Experts (R. 181 – R. 188)

Experts (R 181 – R. 188)

Court expert ← → **Party experts**

R. 185 – R. 188

Court expert (R. 185 – R. 188):

Appointed after hearing parties (R. 182.1)

The parties may make suggestions regarding the identity of the court expert, his technical background and the questions to be put to him (R. 185.2). The Registry maintains a list of experts (R. 185.9).

The court expert is responsible to the Court and needs to possess the expertise, independence and impartiality required for being appointed as court expert (185.3). He is appointed by order and required upon receipt of the order to confirm in writing that he will present the expert report within the time period specified by the Court (R. 185.6). If an appointed court expert does not present his report within the time period specified or, if extended at the expert's request, the extended period, the Court may appoint another expert in his place. The Court may hold the expert liable for all or part of the costs of appointing and reimbursing another expert (R. 185.8).

The duties of the court expert are stipulated under Rule 186.

Upon presentation of the final report to the Court, parties are invited to comment on it either in writing or during the oral hearing (R. 187).

Regarding the hearing of the expert, reference is made to the hearing of witnesses (R. 188 *juncto* R. 178 – R. 180).

Party experts:

cf. Procedure witnesses (R. 181 *juncto* R. 175 – R. 180)

Chapter 3

Order to Produce Evidence and Communicate Information (R. 190 – R. 191)

Rule 190 – Order to produce evidence. Where a party has presented reasonably available and plausible evidence in support of its claims and has specified evidence which lies in the control of the other party or a third party, the Court may, upon a reasoned request of the party specifying such evidence, order that party to produce such evidence. For the protection of confidential information the Court may order that the evidence be disclosed to certain named persons only and be subject to appropriate terms of non-disclosure (R. 190.1). The order shall specify:

(a) under which conditions, in what form and within what time period the evidence needs to be produced, and

(b) any sanction which may be imposed if the evidence is not produced according to the order (R. 190.4).

If an order to produce evidence is requested during written and interim procedures, the J-R may make such order in these procedures having given the other/third party an opportunity to be heard (R. 190.2-3)

Should a third party be ordered to produce evidence, the interests of that third party shall be duly taken into account (R. 190.5).

An order to produce evidence is subject to the provisions of Rule 179.3 (duties of the witnesses), Rule 287 (attorney-client privilege) and Rule 288 (litigation privilege) (R. 190.6).

If a party fails to comply with an order to produce evidence, the Court takes such failure into account when deciding on the issue in question (R. 190.7).

Rule 191 – Application to order to communicate information. The Court may, in response to a reasoned request of a party, order the other party or any third party to communicate such information in the control of that other party or third party as is specified in Article 67 of the Agreement or such other information as is reasonably necessary for the purpose of advancing that party's case.

Chapter 4
Order to Preserve Evidence and Order for Inspection (R. 192 – R. 199)

1. ORDER TO PRESERVE EVIDENCE (*SAISIE*) (R. 192 – R. 199)

Flowchart: Order to preserve evidence (R. 192 – R. 194)

Application for preserving evidence (R. 192.1) (R. 192.2 Content)

An Application for preserving evidence may be lodged by a party (within the meaning of Article 46) at the division where the applicant has commenced infringement proceedings on the merits. If the application is lodged before proceedings on the merits have been started, it shall be lodged at the division where the applicant intends to start proceedings on the merits

Case not pending (R. 193.1)

Application is dealt with in accordance to (R. 193.1):
- R. 16 (formalities examination)
- R. 17.1(a)-(c)2 (date of receipt, recording Registry, case number, assignment to panel)
- R. 18 (designation of J-R by presiding judge)

Case pending (R. 193.2)

Application shall immediately be
- examined on formalities (cf. R. 16)
- forwarded to the panel or single judge (cf. R. 17.2. and R. 194.3-4)

Flowchart: Order to preserve evidence

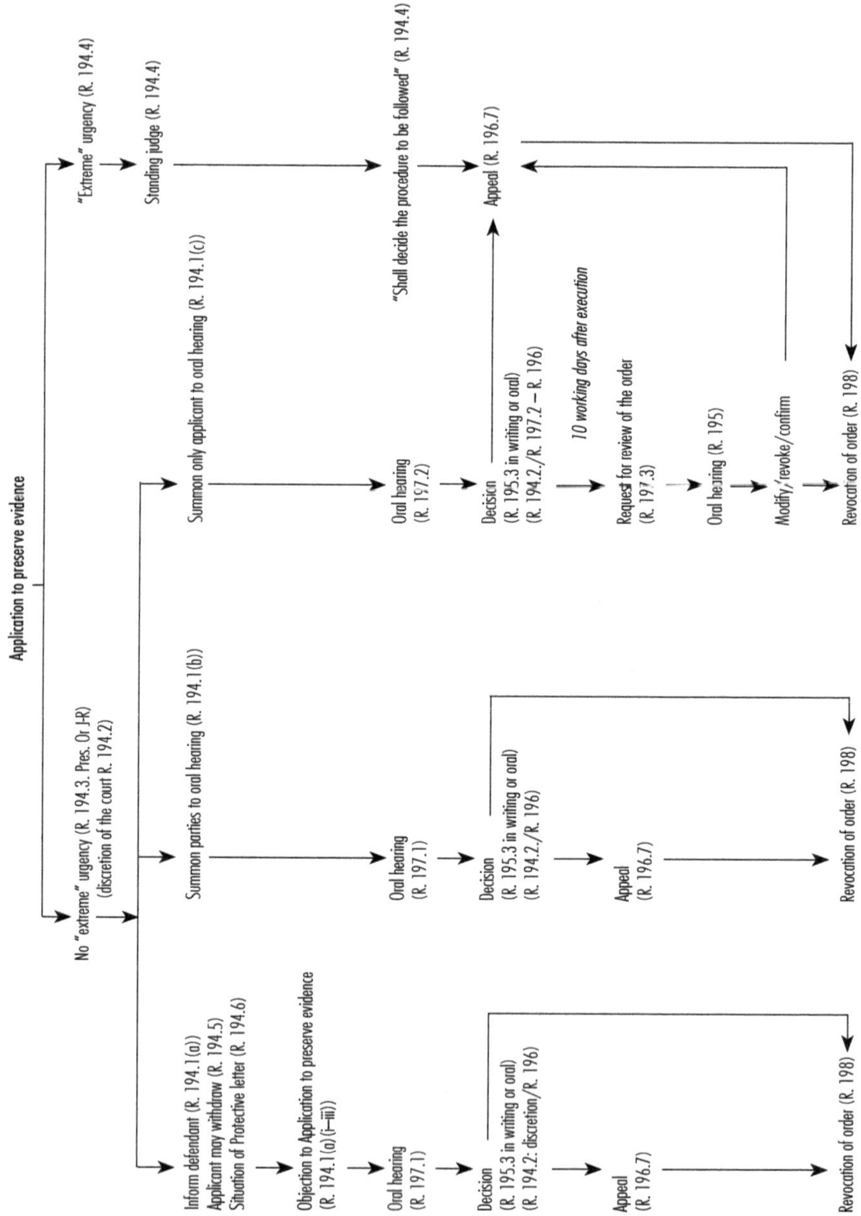

Rule 196 – Decision on the application for preserving evidence. In deciding an application to preserve evidence, the Court can order (R. 196.1)

(a) preserving evidence by detailed description, with or without the taking of samples;
(b) physical seizure of allegedly infringing goods;
(c) physical seizure of the materials and implements used in the production and/or distribution of these goods and any related document.

For the protection of confidential information, the Court may order that any of the above be disclosed only to certain named persons and subject to appropriate terms of non-disclosure.

An order to preserve evidence shall specify that, unless otherwise ordered by the Court, the outcome of the measures to preserve evidence may only be used in the proceedings on the merits of the case (R. 196.2).

The order to preserve evidence shall be enforceable immediately, unless the Court decides otherwise. The Court may set conditions to the enforceability of the order, specifying in particular (a) who may represent the applicant when the measures to preserve evidence are being carried out and under what conditions, or (b) any security which shall be provided by the applicant (R. 196.3).

If necessary, the Court may set penalties applicable to the applicant if these conditions are not observed. (R. 196.3).

The order to preserve evidence shall specify a person who shall carry out the measures ordered and present a written Report on the measures to preserve evidence, all in accordance with the national law where the measures are executed, to the Court within a time period to be specified (R. 196.4). This person specified should be a professional person or expert, who guarantees expertise, independence and impartiality (R. 196.5). Where appropriate and allowed under applicable national law, the person may be a bailiff or assisted by a bailiff. In no circumstances may an employee or director of the applicant be present at the execution of the measures (R. 196.5).

The Court may order the applicant to provide adequate security for the legal costs and other expenses and compensation for any injury incurred or likely to be incurred by the defendant which the applicant may be liable to bear. The Court shall do so where the order to preserve evidence was made without the defendant having been heard. The Court shall decide whether it is appropriate to order the security by deposit or bank guarantee (R. 196.6).

The order to preserve evidence shall indicate that an appeal may be lodged in accordance with Article 73 (R. 196.7).

Rule 198 – Revocation of an order to preserve evidence. An order to preserve evidence is revoked or otherwise ceases to have effect, upon request of the defendant (without prejudice of damages which may be claimed) if within a time period not exceeding 31 calendar days or 20 working days from the date of the order (whichever is the longer), the applicant does not initiate proceedings on the merits of the case before the Court (R. 198.1). Where the measures to preserve evidence are revoked, or where they lapse due to any act or omission by the applicant, or where it is subsequently found that there has been no infringement or threat of infringement of the patent right, the Court may order the applicant, upon request of the defendant, to provide the defendant appropriate compensation for any injury caused by those measures (R. 354.4) (R. 198.2).

2. ORDER FOR INSPECTION

Rule 199 – Order for inspection. The Court may, either of its own motion (but only after hearing the parties) or on a reasoned request by a party, order an inspection of products, devices, methods, premises or local situations *in situ*. For the protection of confidential information, the Court may order that any of the above be disclosed only to certain named persons and subject to appropriate terms of non-disclosure in accordance with Article 34c (R. 199.1).

The rules relating to the order to preserve evidence (R. 192 – R. 197) apply *mutatis mutandis*.

Chapter 5

Other Evidence (R. 200 – R. 202)

Rule 200 – Order to freeze assets. Where a party has presented reasonably available and plausible evidence in support of its claim that a patent has been or is about to be infringed, the Court may, whether before or after proceedings have been commenced, order a party not to remove from its jurisdiction any assets or particular assets located therein nor to deal in any assets, whether located in within its jurisdiction or not (R. 200.1). Rules 192-195 and Rules 197 and 198 shall apply *mutatis mutandis* (R. 200.2).

Flowchart: Experiments ordered by the Court (R. 201)

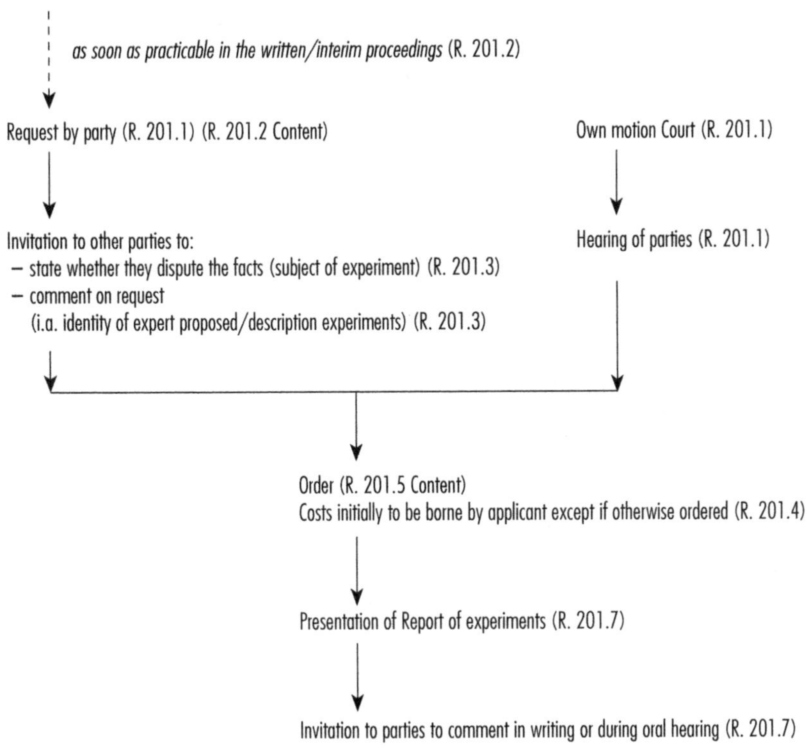

Flowchart: Letters rogatory for hearing of witnesses (R. 202)

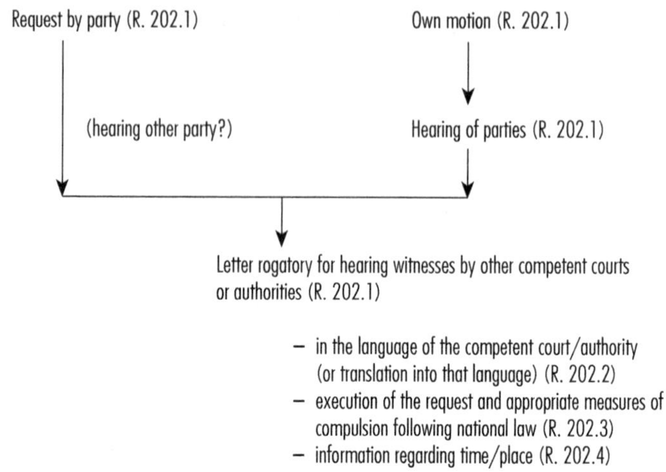

PART 3
PROVISIONAL MEASURES
(SUMMARY PROCEEDINGS)
(R. 205 – R. 213)

Rule 205 – Stages of the proceedings (*summary proceedings*). Summary proceedings before the Court of First Instance consist of a written procedure followed by an oral hearing.

Provisional Measures

As to the extent of the provisional measures, Rule 211 provides the following overview:

(a) injunctions against a defendant;
(b) the seizure or delivery up of the goods suspected of infringing a patent right so as to prevent their entry into or movement within the channels of commerce;
(c) if an applicant demonstrates circumstances likely to endanger the recovery of damages, a precautionary seizure of the movable and immovable property of the defendant, including the blocking of his bank accounts and other assets.

Discretion of the Court

In its discretion, the Court should take into account the following rules:

> 209.2. In exercising its discretion, the Court takes in particular into account:
> (a) whether the patent has been upheld in an opposition procedure before the EPO or has been the subject of proceedings in any other court,
> (b) the urgency of the case,
> (c) whether the applicant has requested provisional measures without hearing the defendant and whether the reasons for not hearing the defendant appear well-founded,
> (d) any Protective letter filed by the defendant; the Court needs to consider summoning parties to an oral hearing if a relevant Protective letter has been filed by the defendant.
>
> 211.2. In taking its decision the Court shall be satisfied with a sufficient degree of certainty that the applicant is the right-holder, that the patent in question is valid and that his right is being infringed, or that such infringement is imminent.
>
> 211.3 In taking its decision on the Application for provisional measures, the Court shall have the discretion to weigh up the interests of the parties.

211.4. The Court may order the applicant to provide adequate security for appropriate compensation for any injury likely to be caused to the defendant which the applicant may be liable to bear in the event that the Court revokes the order for provisional measures. The Court shall do so where interim measures are ordered without the defendant having been heard. The Court shall decide whether it is appropriate to order the security by deposit or bank guarantee. The order shall be effective only after the security has been given in accordance with the Court's decision.

Rule 207 – Protective letter. If a person, entitled to initiate proceedings under Article 27, considers it likely that an Application for provisional measures against him as a defendant may be lodged before the Court in the near future, he may file a Protective letter (R. 207.1). The Protective letter needs to be filed with the Registry in the language of the patent and to contain the elements as detailed under Rule 207.2. Upon filing a Protective letter, a fee needs to be paid in the amount as set out under Rule 207.3.

Flowchart: Protective letter (R. 207)

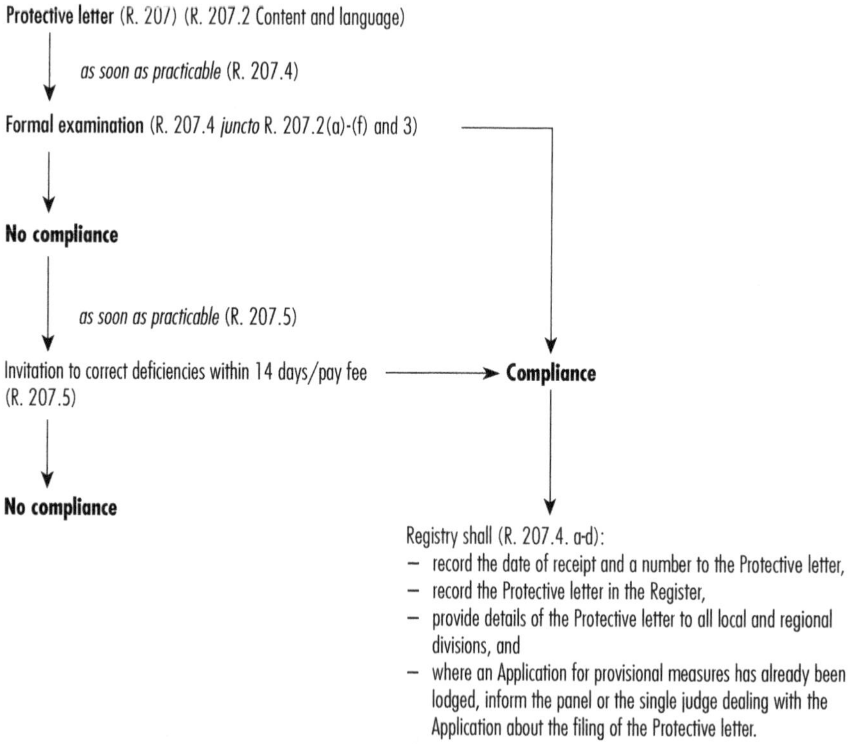

Where an Application for provisional measures is subsequently lodged, the Registrar forwards a copy of the Protective letter to the panel or judge appointed under Rule 208 together with the Application for provisional measures and forwards a copy to the applicant *as soon as practicable* (R. 207.6).

If no Application for provisional measures has been lodged within six months from the date of receipt of the Protective letter, the Protective letter is removed from the Register unless the person who has lodged the Protective letter has prior to the expiry of such period applied for an extension of six months and paid a fee for the extension (R. 207.7).

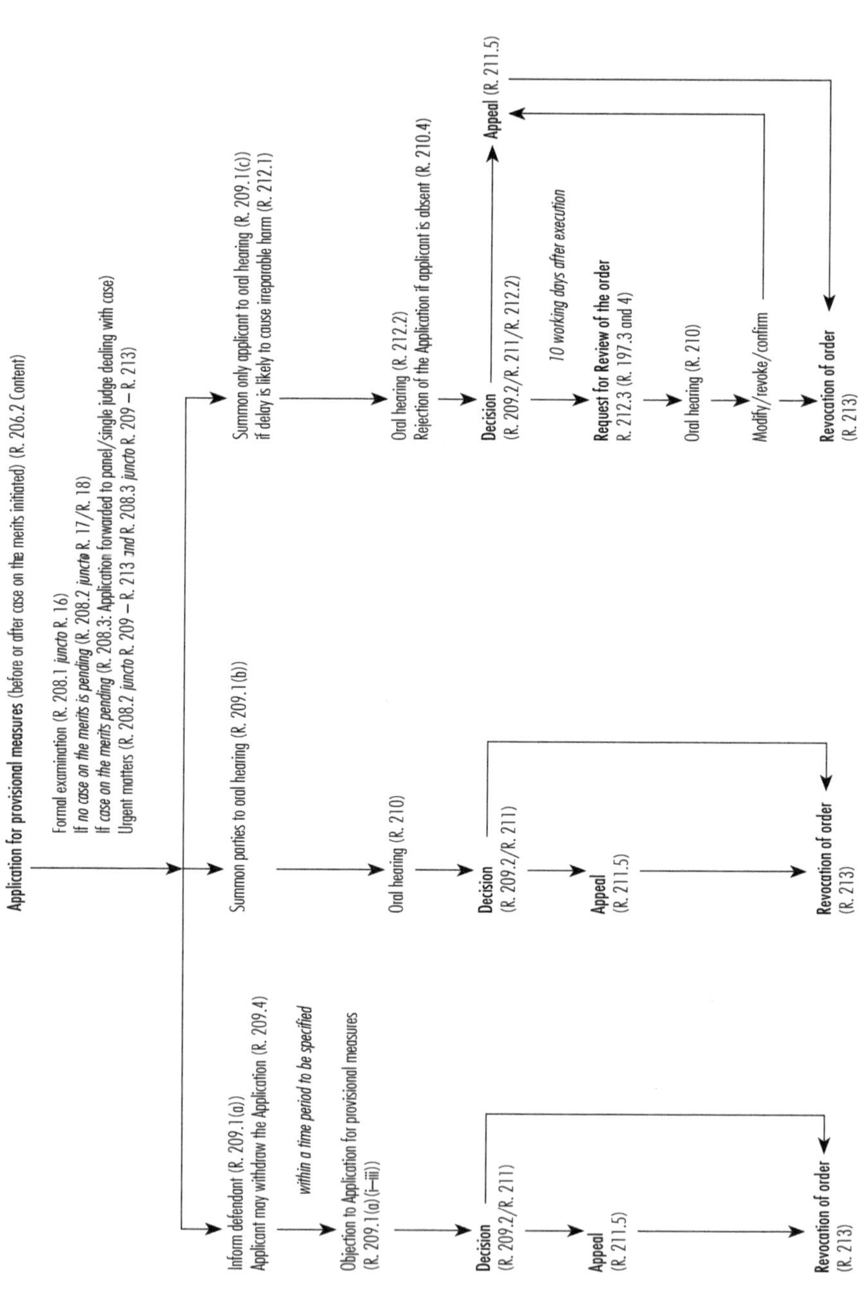

Flowchart: Provisional measures (summary proceedings) (R. 205 – R. 213)

PART 4
PROCEDURES BEFORE COURT OF APPEAL (R. 220 – R. 254)

Rule 220 – Appealable Decisions. The following decisions are appealable (R. 220.1 (a)-(c)):

(a) final decisions of the Court of First Instance,
(b) decisions terminating proceedings as regards one of the parties,
(c) decisions or orders referred to in Articles 49(5), 59, 60, 61, 62, or 67.

Procedural decisions or orders of the Court of First Instance may be appealed with leave of the Court of First Instance (R. 220.2). It should be noted that the members of the Drafting Committee have proposed that Article 73(2)(b)(ii) be altered to allow for leave to be given by the Court of Appeal.

Rule 221 – Application for leave to appeal. The Application for leave to appeal may be lodged by a party adversely affected by a decision or order referred in Rule 220.2 or Rule 157 and this within 15 calendar days of service of the decision or order (R. 221.1).

Flowchart: Overview leave to appeal (R. 221)

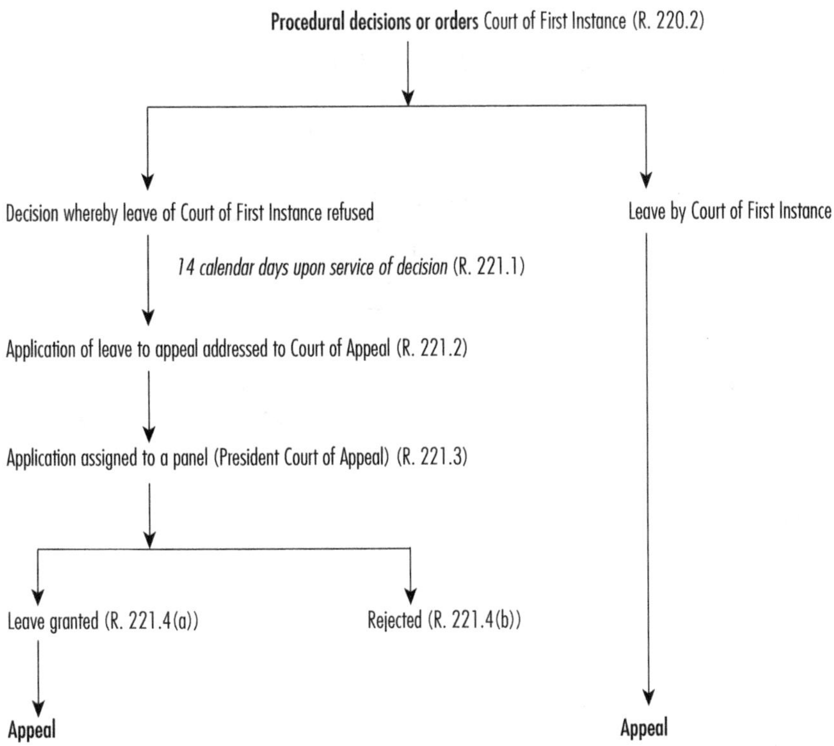

Rule 222 – Subject matter before the Court of Appeal. Requests, facts, evidence and arguments submitted by the parties under Rule 225 (Statement of appeal), Rule 226 (Statement of grounds of appeal), Rule 230 (Statement of Response) and Rule 238 (Reply to a Statement of cross-appeal) constitute the subject matter of the proceedings before the Court of Appeal (R. 222.1).

Requests, facts and evidence not submitted by a party during proceedings before the Court of First Instance may be disregarded by the Court of Appeal. When exercising discretion (R. 222.2), the Court takes in particular into account:

(a) whether a party seeking to lodge new submissions is able to justify that the new submissions could not reasonably have been made during proceedings before the Court of First Instance,
(b) whether the new submissions are highly relevant for the decision on the appeal,
(c) the position of the other party regarding the lodging of the new submissions.

Grounds of appeal which are not raised in the Statement of grounds of appeal are not admissible (R. 222.3).

Rule 223 – Application for suspensive effect

Flowchart: Application for suspensive effect (R. 223)

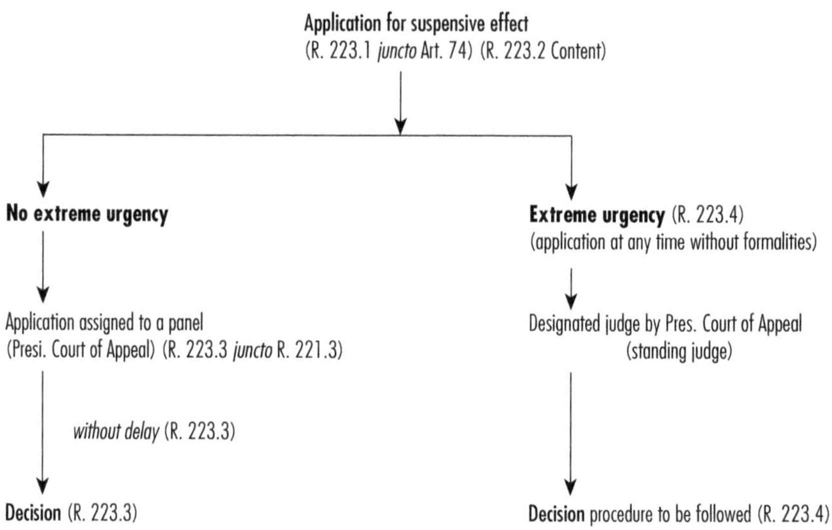

Chapter 1
Written Procedure (R. 224 – R. 238)

(See flowcharts overleaf)

Flowchart: Written procedure (R. 224 – R. 238)

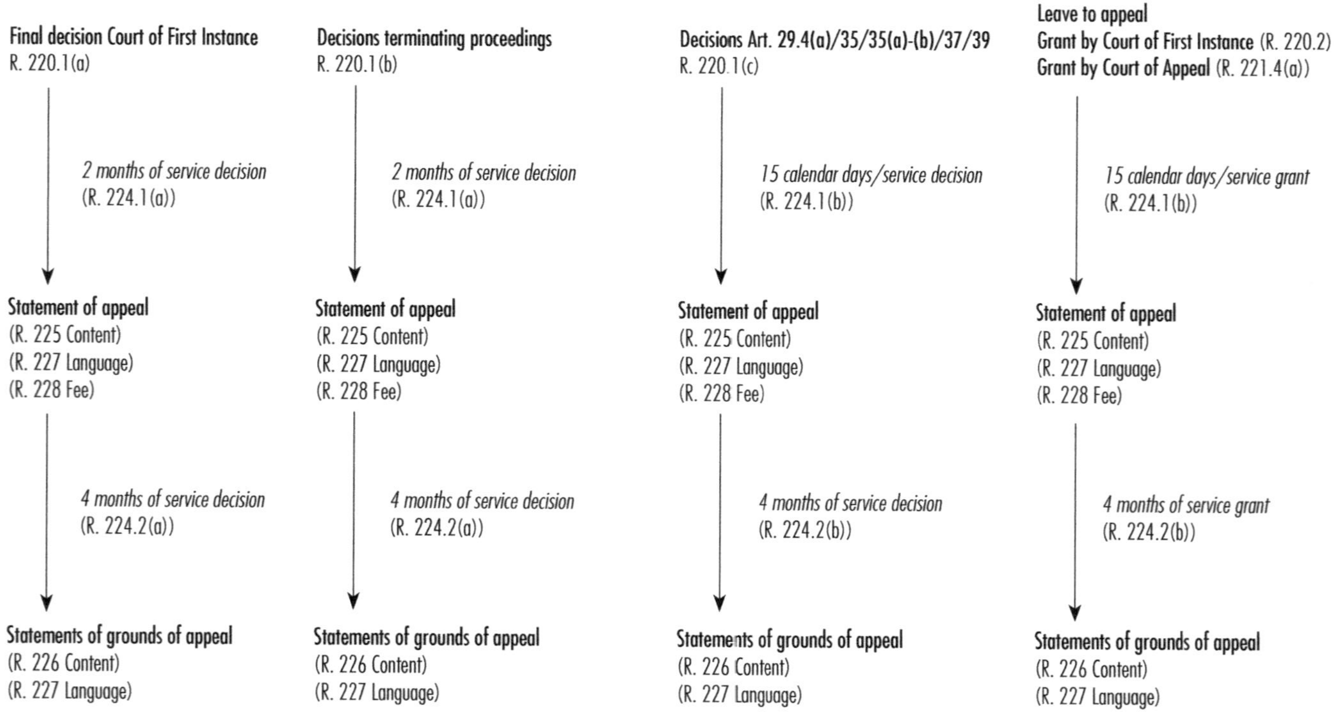

Flowchart: Formal requirements (preliminary examination by registry)

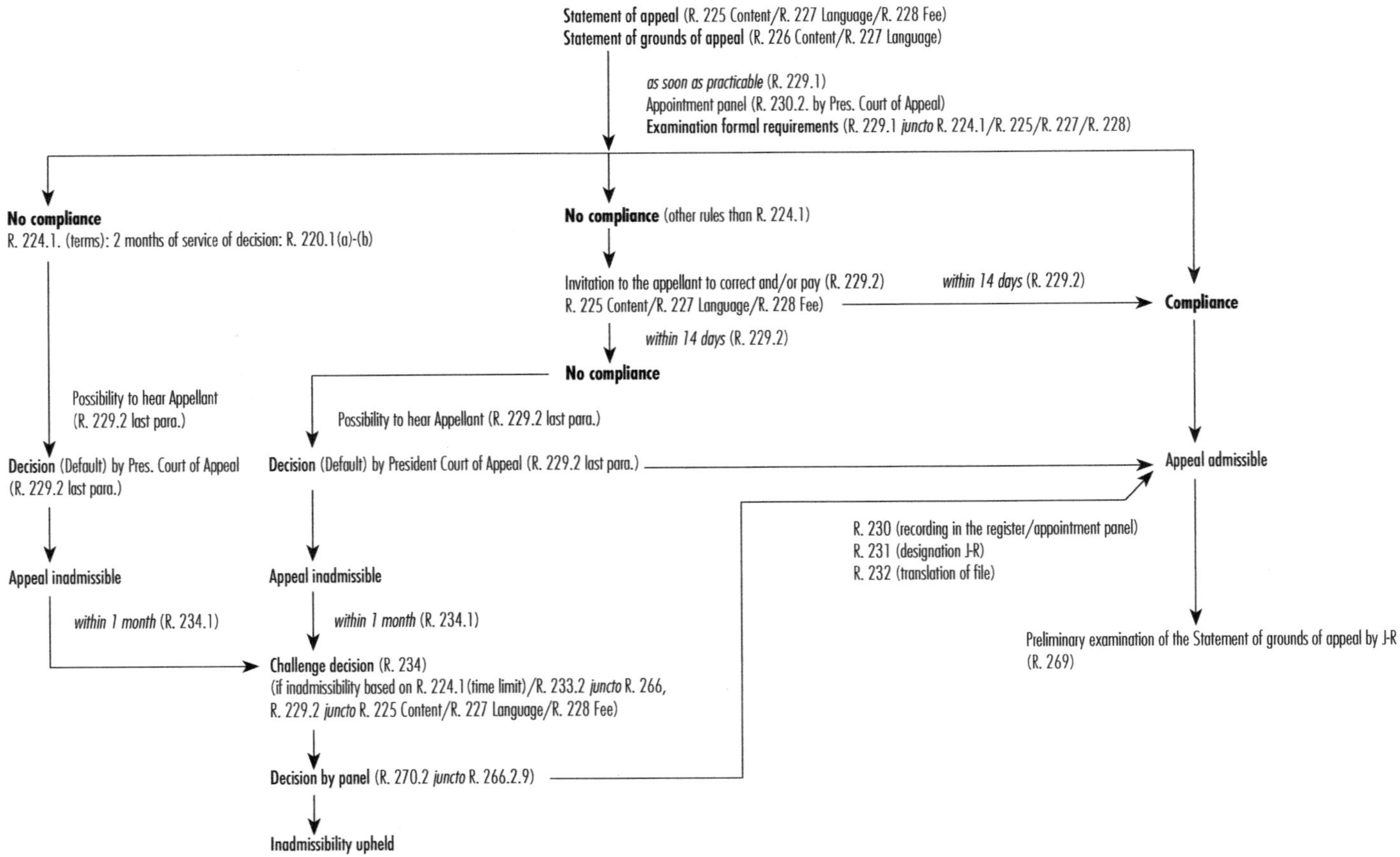

Flowchart: Preliminary examination of the Statement of grounds of appeal (R. 233) by J-R

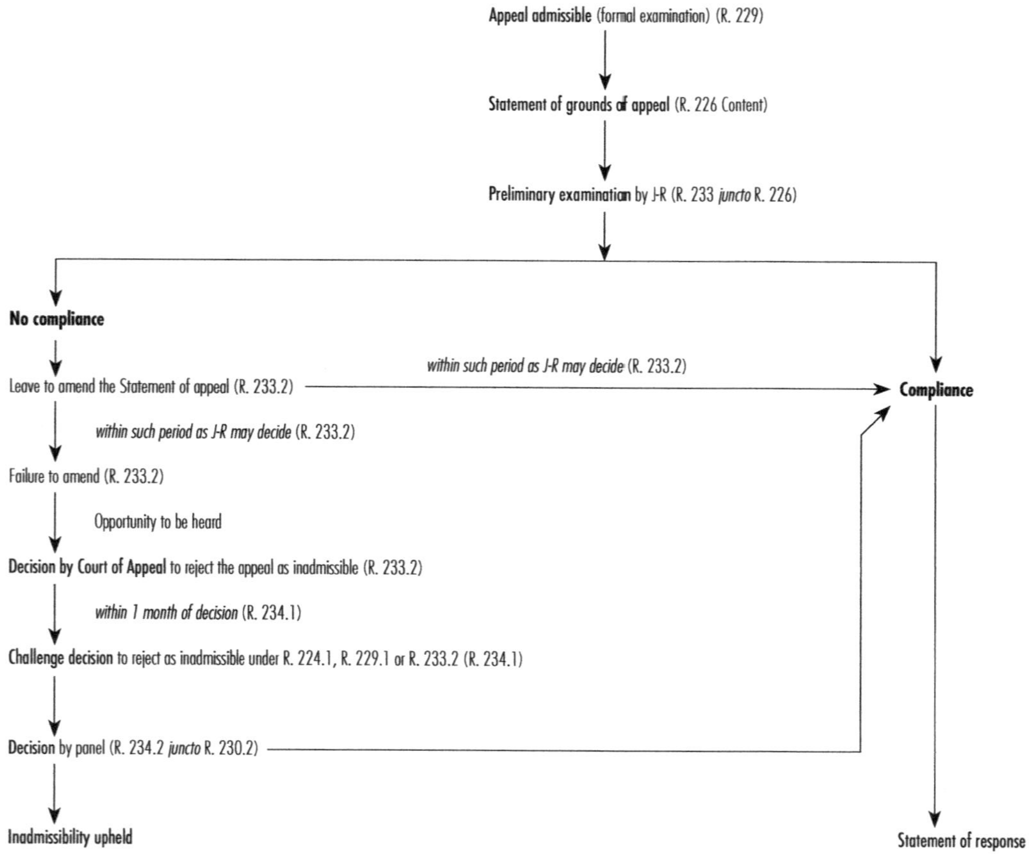

Chapters 1–3

Written Procedure upon Admissibility of Statement of Grounds of Appeals/Interim Procedure/Oral Procedure (R. 235 – R. 241)

(See flowchart overleaf)

Flowchart: Written procedure upon admissibility of Statement grounds of appeals/interim procedure/ oral procedure (R. 235 – R. 241)

Statement of grounds of appeal

↓ *within 3 months of service* (R. 235)

Left branch:

Statement of response
(R. 236 Content)
not including **Statement of cross-appeal** (R. 237)

↓

J-R sets date/time for interim conference (R. 28)

↓

Interim procedure (Role of J-R) (R. 239)
(subject to R. 222 J-R has powers/duties R. 101 – R. 110)

↓ *summons for oral hearing/at least 2 months notice* (R. 239.2)
Presiding judge takes over management (R. 239.2)

Oral procedure (R. 240 – R. 241)
The hearing is held before the panel and directed by presiding judge(R. 240)
The hearing is subject to R. 222 (i.e. subject matter of the proceedings before the Court of Appeal), R. 111 (Role of presiding judge), R. 112 (conduct of oral hearing Court of First Instance), R. 116 (absence of a party), R. 117 (absence of both parties), R. 321 (request by parties to use language in which patent was granted)

If the appeal relates to an **appeal of a cost order** (cf. R. 157) the case is heard by the standing judge alone (with powers of the Court of Appeal) (R. 241)

Right branch:

Statement of response
(R. 236 Content)
including **Statement of cross-appeal** (R. 237)
(compliance R. 225/R. 226/R. 229/R. 233)

↓ R. 237.5: note withdrawal statement of appeal = withdrawal statement of cross-appeal.

within 2 months of service statement of response (R. 238)

Reply to a statement of cross-appeal

↓

J-R sets date/time for interim conference (R. 28)

↓

Interim procedure (Role of J-R) (R. 239)
(subject to R. 222 J-R has powers/duties R. 101 – R. 110)

↓ *summons to appear/at least 2 months notice* (R. 239.2)
Presiding judge takes over management (R. 239.2)

Oral procedure (R. 240 – R. 241)
The hearing is held before the panel and directed by presiding judge(R. 240)
The hearing is subject to R. 222 (i.e. subject matter of the proceedings before the Court of Appeal), R. 111 (Role of presiding judge), R. 112 (conduct of oral hearing Court of First Instance), R. 116 (absence of a party), R. 117 (absence of both parties), R. 321 (request by parties to use language in which patent was granted)

If the appeal relates to an **appeal of a cost order** (cf. R. 157) the case is heard by the standing judge alone (with powers of the Court of Appeal) (R. 241)

Chapter 4

Decisions and Effects of Decisions (R. 242 – R. 243)

Flowchart: Decisions and effects of decisions (R. 242 – R. 243)

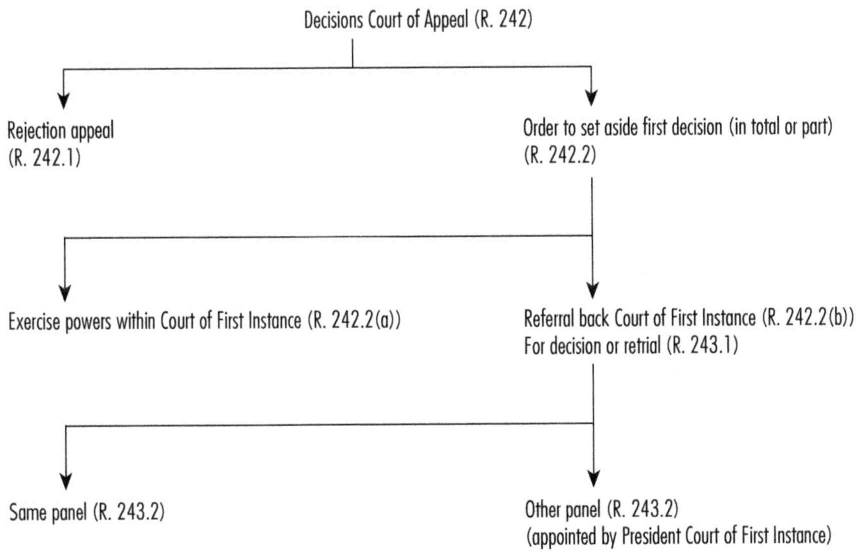

Where a case is referred back to the Court of First Instance, the Court is bound by the decision of the Court of Appeal and its ratio decided (R. 243.3)

Chapter 5
Procedure for Application for Rehearing (R. 245 – R. 254)

Flowchart: Procedure for application for rehearing (R. 245 – R. 254)

Final decision Court of First Instance (for which the time for lodging an appeal has expired) or Court of Appeal

↓

Fundamental procedural defect (R. 247) raised before Court of Appeal (except if impossible) and dismissed (R. 298)
Criminal offence (R. 249)

↓ *within 2 months of service final decision* (R. 245.2(a) *juncto* R. 247)
within 2 months of the date on which the criminal offence has been so held (R. 245.2(c) *juncto* R. 249)
but anyhow *within 10 years of service of final decision* (R. 245.2(c))

Application for rehearing (R. 246 Content) (R. 250 Fee)
R. 251: The lodging of an Application for rehearing shall not have suspensive effect unless the Court of Appeal decides otherwise

↓

Examination of formal requirements by Registry (R. 352)

↓

Recording in the Register (box under R. 250 referring to R. 230.1)

↓

Assignment of the case by President (R. 253)
Appointment of the J-R (R. 253)

↓

Examination of the Application for rehearing by J-R (R. 254)

Flowchart: Examination formal requirement (R. 252)

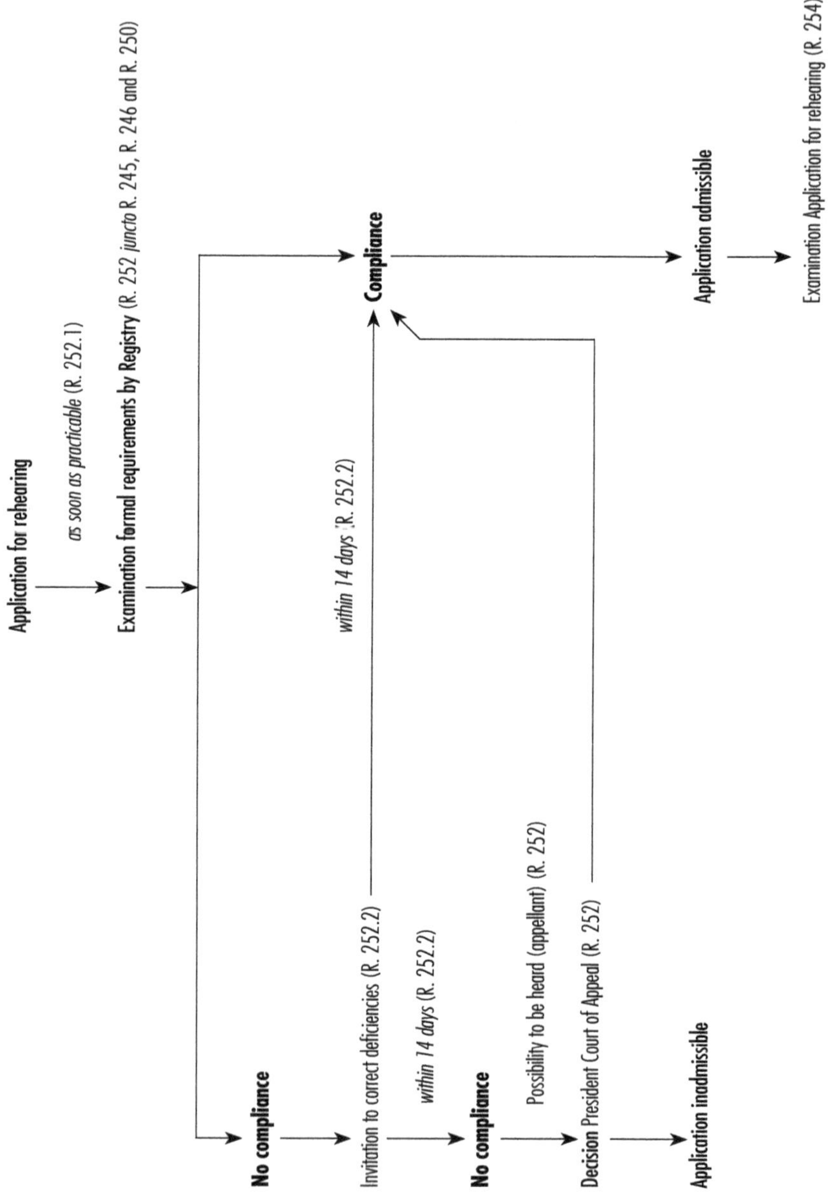

PART 5
GENERAL PROVISIONS (R. 260 – R. 365)

Chapter 1

General Procedural Provisions (R. 260 – R. 266)

The general procedural provisions to be applied throughout the specific provisions of the Rules of Procedure are detailed in this chapter.

Rule 260 – Examination by the Registry of its own motion. The Registry examines, *as soon as practicable* in the proceedings, of its own motion, whether an opt-out has effect for the patent or patents concerned (R. 260.1).

In the event that the Registry notes that two or more actions between the same parties and concerning the same patent or patents are initiated before several divisions, it informs *as soon as practicable* the divisions concerned (R. 260.2).

Rule 261 – Date of pleadings. All pleadings bear a date which is the date of receipt of pleadings in electronic form at the Registry.

Rule 262 – Public access to the register. Unless a party requests that certain information be kept confidential and the Court makes such an order, written pleadings, written evidence, decisions and orders lodged at the Court and recorded by the Registry are available to the public for on-line consultation (R. 262.1).

A party may lodge an application with the Court for an order that certain information should be excluded from public access or restricted to certain named persons on the grounds set out in and in accordance with Article 58 (R. 262.2). Such application should contain (R. 262.3):

(a) details of the information alleged to be confidential or otherwise to be restricted;
(b) the grounds upon which the applicant claims the information should be restricted; and
(c) details of the persons to be prohibited from access to the information or conversely to be allowed access.

Prior to making any order, the Court invites written comments from any other party (R. 262.4). The Registrar takes *as soon as practicable* all steps with regard to access to the Registry as may be necessary to give effect to an order of the Court under this Rule (R. 262.5).

Rule 263 – Leave to change claim or amend case. At any stage of the proceedings, a party can apply to the Court for leave to change its claim or to amend its case, including adding a counterclaim (R. 263.1). Such application should explain why such change or amendment was not included in the original pleading. Leave will not be granted if, all circumstances considered, the party seeking the amendment cannot satisfy the Court that (R. 263.2):

(a) the amendment in question could not have been made with reasonable diligence at an earlier stage; and
(b) the amendment does not unreasonably hinder the other party in the conduct of its case.

Leave to limit a claim unconditionally will always granted (R. 263.3).

Rule 264 – An opportunity to be heard. Where the Rules of Procedure provide that a party or parties will be or may be given an opportunity to be heard (before the Court makes an order or takes some action), the Court will request or may request (as the case may be) the parties to provide written submissions within a specified period and/or will invite or may invite the parties to an oral hearing on a fixed date by the Court. The Court can also order that a hearing takes place by telephone or video conference.

Rule 265 – Withdrawal. As long as there is no final decision in a case, a plaintiff can apply for withdrawal of his action. The Court decides after hearing the other party(ies). The application to withdraw is not permitted if the other party(ies) has (have) a legitimate interest in the action being decided by the Court.

Should withdrawal be permitted, the Court will:

(a) give a decision declaring the proceedings closed;
(b) order the case to be removed from the Register; and
(c) issue a costs order in accordance with Part 1, Chapter 5.

Rule 266 – Preliminary reference to the CJEU. At any stage of the proceedings, where a question is raised before the Court which, in its opinion, requires the CJEU to give a ruling before the Court can give judgement, the Court of First Instance may and the Court of Appeal shall of its own motion or at the request of a party an order for a request to the CJEU for a preliminary ruling (R. 266.1).

The order should set out as clearly and concisely as possible the question on which the Court seeks a preliminary ruling. The order should provide in addition the following information (R. 266.2):

(a) the division or the Court of Appeal making the reference;
(b) the parties;
(c) a summary of the proceedings including the essential facts;
(d) an explanation of why a ruling is sought;
(e) the provisions of European Union law in question;
(f) a copy of a decision, if any, by the Court on the question.

If the Court requests the CJEU to apply its urgent procedure, the order needs to set out in addition (R. 266.3):

(a) the matters of fact and law which establish its urgency, and
(b) the reasons why an urgent ruling is appropriate.

The Registrar shall as soon as practicable forward the order and any request to apply the urgent preliminary procedure to the Registrar of the CJEU (R. 266.4).

Unless otherwise decided by the Court, the proceedings are stayed until the CJEU has given a preliminary ruling on the question (R. 266.5).

Chapter 2
Service (R. 270 – R. 279)

1. SERVICE WITHIN THE CONTRACTING MEMBER STATES OR BY AGREEMENT (R. 270 – R. 272)

Rule 270 – Scope of this section. The rules in this section apply where the defendant has provided an electronic address for the purpose of service of the proceedings under Rule 271(1) or (2) or has an address for service for the purpose of any one of the modes of service here provided within the territory of any of the Contracting Member States (R. 270.1).

A statement of claim, irrespective of where it is lodged, may be served in the manner provided on a defendant in the territory of any Contracting Member State (R. 270.2).

For the purpose of Rules 270-275, the term Statement of claim shall, where appropriate, include a Statement of revocation (R. 45), a Statement for a declaration of non-infringement (R. 62), an Application for preserving evidence (R. 192) and an Application for provisional measures (R. 206).

Rule 271 – Service of the Statement of claim. The Registry serves the Statement of claim, Statement of revocation and Statement for declaration on the defendant at an electronic address which the defendant has provided for the purpose of service in the proceedings (R. 271.1).

It is possible to serve the mentioned documents on the electronic address of the representative when (R. 272.2):

(a) the defendant has provided such address; or
(b) a representative acting for the defendant has notified the Registry or the plaintiff that he accepts service of the Statement of claim on behalf of the defendant at an electronic address,

Should service by means of electronic communication not be effected, the Registry will serve the Statement of claim on the defendant by (R. 272.3):

(a) registered letter with advice of delivery, in accordance with the Practice Directions;
(b) fax, in accordance with the Practice Directions; or

(c) any method authorised by the Court under Rule 275.

Service under R. 271.3 is effected at the following place (R. 271.4):
(a) where the defendant is a company or other legal person: at its statutory seat, central administration or principal place of business within the Contracting Member States or at any place within the Contracting Member States where the company or other legal person has a place of business;
(b) where the defendant is an individual: by leaving it with him or at his usual or last known address.

A Statement of claim served in accordance with Rule 271.1, Rule 271.2 and Rule 271.3 is deemed to be served on the defendant (R. 271.5):
(a) where service takes place by means of electronic communication or by fax: on the day where the relevant electronic message was sent or the transmission of the fax was completed (GMT+1);
(b) where service takes place by registered letter with advice of delivery: ten working days after posting, leaving with, delivering to or collection by the relevant service provider.

Rule 272 – Notice of service and non-service of the Statement of claim. The Registry informs the plaintiff of the date on which the Statement of claim is deemed served under Rule 271.5 (R. 272.1). Should the Registry have served the Statement of claim by registered letter with advice of delivery and the Statement of claim is returned to the Registry, the Registry informs the plaintiff thereof (R. 272.2). This rules applies *mutatis mutandis* where the Registry has served the Statement of claim by fax and the fax appears not to have been received (R. 272.3).

2. SERVICE OUTSIDE THE CONTRACTING MEMBER STATES (R. 273 – R. 274)

Rule 273 – Scope of this section. Rules 273 and 274 apply to the service of a Statement of claim, Statement of revocation or Statement for declaration in the event the defendant has not provided an electronic address for service of the proceedings or otherwise may not be served within the territory of the Contracting Member States in a manner provided for under any of the methods prescribed in section 1.

Rule 274 – Service outside the Contracting Member State. Should a Statement of claim, Statement of revocation or Statement for declaration be served outside the Contracting Member States, it may be served by the Registry as follows (R. 274.1):

(a) by any method provided by:
   (i) Regulation (EC) No. 1393/2007 on the service in the Member States of judicial and extra-judicial documents in civil or commercial matters ("the EU Service Regulation") where it applies, or
   (ii) the Hague Convention on the service abroad of judicial and extra-judicial documents in civil or commercial matters 1965 ("the Hague Service Convention") or any other applicable convention where it applies, or
   (iii) to the extent that there is no such convention in force, either by service through diplomatic or consular channels from the Contracting Member State in which the Registry is established; or

(b) by any method permitted by the law of the state where service is to be effected.

The chosen method is conditional on the fact that it is not contrary to the law of the state where service is effected (R. 274.2).

3. SERVICE BY AN ALTERNATIVE METHOD (R. 275)

Rule 275 – Service of the Statement of claim by an alternative method or at alternative place. The Court may, by way of order, permit service by an alternative method or at an alternative place (R. 275.1).

On a reasoned request, the Court may order that steps already taken to bring the Statement of claim to the attention of the defendant by an alternative method or at an alternative place is good service (R. 275.2).

An order under this rule shall specify (R. 272.3):

(a) the method or place of service;
(b) the date on which the Statement of claim is deemed served; and
(c) the period for filing the Statement of defence.

Such order for alternative service under this Rule outside the Contracting Member States needs to be made permitting service in a manner that is not contrary to the law of the state where service is to be effected (R. 275.4).

4. SERVICE OF ORDERS AND DECISIONS (R. 276 – R. 279)

Rule 276 – Service of orders and decisions. Any order or decision of the Court needs to be served on each of the parties in accordance with the provisions of section 1 (Service within a Contracting Member State of by agreement) or section 2 (Service outside the Contracting Member State), as the case may be.

Rule 277 – Decisions by default under Part 5, Chapter 11. If the Court renders a decision by default, it should satisfy that either (R. 277):

(a) the Statement of claim was served by a method prescribed by the internal law of the state addressed for the service of documents in domestic actions upon persons who are within its territory; or
(b) the Statement of claim was actually delivered to the defendant or to his residence or place of business by another method provided for under Chapter 2.

Rule 278 – Service of other pleadings. *As soon as practicable* (after written pleadings have been received at the Registry), the Registry serves the pleadings on the other party by means of electronic communication, in accordance with the Practice Directions (R. 278.1). Where service by means of electronic communication cannot be effected, the Registry serves the written pleadings on the party by (R. 278.2):

(a) registered letter with advice of delivery, in accordance with the Practice Directions;
(b) fax, in accordance with the Practice Directions; or
(c) any method authorised by the Court under Rule 275.

Service under registered letter with advice of delivery needs to be effected at the following place (R. 278.3):

(a) where the party is a company or other legal person: at its statutory seat, central administration, principal place of business or at any place within the Contracting Member States where the company or other legal person carries on its activities and which has a real connection with the claim;
(b) where the party is an individual: at his usual or last known residence.

Rule 279 – Change of electronic address for service. Where the electronic address for service of a party changes, that party must give notice in writing of the change to the Court and every other party as soon as it has taken place.

Chapter 3
Rights and Obligations of Representatives (R. 285 – R. 294)

Rule 285 – Powers of attorney. Except if his representative powers are challenged and the Court orders to produce a written authority, the claim of representative to be representing a party is accepted as such.

Rule 286 – Certificate that a representative is authorised to practise before the Court. Pursuant to Article 48(1), a representative should lodge at the Registry a certificate that he is a lawyer authorised to practise before a court of a Contracting Member State. In subsequent cases, the representative may refer to the certificate previously lodged (R. 286.1).

Pursuant to Article 48(2), a representative should lodge at the Registry the European Patent Litigation Certificate as defined by the Administrative Committee or otherwise justify that he has appropriate qualifications to represent a party before the Court. In subsequent cases, such a representative may refer to the certificate or other evidence of appropriate qualification previously lodged (R. 286.2).

Rule 287 – Attorney-client privilege. Where a client seeks advice from a lawyer he has instructed in a professional capacity, any confidential communication (whether written or oral) between them relating to the seeking or the provision of that advice is permanently privileged from disclosure, whether in court or arbitration proceedings of any nature or in the face of any compulsory information gathering powers of any body (R. 287.1).

This privilege applies to communications between a client and a lawyer employed by the client and instructed to act in a professional capacity and a client and a patent attorney or agent (including a patent attorney or agent employed by the client) who is instructed in his professional capacity to advise on patent matters (R. 287.2).

The privilege extends to the work product of the lawyer or patent attorney or agent (including communications between lawyers and/or patent attorneys or agents employed in the same firm or entity or between lawyers and/or patent attorneys or agents employed by the same client) and to any record of a privileged communication (R. 287.3).

The privilege prevents the lawyer or patent attorney or agent and his client from being questioned or examined about the contents or nature of their communications (R. 287.4).

The privilege may be expressly waived by the client (R. 287.5).

The expression "patent attorney" and "patent agent" bears the meanings given to them by the law of the Contracting Member State in which the individual practises (R. 287.6).[1]

Rule 288 – Litigation privilege. Where a client, or a lawyer or patent attorney or agent instructed by a client in a professional capacity, communicates confidentially with a third party for the purposes of obtaining information or evidence of any nature for the purpose of or for use in any proceedings reasonably anticipated or pending before the Court, such communications will be permanently privileged from disclosure in the same way and to the same extent as provided for in Rule 361 (R. 288.1). The above-mentioned Rule 287.6 applies *mutatis mutandis*.

Rule 289 – Privileges, immunities and facilities. Representatives appearing before the Court or before any judicial authority to which it has addressed letters rogatory (R. 199) enjoy immunity in respect of words spoken or written by them concerning the case or the parties (R. 289.1). Representatives enjoy the following further privileges and facilities (R. 289.2):

(a) papers and documents relating to the proceedings are exempted from both search and seizure;
(b) any allegedly infringing product or device relating to the proceedings are exempted from both search and seizure when brought to the Court for the purposes of the proceedings.

In the event of a dispute, customs officials or police shall seal those papers, documents or allegedly infringing products or devices, and immediately forward them to the Court for inspection in the presence of the Registrar and of the person concerned.

1. Based on recent communication from the Drafting Committee (8 February 2012), it is possible that Rule 287.6 will alter in such in way to include a reference to the expression "lawyer" referring to a person who is qualified to practice as a lawyer and to give legal advice under the law of the state where he practises and who is professionally instructed as a lawyer to give such advice. Further, a new R.287.7 may be included to refer to the expression "patent attorney" indicating that it includes a professional representative before the EPO pursuant to Article 134(1) EPC. As these changes were not formally introduced in the draft used when going into print, they were not included in the definitive text.

The Court may waive the immunity where it considers that a representative is guilty of conduct which is contrary to the proper conduct of proceedings (R. 289.5).

Rule 290 – Powers of the Court as regards representatives. The Court has the powers normally accorded to courts of law, under the conditions laid down in Rule 291 as regards representatives who appear before it (R. 290.1). Representatives who appear before the Court shall strictly comply with any code of conduct adopted for such representatives by the Court (R. 290.2).

Rule 291 – Exclusion from the proceedings. If the Court considers that the conduct of a party's representative towards the Court, towards any judge of the Court or towards any member of the staff of the Registry is incompatible with the dignity of the Court or with the requirements of the proper administration of justice, or that such representative uses his rights for purposes other than those for which they were granted or that such representative is otherwise in breach of any code of conduct adopted pursuant to Rule 290.2, it informs the person concerned. On the same grounds, the Court may at any time, after having given the person concerned an opportunity to be heard, exclude that person from the proceedings by way of order. Such order has immediate effect (R. 291.1). Where a party's representative is excluded from the proceedings, the proceedings are suspended for a period fixed by the presiding judge in order to enable the party concerned to appoint another representative (R. 291.2).

Rule 292 – Patent attorneys' right of audience. For the purposes of Article 48(4), the term "patent attorneys" assisting a representative referred to in Article 28(1) shall mean persons meeting the requirements of Article 134(1) or (3) (a)-(c) EPC or the professional requirements of the Contracting Member State to the Agreement in which the individual practises (R. 292.1).

Such patent attorneys are allowed to speak at hearings of the Court at the discretion of the Court and subject to the representative's responsibility to coordinate the presentation of a party's case (R. 292.2).

Rules 287-291 apply *mutatis mutandis* (R. 292.3).

Rule 293 – Change of a representative. Any change of representative takes effect from the receipt by the Registry of notification that a new representative is in future representing the party concerned. Until the moment where such statement is received, the former representative remains responsible for the conduct of the proceedings and for communications between the Court and the party concerned.

Chapter 4
Stay of Proceedings (R. 295 – R. 298)

Rule 295 – Stay of proceedings. In the following specific situations, proceedings may be stayed (R. 370):

(a) where it is seized of a case relating to a patent which is also the subject of opposition proceedings or limitation proceedings (including subsequent appeal proceedings) before the EPO or a national authority;
(b) where it is seized of a case relating to a supplementary protection certificate which is also the subject of proceedings before a national court or authority;
(c) where an appeal is brought before the Court of Appeal against a decision or order of the Court of First Instance
  (i) disposing of the substantive issues in part only,
  (ii) disposing of an admissibility issue or a Preliminary objection,
  (iii) dismissing an application to intervene (R. 313);
(d) at the joint request of the parties;
(e) pursuant to Rule 37 (application of Art. 33(3));
(f) pursuant to Rule 118 (suspension of the infringement proceedings pending a final decision on the revocation procedure or final decision of the EPO);
(g) pursuant to Rule 136 (stay of the application for a determination of damages);
(h) in particular cases where the proper administration of justice so requires.

Rule 296 – Duration and effects of a stay of proceedings. The stay takes effect on the date indicated in the order to stay or, in the absence of such an indication, on the date of that order. The Court should stipulate what effect the stay has on any existing orders (R. 296.1).

Where the order to stay does not fix the length of the stay, it ends on the date indicated in the order to resume proceedings or, in the absence of such indication, on the date of the order to resume (R. 296.2). While proceedings are stayed, time ceases to run for the purposes of procedural periods. Time begins to run afresh for the purposes of procedural periods from the date on which the stay of proceedings comes to an end (R. 296.3).

Rule 297 – Resumption of proceedings. Any decision referred to in Rule 295.2 or ordering the resumption of proceedings before the end of the stay should be made by reasoned order of the J-R after hearing the parties. The J-R can refer the matter to the panel.

Rule 298 – Accelerated proceedings before the European Patent Office. The Court may of its own motion or at the request of a party request that opposition proceedings or limitation proceedings (including any subsequent appeal proceedings) before the European Patent Office be accelerated in accordance with the proceedings of the European Patent Office. The Court may stay its proceedings in accordance with Rule 295 pending the outcome of such request and any subsequent accelerated proceedings.

Chapter 5

Time Periods (R. 300 – R. 301)

Rule 300 – Calculation of periods. Any period of time prescribed by the Agreement, the Statute or these Rules of Procedure for the taking of any procedural step is laid down terms of full days, weeks, months or years and are calculated taking the following in consideration:

(a) computation shall start on the day following the day on which the relevant event occurred;

(b) when a period is expressed as one year or a certain number of years, it shall expire in the relevant subsequent year in the month having the same name and on the day having the same number as the month and the day on which the said event occurred. If the relevant subsequent month has no day with the same number, the period shall expire on the last day of that month;

(c) when a period is expressed as one month or a certain number of months, it shall expire in the relevant subsequent month on the day which has the same number as the day on which the said event occurred. If the relevant subsequent month has no day with the same number, the period shall expire on the last day of that month;

(d) when a period is expressed as one week or a certain number of weeks, it shall expire in the relevant subsequent week on the day having the same name as the day on which the said event occurred;

(e) day shall mean a calendar day unless expressed as a working day;

(f) calendar days shall include official holidays of the Contracting Member State in which the division concerned or the Court of Appeal is located, Saturdays and Sundays;

(g) working days shall not include official holidays of the contracting Member State in which the division concerned or the Court of Appeal is located, Saturdays or Sundays;

(h) periods shall not be suspended during the judicial vacations.

Rule 301 – Extension and shortening of periods. If a period expires on a Saturday, Sunday or official holiday of the Contracting Member State in which the division or section of the central division concerned or the Court of Appeal is located, this period will be extended until the end of the first following working day (R. 281.1). This rule also applies for documents filed in electronic form that cannot be received by the Court (R. 281.2).

Chapter 6

Parties to Proceedings (R. 302 – R. 320)

1. PLURALITY OF PARTIES (R. 302 – R. 304)

Rule 302 – Plurality of plaintiffs and patents. The Court can hear a plurality of plaintiffs regarding the same patent or in the case of a plurality of patents in separate proceedings (R. 302.1). Should separate proceedings be ordered, the Court decides on the payment of a new court fee (or court fees) (R. 302.2 *juncto* Part 6). Where it is in the interests of justice, the Court may order that parallel infringement or revocation proceedings relating to the same patent (or patents) (and before the same local or regional division or the central division or the Court of Appeal) are heard together (R. 302.3).

Rule 303 – Plurality of defendants. Proceedings may be initiated against a plurality of defendants. In the event the court has competence in respect of all of them, it may separate the proceedings (R. 303.2). Should separate proceedings be ordered and should the Court not decide otherwise, the plaintiffs in the new proceedings need to pay a new court fee (R. 303.2 *juncto* Part 6).

Rule 304 – Court fees in case of a plurality of parties. If the same representative takes the same position for a plurality of parties, these parties are regarded as one party as far as the payment of court fees is concerned.

2. CHANGE IN PARTIES (R. 305 – R. 306)

Rule 305 – Change in parties. On application by a party and upon hearing the parties, the Court can order a person to be added as or ceased to be a party. The Court may substitute a party. (R. 305.1-2). When ordering a person to become a party or to cease to be a party, the Court may make appropriate orders as to payment of court fees and costs as regards to such party.

Rule 306 – Consequences for the proceedings. Should a party be added, removed or substituted, the Court shall give directions to regulate the consequences as to case management (R. 306.1) and determines the extent to which a new party is bound by the proceedings as then constituted. (R. 306.2).

3. DEATH, DEMISE OF INSOLVENCY OF A PARTY (R. 310 – R. 311)

Rule 310 – Death or demise of a party. In principle proceedings are stayed until such a party is replaced by his successor or successors (R. 310.1). Should there be more than two parties to the proceedings, the Court can decide that proceedings between the remaining parties continue and the stay only concerns the proceedings regarding the party that no longer exists (R. 310.2).

If applicable, the Court may file continuation proceedings against a successor or successors of the party that died or ceased to exist (R. 310.3). In such proceeding the Court decides to what extent the successor or successors takes the position of the defendant who has died or ceased to exist in the main proceedings (R. 310.4).

On the basis of the outcome of the continuation proceedings and independently of the costs of the main proceedings, the costs of continuation proceedings will be decided (R. 310.5).

Rule 311 – Insolvency of a party. Should a defendant be declared insolvent under the national law of his residence or principal place of business or, in the absence of residence or principal place of business, his place of business, proceedings can be stayed until the competent national authority or person dealing with the insolvency has decided whether to continue the proceedings or not (R. 311.1). The plaintiff may withdraw the case against an insolvent defendant. Such withdrawal does not prejudice the case against other defendants (R. 311.2).

Any costs order in favour of an insolvent party (under Rule 156) is payable to the competent national authority or person dealing with the insolvency (R. 311.3).

Should the proceedings be continued, the effect of a decision of the Court as regards the insolvent party in the case are determined by the national law of that party (R. 311.4).

4. TRANSFER OF PATENT (R. 312)

If a patent or patent application is transferred, for one or more Contracting Member States, to another proprietor after proceedings have been initiated before the Court, the Court can authorise the new proprietor to take over the proceedings to the extent that the patent has been transferred to him (R. 312.1). No new court fee is payable, even if the new proprietor is represented by a new representative (R. 312.2).

Should the new proprietor not wish to take over the proceedings, any decision in proceedings that have been recorded in the register is binding upon him (R. 312.3).

5. INTERVENTION (R. 313 – R. 317)

Flowchart: Intervention overview (R. 313 – R. 317)

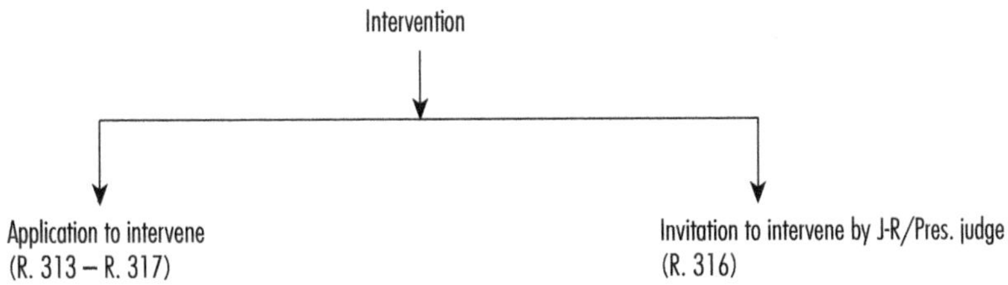

Rules 313–315 – Application to intervene. An application to intervene may be lodged at any stage of the proceedings before the Court of First Instance or the Court of Appeal by any person establishing a legal interest in the result of a case submitted to the Court (R. 313.1). However, the application to intervene is only admissible if it is made in support, in whole or in part, of a claim or remedy sought by one of the parties (R. 313.2).

The application to intervene should be made before the closure of the written procedure (unless the Court of First Instance or the Court of Appeal should order otherwise) (R. 313.2).

Flowchart: Application to intervene (R. 313)

Application to intervene (R. 313.4 Content)

↓ Other parties have the opportunity to be heard

Decision J-R by way of order (R. 314)

↓

Admissible application (R. 315)

↓

Inform parties (R. 315.1(a))
Specify period to lodge Statement of intervention (R. 315.1(b))
Decision on confidential nature of information (R. 314)

↓ *as soon as practicable* (R. 315.2)

Serving of any written pleading served by parties (R. 315.2)

↓

Statement of intervention (R. 315.3 Content)

Inadmissible application

↓

No right to appeal (R. 317)

Flowchart: Invitation to intervene (R. 316)

Own motion J.R. or Presiding Judge (R. 316.1)

↓
– Reasoned request of a party (R. 316.1)
– After consulting the parties (R. 316.1)

Invitation to intervene (R. 316)

↓ *within time period specified* (R. 316.1)

Inform Court whether he wishes to intervene (R. 316.1)

↓ *within 1 month if service of invitation* (R. 316.2)

Application to intervene (R. 316.2)

↓ *within further time period to be specified* (R. 316.2)

Statement in intervention (R. 316.2 *juncto* R. 313.3-4 and R. 315)
An intervener is bound by the decision in the case (R. 316.2)

6. RE-ESTABLISHMENT OF RIGHTS (R. 320)

In the event a time limit for an appeal was not observed by a party or by the Court for a cause which was outside his control and the non-observance of this time limit has had the direct consequence of causing the party to lose a right or means of redress, the relevant panel of the Court can upon the request of that party re-establish the right or means of redress (R. 320).

Flowchart: Application for re-establishment of rights (R. 320)

Time-limit to appeal

↓ *within 1 month of removal of the cause for non-observance of time-limit* (R. 320.2)
in any case *within 3 months of the non-observed time limit* (R. 320.2)

– **Application** for re-establishment of rights (R. 320.3 Content) (R. 320.2 Fee)
– **Performance** of the omitted act together with Application to Re-establishment (R. 320.4)

↓ Right to be heard (R. 320.6)

Decision of the panel by way of order (R. 320.6)
(no grant of re-establishment regarding the time-limits R. 320.2-4) (R. 320.5)

↓

No appeal (R. 320.7)

Chapter 7

Miscellaneous Provisions on Languages (R. 321 – R. 324)

(*see Supplementary part: Language Issues*)

Chapter 8
Case Management (R. 331 – R. 340)

Rule 331 – Responsibility for case management. During the written and the interim procedure, the J-R is responsible for the case management (R. 331.1). He may refer the case to the panel (R. 331.2). After the closure of the interim conference, case management is the responsibility of the presiding judge in consultation with the J-R (R. 331.3). The Registry needs to serve any case management orders on the parties *as soon as practicable* after the decision of the J-R, presiding judge or panel (R. 331.4).

Rule 332 – General principles of case management. Case management consists of:

(a) encouraging the parties to co-operate with each other during the proceedings;
(b) identifying the issues at an early stage;
(c) deciding promptly which issues need full investigation and disposing summarily of other issues;
(d) deciding the order in which issues are to be resolved;
(e) encouraging the parties to make use of the Patent Mediation and Arbitration Centre and facilitating the use of the Centre;
(f) helping the parties to settle the whole or part of the case;
(g) fixing timetables or otherwise controlling the progress of the case;
(h) considering whether the likely benefits of taking a particular step justify the cost of taking it;
(i) dealing with as many aspects of the case as the Court can on the same occasion;
(j) dealing with the case without the parties needing to attend in person;
(k) making use of available technical means; and
(l) giving directions to ensure that the hearing of the case proceeds quickly and efficiently.

Rule 333 – Review of case management orders

Flowchart: Review of case management orders (R. 333)

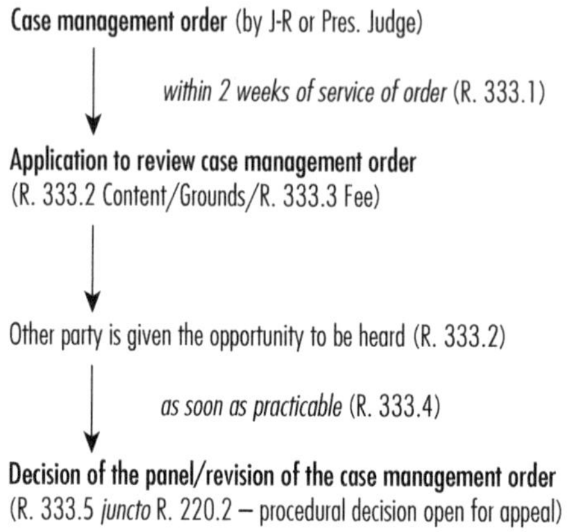

Rule 334 – Case management powers. In order to perform the mentioned actions, and except where the Agreement, the Statute, or the Rules of Procedure provide otherwise, the case manager (be it the J-R, the presiding judge or the panel) may (R. 334):

(a) extend or shorten the period for compliance with any rule, practice direction or order;
(b) adjourn or bring forward the interim conference or the oral hearing;
(c) communicate with the parties to instruct them about wishes or requirements of the Court;
(d) direct a separate hearing of any issue;
(e) decide the order in which issues are to be decided;
(f) exclude an issue from consideration;
(g) dismiss or decide on a claim after a decision on a preliminary issue makes a decision on further issues irrelevant to the outcome of the case;
(h) dismiss a pleading summarily if it has no prospect of succeeding;
(i) consolidate any matter or issue, or order them to be heard together;
(j) make any order pursuant to Rules 103-109.

Rule 335 – Varying or revoking orders. A power of the Court to make a case management order includes a power to vary or revoke such order.

Rule 336 – Exercise of managing powers. The Court may exercise its case management powers on the application by a party or of its own motion, unless otherwise provided.

Rule 337 – Orders of the Court's own motion. Should the Court propose an order of his own motion, it may do so but only after hearing the parties.

Rule 340 – Connection; joinder. In the interests of proper administration of justice, a presiding judge of the local or regional division where the cases are pending (after consultation with any other relevant presiding judge), the President of the Court of First Instance where the cases are in different divisions or the President of the Court of Appeal where the cases are pending may, at any time, after hearing the parties, order that two or more cases are, on account of the connection between them, joined. The cases may subsequently be disjoined.

Chapter 9
Rules Relating to the Organisation of the Court (R. 341 – R. 346)

Rule 341 – Precedence. With the exception of the President of the Court of Appeal and the President of the Court of First Instance, the judges rank in precedence according to their seniority in Court (R. 341.1). Where there is an equal seniority in office, precedence shall be determined by age (R. 341.2). Retiring judges who are reappointed shall retain their former precedence (R. 341.3). Unless otherwise agreed by the panel, the most senior judge is the presiding judge (R. 341.4).

Rule 342 – Dates, times and place of the sittings of the Court. The President of the Court of Appeal, on a proposal from the Presidium,[2] fixes the dates and times of the sittings of the Court (R. 342.1). The Court can hold one or more particular sittings in a place other than that in which it has its seat. (R. 342.2)

Rule 343 – Order in which cases are to be dealt with. Cases are dealt with in the order they become ready for hearing (R. 343.1) The presiding judge of a local or regional division, the President of the Court of First Instance or the President of the Court of Appeal may:

(a) direct that a particular case be given priority and that time limits provided for in these Rules be shortened; or
(b) after hearing the parties, in particular with a view to facilitating an amicable settlement of the dispute, either on his own initiative or at the request of one of the parties, defer a case to be dealt with later (R. 343.2).

---

2. The Presidium shall be responsible for the management of the Court (Art. 15.2 Statute). The Presidium shall be composed of the President of the Court of Appeal, who shall act as chairperson, the President of the Court of First Instance, two judges of the Court of Appeal elected from among their number, three judges of the Court of First Instance who are full-time judges of the Court elected from among their number, and the Registrar as a non-voting member (Art. 15.1 Statute).

Rule 344 – Deliberations. Deliberations, presided over by the presiding judge, are held in closed sessions (R. 344.1-2) and this as soon as possible after the closure of the oral hearing (R. 344.3).

Rule 345 – Composition of panels and assignment of cases. The presiding judge of each local or regional division (being the judge in the division appointed by the Praesidium as the presiding judge of the division) shall allocate (in conformity with Art. 8 – R. 345.2) the legally qualified judges assigned to his division to its panels for the duration of one year. He shall previously consult all judges of the division. The allocation shall be subject to the approval of the President of the Court of First Instance (R. 345.1).

Pending cases in the division shall be assigned to the panels by the Registrar following a case-distribution scheme established by the presiding judge of the division for the duration of one calendar year, preferably distributing the cases accordingly to the date of receipt of the cases at the division (R. 345.3).

Regarding the establishment of the case-distribution scheme, Rule 345.1 shall apply *mutatis mutandis*.

Each panel may delegate to one of more judges of the panel (R. 345.4):

(a) the function of acting as a single judge; or
(b) the function of acting for the panel in the Procedures of Part 1 Chapter 4 (Procedure for the determination of damages and compensation, including the procedure for the laying open of books) and Chapter 5 (Procedure for cost orders). These functions may be delegated to the J-R who has prepared the case for the oral hearing.

The presiding judge of the division shall designate a judge assigned to his division as a standing judge for urgent cases. The assignment may be limited to certain periods of time (R. 345.5).

If all parties agree to having the case heard by a single judge, the presiding judge on the panel to which the case is allocated shall assign the case to a legally qualified judge on the panel (R. 345.6).

Rule 345.1-6 apply *mutatis mutandis* to the central division. All references to the presiding judge of the division shall, regarding the central division, refer to the President of the Court of First Instance (R. 345.7).

Rule 345.1-6 apply *mutatis mutandis* to the Court of Appeal. All references to the presiding judge of the division shall, regarding the Court of Appeal, refer to the President of Court of Appeal (R. 345.8).

Rule 346 – Settling difficulties arising as to the application of Article 7 of the Statute.[3] If a judge of the Court of First Instance, during his term of office, does not respect the obligations arising from his office, pursuant to Article 7(1) and (2) of the Statute, the President of the Court of First Instance, after hearing the judge, may formally in writing put the judge on notice of such failure. If the judge continues not to fully respect the obligations of his office, the President of the Court of First Instance shall ask the Presidium to decide on the consequences of such failure (R. 346.1). The Rule shall also apply to a judge of the Court of Appeal. The President of the Court of Appeal shall perform the functions attributed in that Rule to the President of the Court of First Instance (R. 346.2).

If a judge of the Court, after having ceased to hold office, does not behave with integrity and discretion as regards the acceptance of appointments or benefits, the President of the Court of First Instance or the President of the Court of Appeal may ask the Presidium to decide on the consequences of such behaviour (R. 346.3).

Should a party object to a judge taking part in proceedings pursuant to Article 6(4) of the Statute, the presiding judge of the local or regional division to which the judge is allocated or, if the case is pending before the central division, the President of the Court of First Instance shall, after hearing the judge concerned, decide whether the objection is admissible having regard to Article 5(2) of the Statute (R. 346.4). If the objection is admissible, the presiding judge of the division or the President of the Court of First Instance, as the case may be, shall refer the case to the Presidium which shall hear the judge concerned and shall decide whether the objection shall stand or not (R. 346.5).

Rule 346.4-5 apply to a judge of the Court of Appeal. The President of the Court of Appeal performs the functions attributed in the Rules to the President of the Court of First Instance (R. 346.6).

---

3. Article 7 Statute: Impartiality (only referred to articles are cites hereunder):

(1) Immediately after taking their oath, judges shall sign a declaration by which they solemnly undertake that, both during and after their term of office, they shall respect the obligations arising therefrom, in particular the duty to behave with integrity and discretion as regards the acceptance, after they have ceased to hold office, of certain appointments or benefits.

(2) Judges may not take part in the proceedings of a case in which they:
   (a) have taken part as adviser;
   (b) have been a party or have acted for one of the parties;
   (c) have been called upon to pronounce as a member of a court, tribunal, board of appeal, arbitration or mediation panel, a commission of inquiry or in any other capacity;
   (d) have a personal or financial interest in the case or in relation to one of the parties; or
   (e) are related to one of the parties or the representatives of the parties by family ties.

(3) …

(4) Any party to an action may object to a judge taking part in the proceedings on any of the grounds listed in paragraph 2 or where the judge is suspected, with good reason, of partiality.

(5) …

Chapter 10

Decisions and Orders (R. 350 – R. 354)

Rule 350 – Decisions. Decisions should contain (R. 350.1):

(a) the statement that it is a decision of the Court;
(b) the date of its delivery;
(c) the names of the presiding judge, the J-R and other judges taking part in it;
(d) the names of the parties and of the parties' representatives;
(e) an indication of the claim, order or remedy sought by the parties;
(f) a summary of the facts;
(g) the grounds for the decision.

The order of the Court consequential upon the decision (other than costs) including any order giving immediate effect to an injunction, needs to be appended to the decision. The order should comply with Rule 351 (see hereunder) (R. 350.2)

Any dissenting opinion needs to be part of the Court's decision (R. 350.3). The decision of the Court of First Instance needs to contain a summary of the requests and facts submitted by the parties and a statement of the facts and arguments on which the Court bases its decision (R. 350.4). The decisions are recorded in the Register (R. 350.5).

Rule 351 – Orders. Orders should contain (R. 351.1):

(a) the statement that it is an order of the J-R, of the presiding judge, of a President of the Court or of the Court;
(b) the date of its adoption;
(c) the names of any judge taking part in its adoption;
(d) the names of the parties and of the parties' representatives;
(e) the operative part of the order.

Where an order must be reasoned, it further contains (R. 351.2):

(a) a statement of the forms of order sought by the parties;
(b) a summary of the facts; and
(c) the grounds for the order.

Rule 352 – Binding effect. Decisions and orders may be made subject to rendering a security by a party(ies) to the other party(ies) for legal costs and other expenses and compensation for any damage incurred or likely to be incurred by the other party(ies) if the decisions and orders are subsequently revoked.

Rule 353 – Rectification of decisions. Clerical mistakes, errors in calculation and obvious slips in the decision may be rectified by way of order, of its own motion or on application by a party made within one month of service of the decision to be rectified.

Rule 453 – Enforcement. Decisions and orders of the Court are directly enforceable from their date of delivery in each Contracting Member State in accordance with the enforcement procedures and conditions governed by the law of the particular Contracting Member State where enforcement takes place (R. 453.1). Regarding the enforceability, reference should also be made to Rule 118.9 where it is stated that orders are only enforceable to the defendant after the plaintiff has notified the Court which part of the order he intends to enforce and of the notice has been served on the defendant by the Registry. Further, the enforceability may be subject to the rendering of a security (R. 352). Also in those non-Contracting Member States which are Member States of Regulation (EC) No. 44/2001 or the Lugano Convention, decisions and orders of the Court need to be enforced (R. 354.2).

Decisions and orders of the Court are enforceable in States that are not Contracting Member States or Member States of the Regulation or Convention referred to in Rule 354.2 in accordance with the law of that state (R. 354.3).

In the event an enforceable decision or order of the Court is subsequently varied or revoked the Court may order the party which has enforced such decision or order, upon the request of the party against whom the decision or order has been enforced, to provide appropriate compensation for any injury caused by the enforcement. Rule 125 shall apply *mutatis mutandis* (R. 354.4).

Further, the court's orders may provide for periodic penalty payments payable to the Court in the event that a party fails to comply with the terms of the order or an earlier order. The value of such payments is be set by the Court having regard to the importance of the order in question (R. 354.5).

Chapter 11
Decision by Default (R. 355 – R. 357)

Rule 355 – Decision by default (Court of First Instance)

Flowchart: Decision by default (Court of First Instance) (R. 355)

Decision by default (if failure to take step within time limit (R. 355.1)

Enforceable except if (R. 355.2):

- Court grants a stay of enforcement until it has given its decision on any Application under R. 356
- Court makes enforcement subject to the provision of security which is released if no Application is made or if the Application fails

↓ *within one month of service of the decision* (R. 356.1)

Application to set aside a decision (R. 356.1).

The application should comply with the requirements regarding the contents of the Statement of defence (cf. R. 24) or the contents of the Defence to the counterclaim for revocation (cf. R. 29) as the case may be together with the party's explanation for the default. (R. 356.2).

If the provisions of Rule 356.2 are met the Application shall be allowed and a note of allowance shall be included in any publication of the decision by default (R. 356.3).

Rule 357 – Decision by default (Court of Appeal). The above Rules (R. 355 and 356) also apply where a respondent on whom a Statement of appeal and a Statement of the grounds of appeal have been duly served fails to lodge a Statement of response or where a party fails to file a Reply to a Statement of cross-appeal or translations ordered by the J-R (R. 357.1). If the respondent fails to lodge a Statement of response and fails to lodge an Application to set aside pursuant to Rule 356, the Court of Appeal considers the merits of the appeal and, if the appeal is well-founded, it gives a reasoned decision (R. 357.2).

Rules 355 and 356 do not apply in the event a party fails to comply with the time limits set in Rules 324.1 (R. 357.3).

Chapter 12

Actions Bound to Fail or Manifestly Inadmissible (R. 360 – R. 363)

Rule 360 – No need to adjudicate. If the Court finds that an action has become devoid of purpose and that there is no longer any need to adjudicate on it, it may at any time, of its own motion, after giving the parties an opportunity to be heard, dispose of the action by way of order.

Rule 361 – Action manifestly bound to fail. Where it is clear that the Court has no jurisdiction to take cognisance of an action or where the action or defence is, in whole or in part, manifestly inadmissible or manifestly lacking any foundation in law, the Court may, after giving the parties an opportunity to be heard, give a decision by way of order.

Rule 362 – Orders dismissing manifestly inadmissible claims. Orders under Rules 360 and 361 need to be taken by the panel upon the recommendation of the J-R (R. 362.1). Where the decision is taken by the Court of First Instance, pursuant to Rules 360 and 361, it is a final decision within the meaning of Rule 220.1(a) (R. 362.2).

Rule 363 – Absolute bar to proceeding with an action. The Court may at any time, of its own motion, after giving the parties an opportunity to be heard, decide that there exists an absolute bar to proceeding with an action, for example because of the application of the principle of *res judicata*. The Court needs to give its decision by way of a reasoned judgement. Such judgement is a final decision within the meaning of Rule 220.1(a).

Chapter 13
Settlement (R. 365)

Rule 365 – Confirmation by the Court of a settlement. If a settlement is reached, the J-R should be informed. The settlement may, at the request of the parties, be confirmed by decision of the Court (R. 365.1 *juncto* R. 11.2). Such decision may set out the terms of the settlement and order that the details of the settlement are confidential (R. 365.2). The presiding judge provides a decision as to costs either in accordance with the terms of the settlement either, if not agreed upon in the settlement, at his discretion (R. 365.4). The case will be removed from the Register (R. 365.3).

PART 6
FEES AND LEGAL AID (R. 370 – R. 382)

Chapter 1

Court Fees (R. 370 – R. 372)

Rule 370 – Court fees. Rule 370.2(a) lists the fixed fees for actions, counterclaims, declarations and applications before the Court of First Instance and the Court of Appeal.[1] Further, the fees are mentioned for lodging a Protective letter or rehearing. In Rule 370.2(b), the value-based fees are listed.

Rule 371 – Time period for paying fees. The *fixed fees* should be paid at the time of lodging the relevant pleading (R. 371.2 *juncto* R. 15.1, R. 26, R. 47, R. 53, R. 68, R. 132, R. 192.5, R. 206.4, R. 207.3, R. 228) to one of the bank accounts indicated by the Court. The payment needs to indicate the paying party (or its representative) together with the number of the patent (or patents) involved. Proof of payment should be provided together with the relevant pleading (R. 37.2). In cases of urgency, where a payment in advance is not possible, the representative of the party in question can pay the fixed fee within the period set by the Court (R. 371.3).

The *value-based fees* should be paid within 10 working days of service of the order determining the value of the dispute (R. 371.4 *juncto* R. 22, R. 31, R. 57, R. 58, R. 69, R. 104(i) and R. 133).

Should an Application for legal aid been lodged in accordance with Rule 377 (laying out the conditions for granting legal aid), the rules on the obligation to pay the fixed fees under Rule 371.1 shall not apply (R. 371.5).

Rule 372 – Reimbursement of court fees (to be developed)

---

1. **Court of First Instance**: Fee for infringement action, fee for counterclaim for revocation, fee for revocation action, fee for counterclaim for infringement, fee for declaration of non-infringement, fee for action against a decision of the European Patent Office, fee for application to review a case management order, fee for application to preserve evidence, fee for application for provisional measures, fee for application to determine damages, fee for application to determine compensation pursuant to Rule 125, fee for application of re-establishment of rights, fee for application to prolong the period for a Protective letter to be kept on the register and fee for the application to set aside decision by default.

   Court of Appeal: Fee for appeal against final decision, fee for appeal against interlocutory order, fee for lodging a Protective letter and fee for rehearing.

Chapter 2

Legal Aid (R. 375 – R. 382)

Rule 375 – Aim and scope. The court may grant legal aid to a party, who needs to be natural person, in order to ensure effective access to justice (R. 375.1). Such legal aid may be granted in respect of any proceedings before the Court (R. 375.2).

Rule 376 – Costs eligible for legal aid. Subject to Article 71(3), legal aid may cover, besides the costs awarded to the successful party in the event of the applicant losing the case, in whole or in part, the following costs:

- (a) court fees;
- (b) costs of legal assistance and representation regarding
  - (i) pre-litigation advice with a view to reaching a settlement prior to commencing legal proceedings;
  - (ii) commencing and maintaining proceedings before the Court,
  - (iii) all costs relating to proceedings including the application for legal aid.
- (c) other necessary costs related to the proceedings to be borne by a party, including costs of witnesses, experts, interpreters and translators and necessary travel, accommodation and subsistence costs of the applicant and his representative.

Rule 377 – Conditions for granting legal aid. Any natural person shall be entitled to legal aid where:

- (a) due to his or her economic situation, he or she is wholly or partly unable to meet the costs referred to in Rule 376; and
- (b) the case in respect of which the application for legal aid is made has a reasonable prospect of success.

The Administrative Committee defines thresholds above which legal aid applicants are deemed wholly or partly able to bear the costs of proceedings set out in Rule 376. These thresholds may not prevent applicants whose economic situation is above the thresholds from being granted legal aid if they prove that they are in fact unable to pay the costs of the proceedings referred to in Rule

376 as a result of the high level of the cost of living in the Contracting Member State of domicile or habitual residence (R. 377.2).

When deciding on the grant of legal aid, the Court shall, without prejudice to Rule 377.1(a), consider the importance of the case to the applicant but may also take into account the nature of the case when the application concerns a claim arising directly out of the applicant's trade or self-employed profession (R. 377.3).

Flowchart: Examination application for legal aid (R. 378 – R. 381)

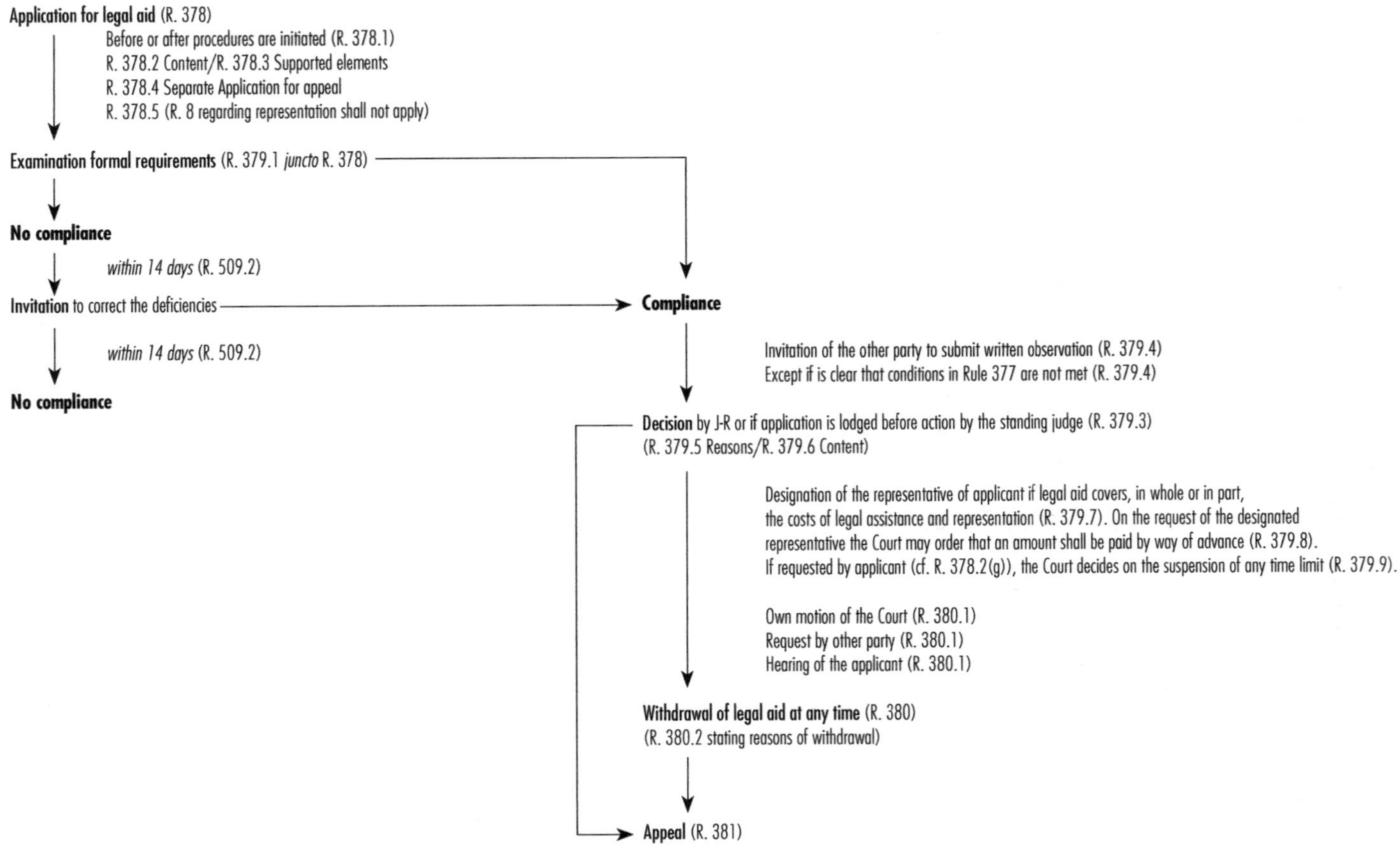

Rule 381 – Appeal. An order wholly or partly refusing or withdrawing legal aid may be appealed to the Court of Appeal if the Court of First Instance grants leave to appeal (or in the event leave is refused, with leave of the Court of Appeal) (R. 221). If such leave is granted the Court may grant legal aid for the conduct of the appeal.

Rule 382 – Recovery. If the Court orders another party to pay the costs of the applicant for legal aid, that other party shall be required to refund to the Court any sums advanced by way of legal aid (R. 382.1). In the event of a shortfall between the costs so ordered and the sums advanced by way of legal aid, the applicant may be required to meet such shortfall from any damages or compensation awarded by the Court or from any sum received by way of settlement. In the event of withdrawal of legal aid under Rule 380, the applicant may be required to refund to the Court any sums advanced by way of legal aid. (R. 382.2).

Supplement
Language Issues

A. AGREEMENT (BACKGROUND)

In Chapter II of the Agreement, the general language arrangements of the proceedings before the Court are stipulated.

A.1. Court of First Instance (Art. 49)

Article 49 deals with the Court of First Instance (making a distinction between a local or regional division on the one hand and a central division on the other hand) while Article 50 tackles the language of the proceedings in appeal.

Article 49(1)-(5) gives the following possibilities relating to language of proceedings before a *local or regional division*:

- the language of proceedings may be an official EU language which is the official language or one of the official languages of the Contracting Member State hosting the relevant division, or the official language(s) designated by the Contracting Member States sharing a regional division (Art. 49(1));
- the language of proceedings may be one or more of the official languages of the EPO so designated by the Contracting Member States as the language of proceedings of their local or regional division (Art. 49(2));
- if the competent panel so approves, parties may agree on the use of the language in which the patent was granted as language of the proceedings; if the panel does not approve, the parties may request that the case be heard by the central division (Art. 49(3));
- with the agreement of the parties, the competent panel may decide (on grounds of convenience and fairness) on the use of the language in which the patent was granted (Art. 49(4));
- at the request of one of the parties and after having heard the other parties and the competent panel, the President of the Court of First Instance may (on grounds of fairness and taking into account all relevant circumstances, including the position of the parties, in particular the

position of the defendant) decide on the use of the language in which the patent was granted as language of proceedings; in such a case the President of the Court of First Instance assesses the need for specific translation and interpretation arrangements (Art. 49(5)).

Article 49(5) states that the language of the proceedings at the *central division* is the language in which the patent concerned was granted.

A.2. Court of Appeal (Art. 50)

Proceedings before the Court of Appeal are dealt with in the following language (Art. 50):

- the language of proceedings before the Court of First Instance (Art. 50(1));
- the language in which the patent was granted and agreed upon between parties (Art. 50(2));
- to the extent deemed appropriate, the Court of Appeal may decide on another official language of a Contracting Member State as the language for the whole or part of the proceedings and subject to agreement by the parties (Art. 50(3)).

A.3. Translation Requirements (Art. 51)

Any panel of the Court of First Instance and Court of Appeal may, to the extent deemed appropriate, dispense with translation requirements (Art. 51(1)). At the request of one of the parties, any division of the Court of First Instance and Court of Appeal need to provide interpretation facilities to assist the parties concerned at the oral proceedings. In the event an infringement action is to be brought before the central division, the defendant has the right to obtain, upon request, translations of relevant documents in the language of the Contracting Member State where he has his residence, or principal place of business or in the absence of residence or principal place of business, place of business in the following cumulative conditions (Art. 51(3)):

- jurisdiction is entrusted to the central division in accordance with Article 33(1) paras 3-4; and
- the language of proceedings at the central division is a language which is not the official language of the Contracting Member State where the defendant has its his residence, or principal place of business, or in the absence of residence or principal place of business, his place of business; and

– the defendant does not have knowledge of the language of the proceedings.

B. RULES

B.1. General

Rule 2 specifies that the language in which a patent was granted means that specific language, and not the language in which a supplementary certificate in respect of the patent was granted.

B.2. Language Issues during Written Procedure

Rule 7 – Language of written pleadings and written evidence. All written pleadings and other documents, including written evidence, need to be lodged in the language of the proceedings, unless the Court or the Rules of Procedure provide otherwise.

Rule 14 – Language of the Statement of claim. The Statement of claim needs to be drawn up:

(a) in one of the languages of the regional division or local division
   (i) which the plaintiff has chosen in accordance with Article 33, or
   (ii) which the parties have agreed to bring the action before in accordance with Article 33(7); or
(b) in the language in which the patent was granted
   (i) where the central division hears the case in accordance with Article 33, or
   (ii) where a Request to use the language in which the patent was granted as language of the proceedings is lodged in accordance with Rules 321 or 323 together with the Statement of claim. An Application under Rule 321.1 or 323.1 needs to specify whether existing pleadings and other documents should be translated and at whose cost. If the parties cannot agree, the J-R or the President of the Court of First Instance, as the case may be, decides in accordance with Rule 321.6 or Rule 323.3 (R. 324); or
(c) in a official language of the EPO designated as the language of proceedings by a Contracting Member State pursuant to Article 49(2).

The language in which the Statement of claim is drawn up is the language of the proceedings, without prejudice to Article 49(3), (4) or (5) or Rules 13.3, 321, 322 or 323 (R. 14.2).

The plaintiff may lodge a translation of the Statement of claim in an official language of the Contracting Member State where the defendant has his residence, or principal place of business or, in the absence of residence or principal place of business, his place of business and request that the translation be served on the defendant (R. 14.3).

Rule 19 – Preliminary objection. The Preliminary objection regarding the language of the Statement of claim (R. 19.1(c)) (Rule 14) should be drawn up

- in the language of the proceedings (R. 19.3(a) *juncto* R. 14.2); or
- in an official language of the Contracting Member State where the defendant has his residence, or principal place of business, or in the absence of residence or principal place of business, his place of business (R. 19.3(b)).

Rule 30 – Application to amend the patent. As mentioned, the Defence to the counterclaim may include an Application by the proprietor of the patent to amend the patent (R. 30). Such Application should contain the proposed amendments of the claims of the patent concerned and/or specification, including, where appropriate, one or more alternative sets of claims (auxiliary requests) (R. 30.1(a)) and this in the language in which the patent was granted. Where the language of the proceedings (R. 14.2) is not the language in which the patent was granted, the plaintiff should to lodge a translation of the proposed amendments in the language of the proceedings (R. 30.1(a)).

Rule 39 – Language of the proceedings before the central division (related to Counterclaim for revocation referred to the central division under Art. 33(3)(b)). Where the language of the proceedings before the regional division or the local division which referred the Counterclaim for revocation to the central division is not the language in which the patent was granted, the J-R may order the parties to lodge, within a period of 21 days, a translation in the language in which the patent was granted of any written pleadings and such other documents lodged during the written procedure as the J-R may direct (R. 39.1). The period may be extended by the J-R on a reasoned request by a party. Where appropriate, the J-R may specify in his order that only excerpts of parties' written pleadings and other documents need to be translated (R. 39.2). Where the language of the proceedings before the regional division or the local division is the language in which the patent was granted, the pleadings served in accordance with Rules 24, 25, 29, 30 and 32 shall stand (R. 39.3).

Rule 41 – Written procedure when the central division deals with the case under Article 33(3)(c). Regarding this procedure, Rule 41(d) states that Rule 39 applies *mutatis mutandis*: the J-R may order that the parties lodge a translation in the language in which the patent was granted of any written pleadings lodged during the written procedure. Where appropriate, the J-R may specify in his order that only excerpts of parties' written pleadings and other documents need to be translated. Otherwise the pleadings lodged during the written procedure will stand (R. 41(d)).

Rule 42 – Written procedure when the central division deals with the case under Article 33(3)(b). When a case is referred to the central division under Article 33(3)(b), the language regime is dependent on whether the language of the proceedings before the regional division is the language in which the patent is granted or not:

R. 42(c) Where the language of proceedings before the regional division which referred the case to the central division *is not the language* in which the patent was granted, the J-R may order the parties to lodge, within a period of 21 days, a translation in the language in which the patent was granted of any written pleadings and such other documents lodged during the written procedure prior to the referral of the case as the J-R may direct. The period may be extended on a reasoned request by a party. Where appropriate the J-R may specify in his order that only excerpts of the parties' written pleadings and other documents need to be translated.

R. 42(d) Where the language of proceedings before the regional division *is the language* in which the patent was granted, the pleadings served before the referral of the case will stand.

Rule 46 – Language of the Statement for revocation. The Statement for revocation should be drawn up in the language in which the patent was granted (R. 46.1). Where the parties have agreed to bring the action before a local or a regional division in accordance with Article 33(7), the Statement for revocation should be drawn up in one of the languages referred to in Rule 14.1(a)(ii) or (b)(ii) or (c) (R. 46.2). Reference is made to Rule 14.2-3 which applies *mutatis mutandis*.

Rule 88 – Application to annul or alter a decision of the Office. The application should be lodged in the language in which the patent was granted (R. 88.1).

B.3. Language during Interim Procedure

Rule 105 – Telephone conference and video conference. Interim conferences may be held in any language mastered by parties' representatives (R. 105.3).

B.4. Language Issues during Oral Procedure

Rule 112 – Conduct of the oral hearing. During oral hearings, the Court may give its consent to a witness to give evidence in a language other than the language of proceedings (R. 112.5).

B.5. Language Issues regarding Evidence

Rule 175 – Written witness statement. The written witness statement needs to set out the language in which the witness shall give oral evidence, if necessary (R. 175.2).

Rule 176 – Application for the hearing of a witness in person. The application should set out the language in which the witness shall give evidence (R. 176(c)).

Rule 178 – Hearing of witnesses. With the consent of the Court, a witness may give evidence in a language other than the language of proceedings (R. 178.7).

Rule 192 – Application for preserving evidence. Where this application is lodged after main proceedings on the merits of the case have been started before the Court, the Application needs to be drawn up in the language of the proceedings (R. 192.4). Where the Application is lodged before main proceedings on the merits of the case have been started before the Court, Rules 12 or 43 apply *mutatis mutandis*.

Rule 202 – Letters rogatory. The Court needs to draw up letters rogatory in the language of the competent court or authority or attach to such letters a translation into that language (R. 202.2).

B.6. Language Issues regarding Provisional Measures

Rule 207 – Protective letter. A Protective letter should be filed with the Registry in the language of the patent (R. 207.2).

B.7. Additional Language Issues before the Court of Appeal

Rule 227 – Language of the Statement of appeal and of the Statement of grounds of appeal. The Statement of appeal and the Statement of grounds of appeal needs to be drawn up (R. 227.1.):

(a) without prejudice to Article 50(3) in the language of the proceedings before the Court of First Instance; or
(b) where the parties have agreed in accordance with Article 50(2), in the language in which the patent was granted; or
(c) where the parties have agreed in accordance with Article 50(2), evidence of the respondent's agreement needs to be lodged by the appellant together with the Statement of appeal.

Rule 232 – Translation of file. If the language of the proceedings before the Court of Appeal is not the language of the proceedings before the Court of First Instance, the J-R may order the appellant to lodge, within a time period to be specified, translations into the language of the proceedings before the Court of Appeal of (R. 232.1.):

(a) written pleadings and other documents lodged by the parties before the Court of First Instance, as specified by the J-R;
(b) decisions or orders of the Court of First Instance.

Should the appellant fail to lodge the translations under Rule 232.1 within the period specified, the Court of Appeal may reject the appeal by a decision by default in accordance with Rule 357. The panel may give the appellant an opportunity to be heard beforehand (R. 232.2).

The appellant may request that documented costs of translations be taken into account when the Court fixes the amount of costs in accordance with Part 1, Chapter 5 (R. 232.3).

B.8. Miscellaneous Provisions on Languages (R. 321 – R. 324)

Flowchart: Change of language of the proceedings (R. 321 – R. 324)

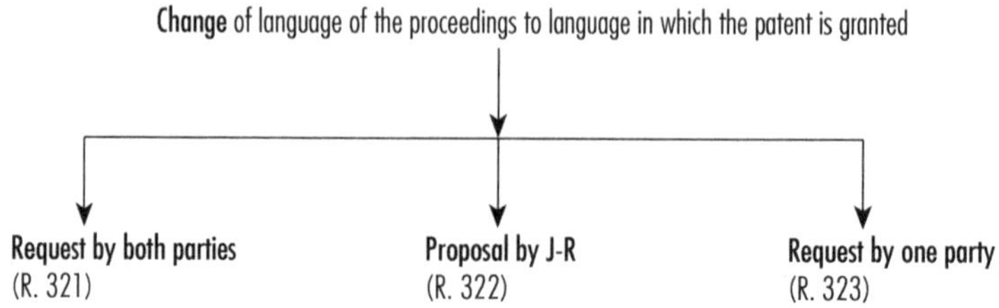

Rule 321 – Request by both parties to use of the language in which the patent was granted as language of the proceedings

Flowchart: Request by both parties to use of the language in which the patent was granted as language of the proceedings (R. 321)

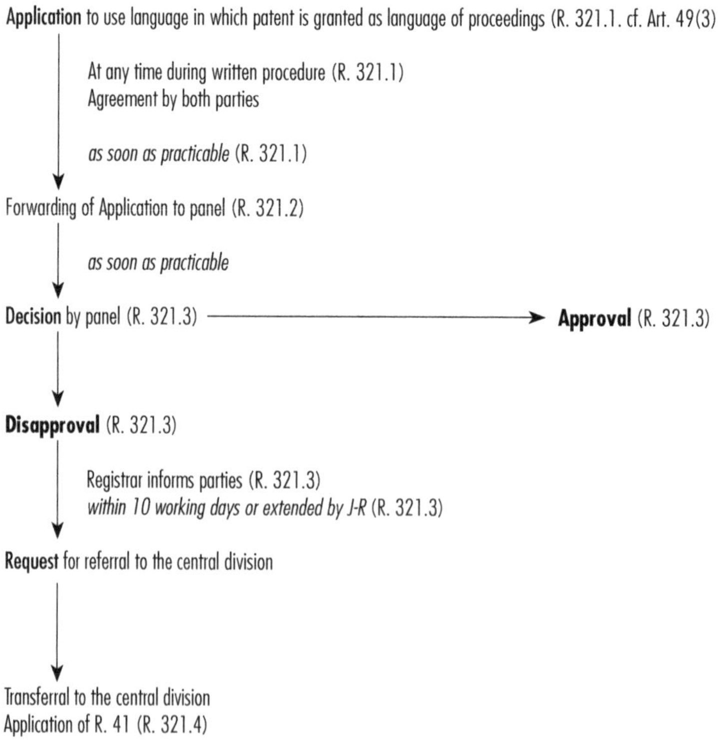

Where:

(a) a Statement of claim is drawn up in the language in which the patent was granted, in accordance with Rule 14.1(b)(ii);
(b) an Application by both parties to use the language in which the patent was granted as language proceedings is not allowed; and
(c) the parties do not request the case to be referred to the central division

the plaintiff shall lodge the Statement of claim in a language provided for in Rule 14.1(a), within ten working days (R. 321.5.).

The period of ten working days may be extended by the J-R on a reasoned request by the plaintiff (R. 321 last sentence).

The J-R shall, at the request of a party, specify whether any other pleading or document shall be translated and at whose cost (R. 323.6.)

Rule 322 – Proposal from the J-R to use of the language in which the patent was granted as language of the proceedings. At any time during the written procedure and the interim procedure, the J-R may, of his own motion or on a request by a party after consulting the panel, propose to the parties to change the language of the proceedings (R. 14.2) to the language in which the patent was granted, (in accordance with Article 49(4)). Upon agreement of the parties and panel, the language of the proceedings will be changed (R. 322).

Rule 423 – Request by one party to use the language in which the patent was granted as language of the proceedings

Flowchart: Request by one party to use the language in which the patent was granted as language of the proceedings (R. 323)

Application to use language in which patent was granted (R. 323.1) (cf. Art. 49(5))
– if plaintiff: Application for change of language in the Statement of claim
– if defendant: Application for change of language in the Statement of defence

↓

Forwarding of Application to Pres. Court of First Instance (R. 323.1)

↓

Invitation of the other party to indicate its position (R. 323.2)

↓ *within 10 days of Application*

Indication of position of the other party (R. 323.2)

↓ Consultation of the panel (R. 323.3)

Decision by the President (R. 323.3)
(may be conditional on translation or interpretation arrangement)

Rule 324 – Consequences where the language of the proceedings is changed in the course of the proceedings. An Application under Rule 321.1 or Rule 323.1 should specify whether existing pleadings and other documents should be translated and at whose cost. If the parties cannot agree the J-R or the President of the Court of First Instance, as the case may be, decides in accordance with Rule 321.6 or Rule 323.3.

B.9. Language Issues relating to Application for Legal Aid

Rule 378 – Application for legal aid. The application for legal aid should be drafted in the language of a Contracting Member State (R. 378.2).